Religion and Development

Also by Jeffrey Haynes

AN INTRODUCTION TO RELIGION AND INTERNATIONAL RELATIONS

COMPARATIVE POLITICS IN A GLOBALIZING WORLD

DEMOCRACY AND CIVIL SOCIETY IN THE THIRD WORLD. POLITICS AND NEW POLITICAL MOVEMENTS

DEMOCRACY AND POLITICAL CHANGE IN THE 'THIRD WORLD' (ECPR Studies in European Political Science, No. 21)

DEMOCRACY IN THE DEVELOPING WORLD. AFRICA, ASIA, LATIN AMERICA AND THE MIDDLE EAST

PALGRAVE ADVANCES IN DEVELOPMENT STUDIES

POLITICS IN THE DEVELOPING WORLD. A CONCISE INTRODUCTION

RELIGION AND POLITICS IN AFRICA, LONDON/NAIROBI

RELIGION, GLOBALIZATION AND POLITICAL CULTURE IN THE THIRD WORLD

RELIGION IN GLOBAL POLITICS

RELIGION IN THIRD WORLD POLITICS

THE POLITICS OF RELIGION. A SURVEY

THIRD WORLD POLITICS. A CONCISE INTRODUCTION

TOWARDS SUSTAINABLE DEMOCRACY IN THE THIRD WORLD

Religion and Development

Conflict or Cooperation?

Jeffrey Haynes
Professor of Politics, Department of Law, Governance and International Relations, London Metropolitan University, UK

First published 2007 by
PALGRAVE MACMILLAN
Houndmills, Basingstoke, Hampshire RG21 6XS and
175 Fifth Avenue, New York, N.Y. 10010
Companies and representatives throughout the world

PALGRAVE MACMILLAN is the global academic imprint of the Palgrave
Macmillan division of St. Martin's Press, LLC and of Palgrave Macmillan Ltd.
Macmillan® is a registered trademark in the United States, United Kingdom
and other countries. Palgrave is a registered trademark in the European
Union and other countries.

ISBN 13: 978–1–4039–9790–6   hardback
ISBN 10: 1–4039–9790–X   hardback
ISBN 13: 978–0–230–54246–4   paperback
ISBN 10: 0–230–54246–8   paperback

This book is printed on paper suitable for recycling and made from fully
managed and sustained forest sources. Logging, pulping and manufacturing
processes are expected to conform to the environmental regulations of the
country of origin.

A catalogue record for this book is available from the British Library.

A catalogue record for this book is available from the Library of Congress.

10   9   8   7   6   5   4   3   2   1
16   15 14 13 12 11 10 09 08 07

Printed and bound in Great Britain by
Antony Rowe Ltd, Chippenham and Eastbourne

Contents

List of Abbreviations   vi

Introduction: Religion and Development   1

1   Religious Resurgence, Globalisation, and Good Governance   26

2   Religion and Development: The Ambivalence of the Sacred   53

3   Conflict, Conflict Resolution and Peace-building   75

4   Economic Growth, Poverty and Hunger   101

5   Environmental Sustainability   124

6   Health   150

7   Education   176

Conclusion   205

Notes   222

Bibliography   226

Index   244

List of Abbreviations

ABC	Abstinence, Being Faithful, Condoms
AHE	Asociación Hondureña de la Ecología
AKDN	Aga Khan Development Network
AKF	Aga Khan Foundation
AKRSP	Aga Khan Rural Support Programme
ARC	Alliance of Religions and Conservation
ART	antiretroviral therapy
BCCs	Basic Christian Communities
BJP	Bharatiya Janata Party / Indian People's Party
CGAP	Consultative Group to Assist the Poor
CIESIN	Center for International Earth Science Information Network
CRSP	Coastal Rural Support Programme
CSWs	commercial sex workers
DDVE	Development Dialogue on Values and Ethics
E-9	Education-9
EFA	Education for All
EFZ	Evangelical Fellowship of Zambia
EMO	Environmental Movement of Olancho
EMRDA	Ethiopian Muslim Relief and Development Association
EPA	Environmental Protection Act
FAO	Food and Agriculture Organisation
G7	Group of 7
GNP	Gross National Product
HIPC	Heavily Indebted Poor Countries
HIV/AIDS	human immunodeficiency virus / acquired immunodeficiency syndrome
IDB	Inter-American Development Bank
IDUs	injecting drug users
IFIs	international financial institutions
IIRO	International Islamic Relief Organisation
ILO	International Labour Organisation
IMF	International Monetary Fund
IPCC	Intergovernmental Panel on Climate Change
ISESCO	Islamic Educational, Scientific and Cultural Organisation
JDC	Jubilee Debt Campaign

LACC	Latin America ChildCare
MCDF	Muslim-Christian Dialogue Forum
MDGs	Millennium Development Goals
MSC	Muslim Supreme Council
NAS	National Academy of Sciences
NCERT	National Council for Educational Research and Training
NFF	National Forum of Fishworkers
NGOs	non-governmental organizations
N&WG	Nuns and Wat Grannies
OECD	Organisation for Economic Cooperation and Development
OIC	Organisation of the Islamic Conference
PIEDAD	Programa Integral de Educacion de Las Asambleas de Dios
PLWHA	People Living with HIV and AIDS
PRSP	Poverty Reduction Strategy Paper
RACHA	Reproductive and Child Health Alliance
RENAMO	Mozambican National Resistance
RSS	Rastriya Swayansevak Sangh / National Volunteer Corps
SAPs	structural adjustment programmes
SIPA	School of International and Public Affairs
SIT	School for International Training
SLVF	Swami Lakshmanacharya Vishwa Santi Foundation
SSM	Sarvodaya Shramadana Movement
TERI	Tata Energy Research Institute
TNCs	transnational corporations
UNDP	United Nations Development Programme
UNEP	United Nations Environmental Programme
UNFPA	United Nations Fund for Population Activities
UNICEF	United Nation's Children's Fund / United Nations International Children's Emergency Fund
UNTAC	United Nations Transitional Authority in Cambodia
UNESCO	United Nations Educational, Scientific and Cultural Organisation
USAID	United States Agency for International Development
VBS	Vidya Bharati Sansthan / Indian Organisation for Education
WCC	World Council of Churches
WFDD	World Faiths Development Dialogue
WTO	World Trade Organisation

Introduction: Religion and Development

After World War II, most Western governments and development agencies saw religion as part of the development problem, not as a potential aspect of its resolution. More recently, this negative consensus about religion has fractured, partly as a result of the widespread failure of secular development trajectories to achieve widespread poverty reduction or reductions of inequality and injustice in the developing world. As a result, the emphasis of development thinking has shifted to include various religious expressions that are now widely seen as potentially important components of achieving development gains, although those associated with 'religious extremism' are not. Primarily concerned with the holistic human development dimension, visions of development from faith perspectives differ significantly from those expressed historically by secular development organisations, which often appear to be singularly concerned with 'economic development' to the exclusion of other aspects of development. From a generally religious perspective, such development programmes and policies often appeared to be what Goulet calls 'one-eyed giants', because they 'analyse, prescribe and act *as if* man could live by bread alone, *as if* human destiny could be stripped to its material dimensions alone' (Goulet 1980).

In this introductory chapter, we trace the evolution of the idea that faith-based organisations[1] can play a significant role in delivery of development goals in the developing world. Things have not always been this way. Sixty years ago, 'development' and 'religion' were regarded in the West as emphatically separate concerns. This was because the notion of development was closely tied to both secularisation and modernisation, conditions from which religion had been progressively excluded over time in the West (Haynes 1998). Religion

1

was widely regarded as being concerned with 'mere' spirituality, perceived by most Western academics, governments and development practitioners as irrelevant or antipathetic to the achievement of development goals, primarily understood as being concerned with material improvements.

In much Western thinking, the way to achieve substantial development improvements in the developing world focused squarely on the injection of large quantities of 'development aid'. The American president, Harry Truman, set the tone in his inaugural speech in 1949. Set against the deepening of the Cold War divide, Truman announced what he called a 'bold new' programme. His aim was to use development aid in tandem with the West's primary development advantage – swift scientific-industrial progress – to facilitate the development of the 'underdeveloped regions' (Holenstein 2005: 17). He hoped that this would enable them to kick-start their own development, a strategy that would not only, it was hoped, end the scourge of poverty in the poor countries but also bind them ideologically and financially to the United States at the beginning of the Cold War. Truman's call went out to the Western industrialised countries, asking them to join with the USA, a strategy well captured in the choice of words adopted in a Swiss Foreign Ministry memorandum of 1950: 'Basically it is to win the hearts and minds of people who are threatened by Communism or possibly drawn to it through misery' (quoted in Holenstein 2005: 17).

In short, the perceived technical and cultural backwardness of non-Western cultures in the developing world shaped the strategy of Western development aid in the decades after World War II. According to this emphatically secular doctrine of salvation, people living in underdeveloped countries should be saved from their backwardness through the application of both capital and modern western technology (Holenstein 2005: 17). This perception of the notion of development completely excluded any role for religion.

Three recent developments – deepening globalisation, pervasive calls for better governance and widespread religious resurgence – have encouraged the belief that religion can play an important role in the achievement of desirable development outcomes in the developing world (Beyer 2006). Globalisation is a key focus because of its economic, social and developmental ramifications. This includes the economic range and clout of transnational corporations and a perception that they are taking economic power from governments – and thus from citizens and their efforts to control their own fates (Haynes 2005a). Globalisation is also associated in many faith views with growing impoverishment of already poor people in many parts of the developing world (Thomas 2005). These circumstances encourage religions to try to use their own resources to ameliorate developmental imbalances that in many faith views are often exacerbated by economic globalisation. As a result, there is now a widespread faith concern with the developmental dimensions of the impact of economic globalisation. This is manifested in various ways, including: increased religious involvement in development initiatives, as well as new religious fundamentalisms and support for anti-globalisation activities, such as anti-World Trade Organisation protests and North/South economic justice efforts (Spickard 2001). Collectively, these reactions underline that religious responses to economic globalisation increasingly include a stress on social interests that go way beyond the confines of what might be called conventional religious concerns.

Demands for greater developmental justice from faith-based organisations dovetails with the wider call from both citizens and international agencies, including the United Nations and the World Bank – for better governance (Cleary and McConville 2006). The overall thrust of such demands is to highlight the realisation that, especially in the developing world, governments cannot hope to achieve all development aspirations on their own, partly as a result of widespread resource shortages. There is now greater awareness of the potential of non-state entities, including faith-based organisations, to augment the state's developmental abilities. That faith-based entities are now increasingly involved in various aspects of governance is also due to the fact not only that there is a well documented religious resurgence in many parts of the world (Berger 1999), but also that opinion polls in sub-Saharan Africa and elsewhere in the developing world emphasise that religious leaders are often among the most trusted individuals in society (Ferret 2005). Overall there is now widespread acceptance that desired development outcomes can more likely be achieved if the energies and abilities of various non-state actors – including faith-based organisations – can be tapped into.

The focus on the role religious actors can play in development has coincided with renewed interest in 'human development', a concept that often includes concern with life's spiritual dimension. Once, 'development' meant little more than *economic* development *tout court*, a generalised notion of economic growth over time. Recently, 'the concept of human development has come into vogue, emphasising aspects of people's lives that go beyond the economic dimension'

(Ellis and ter Haar 2005: 1), including: health, education, literacy, social relationships, and 'quality of life'. The United Nations Development Programme (UNDP) notes that 'human development' is a 'complex concept of development, based on the priority of human well-being, aimed at ensuring and enlarging human choices leading to greater equality of opportunities for all people in society and empowerment of people so that they participate in – and benefit from – the development process' (Human Development Report 1996: 5).

The concept of 'human development' can be understood in various ways. Politically and economically, human development is concerned with stability, security and the relative prosperity of citizens. Socially, it relates to literacy, education, social relationships and, more vaguely, 'the quality of life'. Morally, it involves development of conscience, moral awareness, and will and capacity to act according to societal and cultural knowledge of what is judged to be right – and in the developing world this overlaps considerably with religious and spiritual dimensions of life. Finally, psychologically, human development is to do with mental health, self-esteem, success in significant relationships, and happiness. In short, the idea of human development is a broad category focusing on societal stability, security and relative prosperity, with political, economic, social, moral and psychological dimensions. For many usually secular development professionals, however, human development has long been an add-on, an 'optional extra', peripheral to a more pressing concern: finding ways to generate economic growth and then to distribute the resulting wealth among a country's population according to varying ideas of what is just and equitable. Now, however, many agree that things have changed quite dramatically: secular development professionals often now seek to try to make the idea of human development a reality by including various factors, including the spiritual dimension of life, in their considerations (Kollapen 2005).

This is not to suggest that faith-based organisations have been uninterested or unconcerned with human development in the past, having traditionally played a significant role in many aspects of development, including: education, social welfare, charitable work, and humanitarian relief (Haynes 1993; Dark 2000). Yet, they were often explicitly excluded from national development programmes by modernisation processes often led by secular states in many parts of the developing world. Now, however, numerous non-governmental organisations with a religious base or affiliation are now increasingly active in various development fields, often cooperating with secular development bodies in joint efforts. Whether religious or secular, these entities now ask similar questions:

- At the start of the 21st century, what should be the key developmental priorities?
- How can faith-based organisations assist and deepen cooperative processes, helping deliver development priorities and goals?
- What role does religion have in helping define and refine those goals, including their spiritual dimension?
- What can religion do in helping resolving conflicts in the developing world?

The focus of this book is on the dual nature of religion's involvement in development. We shall see that it can be both constructive and destructive. To examine the issue we look at the involvement in development of four major world religions – Islam, Christianity, Hinduism and Buddhism in sub-Saharan Africa, (East, South East and Central) Asia, and Latin America. We do not explicitly focus on the Middle East in this book for two main reasons: (1) the issues are complex enough in the regions that we do focus upon without adding an additional layer of complexity, and (2) the Middle East region is often said to have qualitatively different characteristics compared to other developing regions, notably the importance of oil and particularistic – typically undemocratic – political systems (Mansfield and Pelham 2003; Fisk 2005; Khan 2006).

In the remainder of this introductory chapter, we examine (1) evolution of the theory and practice of development, (2) ways to understand and define religion, and (3) why religion is now a 'hot topic' in development discourses.

Theory and practice of development

'Development' has long been a vague yet predictive term, struggling to acquire a precise meaning. Sixty years ago, however, that is, immediately after World War II, things seemed clearer: development was widely seen as a relatively unproblematic, self-evident and prophetic concept. The issue of 'development' and how to achieve it was of great relevance not only to war-torn Europe but also in relation to the large group of 'developing' (or 'Third World') countries that emerged from colonial rule over the next 30 years, especially in Africa, Asia and the Caribbean. For this growing group of countries, a key issue was how to advance from a position of 'underdevelopment' to one of being a 'developed', that is, to achieve the status of a 'modern' state. In other words, how would they manage to emulate the developed status of many countries in Europe and North America and achieve modernity? On the one hand, there was the Western developmental model – but it was not the only one on offer. On the other hand, some developing countries looked not to the West but to the communist East and the alternative model provided by the Soviet Union and its Central and Eastern European allies, including East Germany and Hungary: communist states pursuing a different development path. Yet, while differing in fundamental respects, both 'capitalist' and 'communist' development models concurred on one important point: religion's social, political and economic standing needed to be reduced or even eliminated in order to usher in both development and modernity.

The study of development and how to achieve it – 'development studies' – emerged in the decades following World War II, when the idea of development first appeared on the international agenda. Initially, as Ellis and ter Haar note:

> development was seen as an integrated approach in which all aspects of society would have their role in the strategic aim of making people more productive and able to live longer and healthier lives. For several decades, both liberal and Marxist experts saw states as playing the central role in the process of development through their commanding position in the governance of society (Ellis and ter Haar 2005: 1).

It was believed to be the job of government to inaugurate and deliver the necessary and specific policies and programmes to bring about development. Initially, problems of underdevelopment were regarded primarily as technical issues that could be resolved by trained administrators who, producing the necessary policies and programmes and with the appropriate budget, would work to achieve the state's developmental goals. Dedicated state officials were expected to implement the necessary policies, in line with relevant statements, policies and programmes produced by government, and within budget. In short, governments were regarded as the primary agents of development, responsible for improving the material well-being of all their citizens (Calvert and Calvert 2001).

The primary role of the state in development is now questioned, not only by many development practitioners and academics specialising in the study of human development but also by international development agencies, including the largest, the World Bank, as well as civil societies in many developing countries (Haynes 2005a). While there are various views regarding the best ways of achieving human development, there is an emerging consensus that religion's developmental potential has long been under-utilised. This reflects a widespread agreement that development is a complex process, difficult to attain, and a realisation that it is necessary to look to various non-state, including faith-based, entities to maximise chances of achieving it. In the next section we trace the various stages of thinking about development and how to achieve it after World War II, in order to understand the initial denial and now acceptance of the developmental importance of many faith-based organisations.

Models of development: modernisation, 'basic needs' and structural adjustment programmes

Thinking about development in relation to the developing world went through three main stages between the 1950s and 1990s. First, during the 1950s and 1960s, when dozens of culturally, politically, and economically disparate post-colonial countries emerged, mainly in Africa, Asia and the Caribbean, the West's chosen strategy to achieve development was primarily via the application of appropriate levels of development aid. Second, during the 1970s, substantial oil price rises both underlined and hastened developmental polarisation, with richer developing countries – such as South Korea, Taiwan and Singapore – on the whole managing to cope. On the other hand, most non-oil producing developing countries – especially in Africa – failed to do so, and found their international debts fast rising. The West's development focus at this time was on a 'basic needs' strategies where, it was envisaged, development goals would be achieved via a strategy to ensure that *all* people had access to necessary 'basics', including: clean water, basic healthcare, and at least primary education. This strategy generally failed, however, for two main reasons: first, the developmental issue became subsumed into the wider Cold War ideological division, with government-disbursed development funds not necessarily going to the most developmentally deserving cases – but often instead to allies of the key aid providing countries; and, second, because of the frequent unwillingness of ruling elites and their supporters in many developing countries to facilitate the necessary financial transfers upon which the successful delivery of basic needs strategy fundamentally hinged (Taylor 2005; Shaw 2005).

The third phase followed in the 1980s. Increased developmental polarisation in the developing world led to renewed Western attempts to encourage developing countries to reform their economic policies in order to try to stimulate increased economic growth. Western governments, especially those of the USA, Britain and Germany, and international development agencies, including the World Bank and International Monetary Fund (IMF), believed that unacceptable levels of state meddling, incompetence and poor policies had fatally undermined achievement of development goals in much of the developing world. Their solution was to try to 'roll back' the state, believing that states had often 'tried to do too much', expending much effort and money but achieving little. Private entrepreneurs, bringing both dynamism and energy to seek solutions to development shortfalls, would usefully augment the state's developmental role. In pursuit of this strategy, Western financial assistance was focused on 'structural adjustment programmes' (SAPs) in dozens of developing countries in the 1980s and 1990s. According to Barber Conable, President of the World Bank between 1986 and 1991, SAPs reflected the belief that 'market forces and economic efficiency were the best way to achieve the kind of growth which is the best antidote to poverty' (Conable quoted in Thomas and Reader 2001: 79).

Conable's statement reflected the then current intellectual predominance of neo-liberalism in relation to development thinking. Neo-liberalism was an economic and political philosophy that ideologically underpinned the pro-market and monetarist ideas of various governments, including those of Britain's Margaret Thatcher (1979–90), Germany's Helmut Kohl (1982–98) and, in the USA, the administrations of Ronald Reagan (1980–88) and George H.W. Bush (1988–92). A core belief of neo-liberalism was that to achieve desirable development outcomes, government's role must be diminished, with private capitalists and entrepreneurs 'freed' from state control to apply their energies to economic growth strategies. Under pressure from Western governments and key international financial institutions (IFIs) – especially, the World Bank and the IMF – many developing country governments were strongly encouraged to put in place and develop neo-liberal policies. Outcomes, however, were on the whole disappointing in terms of reducing developmental inequalities (Stiglitz 2006).

The ideological power of neo-liberalism was at its zenith in 1989–91 when the Cold War came to an end and the Eastern European communist bloc spectacularly and swiftly collapsed. The swift disintegration of Europe's communist governing systems not only appeared to offer spectacular evidence of the superior power of capitalism and liberal democracy over communism, but also provided pro-market forces with added ideological momentum. The then dominant neo-liberal development strategy was known as the 'Washington consensus', reflecting the pre-eminence of such ideas among key, Washington, DC-based, opinion leaders: 'the IMF and the World Bank, independent think-tanks, the US government policy community, investment bankers, and so on' (Thomas and Reader 2001: 79). However, critics of the Washington consensus model argued that the studiously pro-market view it endorsed gave insufficient emphasis not only to the essential developmental role of government, the only institution with power to alter prevailing socio-economic realities through application of appropriate policies and programmes, but also to that of relevant non-state actors – both secular and faith-based organisations – that could be influential in helping to deliver human development goals (Taylor 2005).

The renewed focus on non-state actors in relation to development goals in the developing world reflected what many would regard as the abject failure of post-World War II development strategies. After half a century of applied development policies and programmes, and a quarter century of neo-liberal economic policies, over a billion people in the developing world still live on less than one US dollar a day at the end of the 20th century. More than two billion people – a third of the global population – do not have access to potable clean water. Hundreds of millions of individuals, especially women and the poor, lack anything like adequate healthcare or basic educational opportunities. Overall, the global developmental picture is still very gloomy, characterised by rising global poverty and polarising inequality, especially in many developing countries.

At the end of the 20th century, widespread development disappointments in the developing world stimulated the international community, led by the United Nations, to renewed activity to try to address the problems. The international community set itself the challenge of a third millennium 'onslaught' on poverty and human deprivation, with efforts focused on the developing world, especially Africa, where human deprivation and poverty was most pronounced. A new strategy was announced in September 2000, with a deadline of 2015 to achieve eight Millennium Development Goals (MDGs), as noted in Box I.1.

The world's most influential and money-rich developmental agency, the International Bank for Reconstruction and Development, universally known as the World Bank, accepted the need for a significantly

---

Box I.1   The Eight Millennium Development Goals (MDGs)

- Eradicate extreme poverty and hunger
- Achieve universal primary education
- Promote gender equality and empower women
- Reduce child mortality
- Improve maternal health
- Combat HIV/AIDS, malaria, and other diseases
- Ensure environmental sustainability
- Develop a global partnership for development
  (http://www.un.org/millenniumgoals/)

---

different developmental emphasis if the MDGs were to be achieved by 2015. The Bank noted in its *World Development Report 2000/2001* that adjustments would be necessary at both global and national levels. It also claimed that MDG goals, including the promotion of opportunity, were inherently linked to increases in overall economic growth, as were patterns and quality of growth. Yet, while market reforms were believed central in relation to expanding opportunities for poor people in the developing world, reforms were also urgently needed in relation to local institutional and structural conditions (World Bank 2001).

The Bank also emphasised a second concern: the necessity of improving governance, involving 'choice and implementation of public actions that are responsive to the needs of poor people [that] *depend on the interaction of political, social, and other institutional processes*' (emphasis added). That is, the Bank believed it was strongly necessary to encourage the involvement of various societal actors, both secular and faith-based, to try achieve improved development outcomes. Success would depend both on (1) 'active collaboration among poor people, the middle class (sic), and other groups in society', and (2) be linked to wider changes in style and outcomes relating to governance. These reforms were necessary, the Bank averred, so as to make public administration, legal institutions, and public service delivery more efficient and accountable to and for *all* citizens – rather than primarily serving the interests of a privileged few with best access to the 'levers of power' (World Bank 2001: 7). In short, the Bank accepted that to deliver enhanced participation in development required the inclusion of ordinary people and their representative organisations in decision-making structures and processes at various levels, from the local to the national. While the Bank did not specifically mention faith-based organisations in the *2000/2001 Report* there was a clear inference to its recommendations for better developmental outcomes: to achieve the MDGs in the short time span allotted – just 15 years – would require utilisation of all currently under-used human resources, including those of faith-based organisations.

Marshall and Keough pose the following question: 'How can development agencies and governments constructively integrate faith groups' perspectives on "poverty reduction" into their programs and policies when many faith groups do not view poverty reduction as the central question in the creation of more fulfilling, sustainable lifestyles?"' (Marshall and Keough 2004: 10). While the answer was not immediately clear, there was strong support for initiatives to involve faith-based organisations from the highest echelons of the Bank. At the time of the announcement of the MDGs, the World Bank was under the leadership of James D. Wolfensohn, a man of strong personal religious convictions. Wolfensohn noted that

> This is a powerful idea – to tap the strengths of religions as development actors. Consider economics, finance and administration as disciplines that are deeply ethical at the core ... they are about poverty reduction and employment creation. A vision without a task is boring. A task without a vision is awfully frustrating. A vision with a task can change the world (Wolfensohn n/d).

Wolfensohn, president of the Bank between 1995 and 2005, was instrumental in establishing the World Faiths Development Dialogue (WFDD),[2] engaging in an exchange of ideas about development with the World Council of Churches (WCC),[3] and helping establish The Development Dialogue on Values and Ethics (DDVE), a self-contained unit within the Human Development Network Vice-Presidency. The DDVE was established in 1998, following meetings between Wolfensohn and the then Archbishop of Canterbury, Dr George Carey. Its purpose was to be 'primarily responsible for engaging with faith institutions around development issues and working with other institutions and leaders who are addressing the complex ethical issues around globalization' (www.worldbank.org/developmentdialogue).

Marshall and Marsh (2003) report on a meeting held in Canterbury, England in October 2002, hosted by Wolfensohn and Carey, which centred on a range of human development issues. The gathering brought together an impressive group of leaders from some of the world's faith communities, key development organisations, and from the worlds of entertainment, philanthropy and the private sector. Couched within the context of the MDGs, the leading themes of the meeting were poverty, HIV/AIDS, gender, conflict, and social justice. Participants spoke on the various dimensions of and developmental ramifications of globalisation, as well as on its differential impact on rich and poor countries. It was noted that poverty, HIV/AIDS, conflict, gender concerns, international trade and global politics bind all the world's countries and peoples into a global community, emphasising the urgency of shared responsibility and partnership.

The DDVE initiative was led by a senior World Bank figure, Katherine Marshall.[4] In a speech delivered in June 2005, Marshall stated that the Bank did not believe 'that religion and socio-economic development belong to different spheres and are best cast in separate roles – even separate dramas'. Her observation was based on recognition that around the world many faith-based organisations and secular development agencies have similar key concerns, including: how to improve (1) the lot of materially poor people, (2) the societal position of those suffering from social exclusion, and (3) unfulfilled human potential in the context of glaring developmental polarisation within and between countries. In other words, while religion has often in the past been understood as 'other-worldly' and 'world-denying', Marshall notes that there is now much agreement both in the World Bank and within other secular development agencies that increased cooperation with faith-based organisations can usefully contribute to the achievement of developmental goals, not least because issues of right and wrong and social and economic justice are central to the teachings of the world religions (see below). As a result, the Bank sought to develop increased engagement with faith-based organisations under a general rubric, 'Shaping the Agenda – Faith & Development', and featuring three main areas of dialogue:

- Building bridges – stronger, bolder partnerships;
- Exploring a more 'comprehensive', 'holistic', and 'integrated' vision of development;
- Transforming dialogue into practice and action (http://web.world-bank.org/WBSITE/EXTERNAL/EXTABOUTUS/PARTNERS/EXTDEV-DIALOGUE/0,,menuPK:64193238~pagePK:64192526~piPK:64192494~theSitePK:537298,00.html).

In addition to World Bank initiatives, other secular development agencies were also active in developing dialogue with faith-based organisations from the early 2000s. Both the International Labour Organisation (ILO) and the IMF developed a relationship with the WCC. The Inter-American Development Bank (IDB), an affiliate of the World Bank, not only began an initiative entitled, 'Social Capital, Ethics, and Development' but also 'approached religious leaders to try to win the backing of their moral authority ...for its campaign in Latin America against corruption' (Tyndale 2004: 2). In addition, the United Nations Fund for Population Activities (UNFPA) worked on relations with various faith leaders, including Muslim Imams in Africa and Bangladesh ('Married adolescents ignored in global agenda, says UNFPA', 2004) The UNFPA also collaborated positively with religious leaders in Africa and, via a dialogue characterised by sensitivity and respect, educational programmes and programmes for women's empowerment were instituted. As Tyndale notes, such collaborations are only possible when both sides are ready to acknowledge that they have not got the whole answer (Tyndale 2004: 6).

In summary, various secular development agencies – including the World Bank, IMF, ILO and several UN agencies – sought to engage with faith-based organisations in initiatives designed to improve developmental outcomes for the world's poorest people. This followed a realisation that both secular and faith entities often shared similar development concerns, especially commitment to poverty alleviation as the crucial first stage in a wider and deeper process of human development. Their common ground linked them to a growing consensus that underpinned both the 2000 Millennium Declaration and the MDGs, the focal point of a United Nations Summit held in 2000 (Marshall 2005a, 2005b).

Having discussed the concept of development and the current engagement of some secular development agencies with faith-based organisations, it will now be useful to examine, first, the concept of religion and, second, how the four world religions featured in this book share many similar concerns about development issues.

Defining and conceptualising religion

First, we examine the term 'religion'. Although Huntington claims that, '[i]n the modern world, religion is central, perhaps *the* central, force that motivates and mobilizes people...' (Huntington 1996: 27), defining and conceptualising religion is a notoriously difficult task. Thinking of religion in relation to the developing world, the first problem is that the term, 'religion', is 'Eurocentric in nature' (Holenstein

2005: 7). This is because most languages of non-European cultures do not have an exactly corresponding equivalent term, whether semantically or in regard to content. Consequently, there is no conception of religion that can safely be used in inter-cultural and/or inter-religious contexts outside of Europe and the West more generally. It is necessary to take into account a more complicated set of relationships involving religion and culture than that inherent in most Western concepts and forms of language. Throughout the developing world, it is implausible to believe that the religious factor can be isolated from life's general context. This is because, irrespective of which faith we refer to, religions provide necessary concepts and ideas to answer people's existential questions; this turns into religiousness within individuals as meaning meets human needs.

There is a lack of agreement in defining religion among Western analysts. Marty (2000) begins his discussion of religion by listing 17 different definitions, before commenting that: 'Scholars will never agree on the definition of religion'. He himself does not attempt to offer a precise meaning – but does identify five 'phenomena that help describe what we're talking about ... [that] help point to and put boundaries around the term'. For Marty, religion

- Focuses our 'ultimate concern';
- Builds community;
- Appeals to myth and symbol;
- Is enforced through rites and ceremonies;
- Demands certain behaviour from its adherents (Marty 2000: 11–14).

These points collectively suggest that religion can usefully be thought of as: (1) a system of beliefs and practices – often but not necessarily related to an ultimate being, beings, or to the supernatural, and (2) involving that which is sacred in a society, including beliefs and practices which are widely regarded as inviolate. For purposes of social investigation, religion may also be approached (1) from the perspective of a body of ideas and outlooks – that is, as theology and ethical code, (2) as a type of formal organisation – that is, an ecclesiastical 'church', and/or (3) as a social group – that is, faith-based organisations. Religion can affect the world in two basic ways: by what it *says* and by what it *does*. The former relates to doctrine or theology, the latter to religion's importance as a social phenomenon and mark of identity, working through a variety of modes of institutionalisation, including church-state relations, civil society and political society (Aquaviva 1979; Haynes 1998).

While religions often differ greatly in terms of their beliefs and content, they can be divided into two broad categories: theistic – where a God or gods are worshipped – and non-theistic. The theistic religions can be divided further into a monotheistic group – where one God is worshipped – and a polytheistic group, where more than one god is the focus of attention. All three Abrahamic religions,[5] Christianity, Islam and Judaism, as well as Sikhism which derives from Hinduism, are theistic. In addition, there are numerous polytheistic religions, including: Shinto (Japan), the Native American Toltec tradition, and various expressions of new neo-paganism now emerging and developing in some parts of Europe (Ratzinger and Pera 2006). Notable non-theistic religions include: Buddhism, Jainism, and Taoism. Hinduism is both polytheistic *and* monotheistic. Most Hindus would probably contend that the religion's numerous deities are actually different manifestations of the One God. On the other hand, Hinduism is also non theistic in the sense that the metaphysics of Hindu Vedanta is almost identical to that of Buddhism (Knott 2000).

The issue of how many gods a religion has is not the key concern when we think of the involvement of faith-based organisations in human development. Most religious people would probably agree that true development is impossible without corresponding spiritual advancement, or, as Hindus would put it: 'all human activities are part of the sacred pattern of the universe' (International Consultancy on Religion Education and Culture 1998). More generally, as Tyndale notes, 'the collective wisdom of the world's major religions makes quite clear that unless more than a mere improvement of people's material conditions is aspired to, even that goal will fail. Human beings cannot, as the Christians teach, "live by bread alone"' (Tyndale 2001: 1). This suggests that there is a common metaphysical thread running through the world's major religions, encompassing a shared sense of 'oneness' of name and form that is believed to permeate our world. This sense of 'oneness' is 'described as the "Great One" in the Dead Sea Scrolls and as God the Father in Christianity. It is referred to as *Sunyata* in Buddhism and as *Brahman* in Hindu Vedanta. ... [T]his concept of oneness occurs in so many different locations in the holy books and verbal transmissions of all the religions of the world' (MacDowell and Utukuru 2005).

In conclusion, religions are often fervently interested in how to achieve better human development. This is reflected in the fact that many share a common concern of crucial importance to human development: poverty alleviation. In addition, as the Catholic theologian, Hans Küng points out, all major religions share certain core ethical principles. This underlines that they have in common a sense of the value of the human being that is independent of specific religions and confessions. Küng's hope is that the construction of what he calls a 'world ethos', that is a global ethic, will elevate these commonalities at their heart while stimulating them to arrive at an understanding about what they hold in common (Holenstein 2005: 23–4). In sum, the involvement of religions in human development takes us beyond the merely material aspects of development to include a more intangible, spiritual aspect that some see as evidence of their shared and collective concerns.

Articulating human development: basic beliefs of Buddhism, Christianity, Hinduism, and Islam

To fill in any gaps in the reader's basic knowledge of the major world religions which feature in this book, the second part of this section briefly examines some of their basic beliefs. This will facilitate understanding of how religious beliefs inform the behaviour of faith-based organisations in relation to human development. Prior to that, in the first part of the section, we identify and briefly discuss five areas of common concern in the world religions that are all related to the achievement of human development goals: fighting poverty; service provision; popular regard for religious leaders; faith communities as community organisations; and ethical and moral issues.

Fighting poverty is a key issue for each of the world religions on which we focus in this book. Buddhism, Christianity, Hinduism and Islam are all centrally concerned with three sets of deprived people, often in practice the same people: those who are excluded, those who suffer and those who are materially poor. As a result, there is a clear overlap in areas of concern, interest and engagement among not only these world faiths but also secular development organisations. Not only at the Millennium Summit in 2000, but also in earlier summits since the 1980s, there was frequent and clear concern expressed about the plight of the poorest of the poor, sometimes termed 'the lowest 40 percent' (www.un.org/millennium/summit.htm). For many religious people, the sense of a common bond between the faith traditions and the development world is a very compelling inspiration for dialogue and action.

Second, there is the area of faith-based organisations' of often exten-sive service provision in many parts of the developing world. This is a crucial issue from the point of view of the secular development agen-cies and attainment of human development goals, in relation not only to the achievement of improvements in both education and health but also in relation to provision of humanitarian relief, social safety nets for the poor and deprived in society, and support for children without parents and the disabled. These concerns are not only all crucial aspects of many ancient traditions but, as we shall see in forthcoming chapters, are also key concerns for numerous faith-based organisations.

Third, according to many recent analyses and polls – such as, the 'Voices of the Poor' work done by the World Bank and the Latinobarómetro poll – most people in the developing world have higher trust levels for faith-based organisations, compared to secular institutions, including: politicians, governments, and the police (Narayan *et al* 2000). The key point here is that in order to do effective development work with communities in the developing world, the building of trust is crucial if initiatives are to have any chance of success, and building on and working with the trust placed in faith-based organisations is very important.

Fourth, faith-based organisations have often unrivalled coverage and depth of presence among communities in the developing world, implying a pronounced – usually, unrivalled – ability to reach and talk to people. As faith-based organisations are ubiquitous in most parts of the developing world, often with the status of the most significant community organisations, especially in places where governments and infrastructures are weakest, their potential and in many cases actually developmental role can be hugely significant, as we shall see in later chapters.

Finally, and this is usually seen as perhaps the most complex issue in relation to faith involvement in development, faith-based organisa-tions have for long periods sought to address some of the most complex ethical and moral issues that societies face. The business of development does not escape this concern, as it confronts many such issues. This is because development necessarily implies and involves often profound transformation, with major and often abrupt depar-tures from traditional ways, and related changes in individual and soci-etal behaviour. Faith-based organisations often face a difficult trade off: how to reconcile ancient, culturally-based wisdom with the changes necessary for improvements in development outcomes for example in relation to education, health and gender issues. In addition, dealing with issues of corruption, for example, often leads to intense dialogue between secular development agencies and faith-based organisations, with discussions often centring on finding the best ways to deal with what, all parties would agree, 'is a very complex set of behaviours and incentives that affect people in so many parts of the world, rich and poor, and that bind them together across national boundaries in intricately elaborate ways' (Marshall 2006).

Next we look at core beliefs of Buddhism, Christianity, Hinduism and Islam.

Buddhism

The Dalai Lama, leader of Tibetan Buddhism living in exile in India as a result of China's takeover of the country, has remarked that: 'Every religion emphasizes human improvement, love, respect for others, sharing other people's suffering. On these lines every religion had more or less the same viewpoint and the same goal' (quoted in Hirohita 2002).

Around the world, there were an estimated 708 million Buddhists in 2005 (http://www.buddhanet.net/e-learning/history/bstatt10.htm). Buddhism is divided into three main schools: Mahayana (56%), Theravada (38%) and Vajrayana (6%). Rather than a religion as such, Buddhism is both a philosophy and moral practice, whose overall purpose is to work towards the relief of suffering in existence by ridding one of desire. Buddhism is based on the teachings of the Buddha, Siddhartha Gautama (in the Sanskrit form; Siddhattha Gotama in the Pāli form), who lived between approximately 563 and 483 BCE. While there are very large differences between different Buddhist schools of thought they all share an overall purpose and aim: to liberate the individual from suffering (*dukkha*). While some interpretations stress stirring the practitioner to the awareness of *anatta* (egolessness, the absence of a permanent or substantial self) and the achievement of enlightenment and Nirvana, others (such as the 'Tathagatagarbha' sutras) promote the idea that the practitioner should seek to purify him/herself of both mental and moral defilements that is a key aspect of the 'worldly self' and, as a result, break through to an understanding of the indwelling 'Buddha-Principle' ('Buddha-nature', also termed the 'True Self') and thus become transformed into a Buddha. Some Buddhist interpretations beseech *bodhisattvas* (that is, enlightened beings who, out of compassion, forgo Nirvana in order to save others) for a favourable rebirth. Others, however, do none of these things. What most, if not all, Buddhist schools also encourage followers to undertake both good and wholesome actions, and consequently not do bad and harmful actions.

Buddhism began in India, and gradually spread throughout Asia to Central Asia, Tibet, Sri Lanka and South-East Asia, as well as to China, Mongolia, Korea, and Japan in East Asia. At the current time, several Asian countries have majority Buddhist populations: Thailand (95% Buddhist), Cambodia (90%), Myanmar (88%), Bhutan (75%), Sri Lanka (70%), Tibet (an autonomous region of China; 65%), Laos (60%), Vietnam (55%). Other Asian countries with significant Buddhist populations include: Japan (50%) and Taiwan (43%). In recent years, in South-East Asia, where economic development has generally taken a Western-style secular route: focusing often single-mindedly on economic growth without adequate consideration for environmental sustainability, social justice, cultural diversity and spiritual well-being. This 'economic growth at all costs' approach has however created much existential suffering among many people in these countries, many of which are traditional Buddhist societies. In response, a 'socially engaged' Buddhism has emerged in recent years, whose frame of reference involves a critical embrace of traditional values and cautious critical selection and integration of appropriate values from modernisation. Socially engaged Buddhism is an attempt to renew ancient wisdom using Buddhism as a guideline to confront contemporary suffering in an inclusive way. It advocates changing one 's consciousness side-by-side with transforming structural violence in society (Hutanuwatr and Rasbach 2004).

Christianity

There were an estimated 2.12 billion Christians in 2005 (Center for the Study of Global Christianity 2006), found in probably every country in the world, with major populations in Europe, the Americas, Africa and parts of Asia. Christianity is a faith with foundations in the teachings of Jesus, regarded by Christians as the Son of God. Jesus is the second component of a Trinity, comprising: God the Father, Jesus the Son, and the Holy Spirit. Christians believe that Jesus's life on earth, his crucifixion, resurrection, and subsequent ascension to heaven are signs not only of God's love for humankind but also his forgiveness of human sins. Christianity also includes a belief that through faith in Jesus individuals may attain salvation and eternal life. These teachings are contained within the Bible, especially the New Testament, although Christians also accept the Old Testament as sacred and authoritative Scripture.

The ethics of Christianity draw to a large extent from the Jewish tradition as presented in the Old Testament, notably the Ten Commandments. There is however some difference of interpretation between them as a result of the practice and teachings of Jesus. Christianity can be further defined generally through its concern with the practice of corporate worship and certain rites. These include the use of sacraments – including the traditional seven rites that were instituted by Jesus and recorded in the New Testament and that confer sanctifying grace (the Eastern Orthodox, Roman Catholic, and some other Western Christian churches) and in most other Western Christian churches, by two rites: Baptism and the Eucharist, instituted by Jesus to confer sanctifying grace.

Since Pope Paul VI's encyclical, Populorum Progressio (1967; http://www.vatican.va/holy_father/paul_vi/encyclicals/documents/hf_p-vi_enc_26031967_populorum_en.html), Roman Catholic social teachings have consistently expressed a Catholic view of development. This emphasises the contributions of 'spiritual disciplines and of ethical action to a person's "vocation to human fulfillment", addressed alongside contributions made by markets, public policy, and poverty reduction' (Alkire 2004: 10). Explicit Catholic articulations of concern about human development are also to be found in the radical ideas of liberation theology, a set of ideas that emerged in Latin America in the 1960s. The core of liberation theology is a demand for greater social and economic justice for the poor in the name of Christian values, with explicit reference to the Christian Gospel demands for 'a preferential option for the poor'. This demands that Catholics be involved in the struggle for economic and political justice in the contemporary world – particularly in the developing world, where inequalities and injustices are often pronounced. The tenets of liberation theology were instrumental in bringing together millions of people in Latin America and elsewhere in the developing world in what were known in the former as comunidades de base (English, [Christian] Base Communities). Their aim was to study the Bible and use its relevant passages as a basis to fight against social and developmental injustices. Gustavo Gutierrez, a Peruvian priest, famously articulated liberation theology in his book, A Theology of Liberation. History, Politics and Salvation (1973). Liberation theology fell from favour among many Catholic leaders, including most importantly Pope John Paul II (1979–2005), who criticised both the ideas and their advocates, accusing them of wrongly supporting violent revolution and Marxist class struggle.

Representatives of other religious faiths, including Judaism and Buddhism, have also advanced similar kinds of development interpretations to that of Gutierrez. Distinct liberation theologies have also been articulated by other major faiths. For example, various popular books have focused on a similar people-centred development perspective, for example, Bernardo Klicksberg's *Social Justice: A Jewish Perspective* (2003) and, from a Buddhist perspective, Sulak Sivaraksa and Ginsburg's *Seeds of Peace* (1992).

Hinduism

Hinduism is the Western term for the religious beliefs and practices of most of the 1.1 billion people of India. Of the total global Hindu population of more than 1.2 billion (Center for the Study of Global Christianity 2006), over 90% (more than 800 million) live in India. Other countries with a significant Hindu population include: Nepal (22.5m.), Bangladesh (14.4m.), Indonesia (4.3m.), Pakistan (3.3m.), Sri Lanka (3m.), Malaysia (1.5m.), Mauritius (600,000), Bhutan (560,000), Fiji (300,000), and Guyana (270,000). In addition, the Indonesian islands of Bali, Java, Sulawesi, Sumatra, and Borneo all have significant native Hindu populations.

Hinduism is one of the oldest living religions in the world, unique among the world religions in that it had no single founder but grew over a period of 4,000 years in syncretism with the religious and cultural movements of the Indian subcontinent. Hinduism is composed of innumerable sects and has no well-defined ecclesiastical organisation. Its two most general features are the caste system and acceptance of the Veda – that is, the oldest and most authoritative Hindu sacred texts, composed in Sanskrit and gathered into four collections – as the most sacred scriptures.

Hinduism's salient characteristics include an ancient mythology, an absence of recorded history (or 'founder'), a cyclical notion of time, a pantheism that infuses divinity into the world around, an immanentist[6] relationship between people and divinity, a priestly class, and a tolerance of diverse paths to the ultimate ('god'). Its sacral language is Sanskrit, which came to India about 5,000 years ago along with the Aryans, who came from Central Asia. It is a varied corpus, comprising religion, philosophy, and cultural practice that are both indigenous to and prevalent in India. The faith is characterised by a belief in rebirth and a supreme being that can take many forms and types, by the perception that contrasting theories are all aspects of an eternal truth, and by its followers pursuit of liberation from earthly evils.

For Hindus, the aim is holistic human development and the complete fulfilment of all needs – material, moral and spiritual (Oommen

1992). According to Gupta, Hinduism's transcendental view of reality offers new possibilities to an understanding of the notion of human development. As a result,

> it becomes possible to view different cultural views of development as contextual views derived from the One Supreme Reality. It allows human beings to become instruments of divine expression in new myriad ways. It allows for creative dialogue across cultures and religions with some a-priori notions to begin with but with no apriori end points. Here one can posit the possibilities of new unthought forms and directions of human development. Development, then, becomes an open-ended pursuit rather than some societies catching up with the others (Gupta 2004: 3).

Islam

There were an estimated 1.3 billion Muslims in the word in 2005 (Center for the Study of Global Christianity 2006). Like Christians, Muslims are found in probably every country in the world, with major populations throughout the Middle East, Africa and parts of Asia.

The origins of Islam are found in an allegiance to God, articulated by his prophet Mohammed (c.570–632 CE). Mohammed was born in Mecca (in present day Saudi Arabia) and over a period of 23 years received revelations from an angel (Jibreel, or Gabriel), who Mohammed believed was relaying the word of God. For Muslims, Mohammed was the last in a series of prophets, which included Abraham, Moses and Jesus, who refined and restated the message of God. After Mohammed's death in 632, Muslims divided into two strands, Shia and Sunni. The Shiites are followers of the caliph (that is, leader of an Islamic polity, regarded as a successor of Mohammed and by tradition always male) Abu Bakr and those who supported Mohammed's closest relative, his son-in-law, Ali ibn Abi Talib. Overall, Shiites place more emphasis on the guiding role of the caliph. The Sunnis, on the other hand, are the majority sect within Islam, followers of the *custom* of the caliphate rather than an individual caliph, such as Ali.

About 85–90% of the world's Muslims are Sunni and about 10–15% are Shia. The Shia-Sunni division still persists, although both share most of the key customs of Islam. Both Shiites and Sunnis share five fundamental beliefs:

- *Shahada* (profession of faith in the uniqueness of Allah and the centrality of Mohammed as his prophet;

- *Salat* (formal worship or prayer);
- *Zakat* (giving of alms for the poor, assessed on all adult Muslims as 2.5% of capital assets once a year);
- *Hajj* (pilgrimage to Mecca, which every Muslim should undertake at least once in their lifetime; the annual hajj takes place during the last ten days of the 12th lunar month every year);
- *Sawm* (fasting during Ramadan, the holy 9th month of the lunar year).

According to Ahmad, human development implies within Islam: (1) the idea of an individual improving his or her capabilities and potentials, and (2) progression from a starting point towards an improved position of greater achievement, opportunity and individual and community benefit. Three steps are required to achieve better human development outcomes: define goals one wishes to achieve; identify the factors that influence their achievement; and assess what steps are needed to achieve them. Islam understands that every person is born with some inherent faculties, but how they are moulded and developed depends on an individual's inherent capacities, the environment within which they live, and various external influences.

Within Islam there is much emphasis on 'self-development' – that is, where individuals take the main responsibility to understand the purpose of human life, and for shaping that life in the best possible manner – for the individual, the community and, more generally, the wider society. For the faith's followers, the tenets of Islam provide comprehensive guidance for achieving better human development. Within Islam, two main sources are identified that can significantly influence human development outcomes. On the one hand, inspiration from divine guidance nurtures human development. On the other hand, failing to pay sufficient attention to God's guidance and instead 'succumbing to conspiracies, arising from within or external environment, corrupts human development' leads to human development failures (Ahmad 2003).

Writing from an Islamic viewpoint, Seyyed Hussein Nasr focuses on the link between modernisation and development, and emphasises how important it is for development to be closely concerned with religion. For Nasr, 'non-religious' development will inevitably – and fatally – distract Muslims from what is their 'true' – that is, religious – nature and, as a result, seriously undermine their chances of living appropriately (Nasr 1975). Finally, as Bouta *et al.* note, 'Islam has a direct impact on the way that peace is conceptualised and the way that conflicts are resolved in Islamic societies, as it embodies and elaborates upon its highest morals, ethical principles and ideals of social harmony ... (Bouta *et al.* 2005: 11).

In summary, the world religions with significant followings in the developing world – Buddhism, Christianity, Hinduism and Islam – feature a variety of beliefs and understandings. Yet they share a significant concern with human development, especially a focus on and commitment to poverty reduction, justice and equality.

Conclusion

To attempt to bring together the spheres of religion and human development and then try to discern and interpret significant patterns and trends is not a simple task. In attempting it in this book, we shall emphasise three points. First, there is something of a distinction to be drawn between looking at the relationship in terms of the impact of religion on development, and that of development on religion. At the same time, they are interactive: effects of one stimulate and are stimulated by the other. Overall, however, we are primarily concerned with how religion – especially in the form of faith-based organisations – affect human development outcomes. We shall see that the relationship is both dialectical and interactive: each shapes and influences the other.

Second, *all* religions are both creative and constantly changing; consequently their relationships with other actors – both religious and secular – vary over time. As we saw above the general nature of the relationship between faith-based and secular development agencies and governments has changed significantly in recent years, characterised by much closer relations in the context of the MDGs, announced in 2000.

Third, Gopin suggests that it is very likely that all religions have developed laws and ideas that provide civilisation with cultural commitments to critical peace-related values. These include: empathy, an openness to and even love for strangers, the suppression of unbridled ego and acquisitiveness, human rights, unilateral gestures of forgiveness and humility, interpersonal repentance and the acceptance of responsibility of past error as a means of reconciliation, and the drive for social justice (Gopin 2000: 13).

The remainder of the book is structured as follows. Chapter 1 examines the rise in prominence of faith-based organisations in relation to development outcomes. It seeks to set the scene for later analysis while answering a basic question: Why do faith-based organisations have a higher profile in relation to development issues now compared to two or three decades ago? To answer the question the chapter stresses the interconnections between religious resurgence, 'good governance', and often complex processes of globalisation that are seen to stimulate both increased cooperation and more conflict, with attendant results for human development outcomes.

Chapter 2 has two aims. First, it seeks to ascertain in what ways religion relates to development issues in the developing world, by reference to ideas, practices and experiences. Second, it puts forward a simple typology of faith-based entities active in development in the developing world. One general category of such actors operates at the international level, while another focuses on development outcomes within countries, both nationally and locally. The latter category is subdivided into 'pro-development' or 'anti-development' entities, conventionally identified, although as we shall see such a dichotomy is problematic. This is because such labels are regularly applied in the mostly secular relevant literature, coming at the issue not from a religious perspective but from one that sees development in rather conventional terms, primarily focusing on beneficial development outcomes that increase people's well-being in ways traditionally highlighted in much of the development literature: more and better education, welfare, health, clean water, and so on. As already noted, however, many religious people do not necessarily see development issues in the same materialistic ways. Instead, many highlight the human development aspects of 'development' that for them include both religious and spiritual dimensions.

The third chapter focuses on religion's role in conflict, conflict-resolution and peace-building in the developing world. Overall, it examines how religion can (1) both encourage conflict and peace in the developing world, and (2) offers examples – from Mozambique, Nigeria and Cambodia – of religious peacemakers who are significant in attempts to reconcile previously warring communities and achieve social cohesion, crucial foundations of progress in human development.

Chapters 4–7 turn our attention to the role of faith-based organisations in helping achieve the MDGs by 2015. Chapter 4 examines the relationship between faith-based organisations, economic growth, poverty and hunger. Chapter 5 focuses upon what faith-based organisations are doing in the developing world to increase chances of environmental sustainability. Chapter 6 does the same task in relation to their role in the delivery of improved healthcare, while Chapter 7 looks at faith-based entities' involvement in educational provision for both children and adults. The final chapter, Conclusion, sums up the book's findings in relation to religion's involvement in achievement of human development goals in the developing world regions of sub-Saharan Africa, Asia and Latin America.

1
Religious Resurgence, Globalisation, and Good Governance

[R]eligion is enormously important in guiding the choices of billions of people. Religion influences viewpoints on individual agency and collective responsibility. It profoundly shapes development agendas and people's willingness to be involved in them. In this sense, understanding faith is central to developing policies that will say – and do – something meaningful about poverty (Marshall and Keough 2004: 24).

In our globalised world there is more opportunity than ever before for organisations and groups from different religions to work together on development issues. Nevertheless, there is still relatively little co-operation among people from different religious traditions, either in the practical work they do or at the level of policy discussions, even though they may be saying and doing similar things (WFDD homepage at: http://www.wfdd.org.uk/aboutus.html).

The preceding chapter traced the theory and practice of the concept of development in the decades after World War II. We saw that while for years 'development' was understood principally as a state directed endeavour, in many developing countries outcomes were disappointing. Following the end of the Cold War in the late 1980s and deepening of globalisation in the 1990s, the hitherto exclusively secular focus of development theory and practice underwent a change. Faith-based organisations[1] were encouraged to become key partners – along with secular agencies – in a renewed drive for better human development in the developing world. Efforts were focused in the eight MDGs, announced in 2000 for achievement by 2015. Many faith-based organisations assumed a higher public profile than before in relation to human development. Their rise in prominence came in a wider context of change, reflecting three interlinked developments: religious resurgence; deepening globalisation; and demands for 'good governance' throughout much of the developing world.

This chapter examines the general rise in prominence of faith-based organisations in relation to development outcomes in recent years. It sets the scene for later analysis and seeks to answer a basic question: Why do many faith-based organisations now have higher profiles in relation to development issues compared to two or three decades ago? The chapter stresses interconnections between religious resurgence, 'good governance', and often complex processes of globalisation that are widely seen to stimulate both increased cooperation and more conflict, with attendant results for human development outcomes (Berger 1999; Thomas 2005; Beyer 2006; Haynes 2007).

Explaining religious resurgence

Anybody who had predicted '30 years ago that the 20th century would end with a resurgence of religion, with great new cathedrals, mosques, and temples rising up, with the symbols and songs of faith everywhere apparent, would, in most circles, have been derided' (Woollacott 1995).

In the modern world, religion is central, perhaps *the* central, force that motivates and mobilizes people... (Huntington 1996: 27).

Claims that the world would experience a 'religious resurgence' at the end of the 20th century and the beginning of the 21st would have been widely treated with scepticism a few years ago. Secularisation appeared to have made such inroads into many previously religious societies, particularly in Western Europe, that it was all but inevitable that religion would continue to decline in the modern world through a combination of technological advancement and associated undermining of traditional cultures. According to the theologian Harvey Cox, this meant that growing numbers of people around the world would live in highly secular environments (Cox 1968). In the 1960s, Cox was an influential secularisation theorist who, 20 years later, reversed his position. According to Cox, evidence that religion's influence was growing not declining was to be found primarily in the rise of sundry 'religious grassroots movements', including expressions of religious fundamentalism, as well as Pentecostalism and vehicles of liberation theology (Cox 1984).

Peter Berger, an eminent sociologist of religion who, like Harvey Cox, was once a leading proponent of the secularisation thesis, argued that 'far from being in decline in the modern world, religion is actually experiencing a resurgence ... the assumption we live in a secularized world is false.... The world today is as furiously religious as it ever was' (Berger 1999: 3). According to Berger, processes of 'modernisation' did not weaken religion – but actually strengthened it, often increasing its public significance, especially in the developing world. In recent years, the perception of religion's growing influence has been accepted by a growing number of observers and analysts, with some claiming to see a near-global religious resurgence (Moghadam 2003; Petito and Hatzopoulos 2003; Thomas 2005).[2] Overall, the main claim is that religion's influence is increasing, *contra* the secularisation thesis, with social, political, economic and developmental influence in many parts of the globe, especially the developing world.[3] Berger (1999) contends that religious movements and faith-based organisations have not adapted to secular culture merely in order to survive – but instead have managed successfully not only to develop their own identities but also to retain focus on the supernatural in their beliefs and practices. In response to Berger's claims, Norris and Inglehart comment that 'some of these reported phenomena may have been overstated, but the simplistic assumption that religion was everywhere in decline, common in earlier decades, ha[s] become implausible to even the casual observer' (Norris and Inglehart 2004: 215–16).

Numerous religious actors are now publicly interested in a variety of areas of concern with direct relevance for human development, including: economic growth; conflict, conflict resolution and peace-building; human rights; and social justice. Such concerns are found in a variety of countries, at differing levels of human development and economic growth. They include: the *United States*, especially the continuing vitality of the Religious Right; an evangelical revival in various countries in *Latin America*; new religious emphases in post-Communist *Central and Eastern Europe*; reported renaissance of Islam in the *Middle East* and elsewhere in the Muslim world; and growing evidence that in many *African* and *Asian* countries various religious practices and beliefs thrive (Beyer 2006; Thomas 2005; Haynes 2007).

Why have various religious actors entered or re-entered various – political, social, economic and development – debates? Berger maintains that, despite often significant differences, many share a critique of secularity, believing that human 'existence bereft of transcendence is an impoverished and finally untenable condition' (Berger 1999: 4). This suggests that a common human desire for transcendence – that is, a state of being or existence above and beyond the limits of material experience – is an integral part of the human psyche, and secularity – that is, the condition or quality of being secular – does not allow for this necessary sense of transcendence. Without a sense of transcendence, life for many people is unsatisfactorily empty.

Thomas contends that in the developing world the widespread failure of development and consequent disillusionment with neo-liberal economic policies has led to much 'dissatisfaction with the project of the postcolonial secular state and conflict between religious nationalism and secular nationalism'. He also suggests that religious resurgence has become part of a search for 'roots' identity for many people in post-colonial countries, as they reject the modernising paradigm as an external force and seek an 'authentic' alternative to the failed policies of the West. The implication is that across the developing world religion has been widely politicised by the 'crisis of modernity' and its associated failure to produce development (Thomas 2000: 49).

Many observers agree that widespread feelings of disappointment and emptiness are linked to the effects of modernisation (involving urbanisation, industrialisation and swift technological developments) coupled with declining faith in the redemptive qualities of secular ideologies. As a result, many people experience feelings of loss and sadness rather than achievement – even though their material lifestyles may well be improving (Esposito and Burgat 2002; Sacks 2003; Scruton 2005). Secular development programmes and policies – that undermine 'traditional' value systems in the developing world while often allocating opportunities in highly unequal ways – produced in many people a deep sense of alienation while doing little if anything to improve development outcomes (Haynes 1993). Some people in the developing world responded to political, social, and economic disappointments by turning or returning to religion to give their lives meaning and purpose. In addition, the rise of a global consumerist culture led to expressions of aversion at the soulless-ness of modern life, for many religious groups a key concern (Thomas 2005). The overall result was a resurgence of religion – in countries with differing political and ideological systems, at various levels of economic development, and with diverse religious traditions – often with implications for development outcomes in the developing world.

Resurgent religion does not only relate to personal beliefs but also leads to a desire to grapple with social, economic and political issues. 'Because it is so reliable a source of emotion, religion is a recurring source of social movement framing. Religion provides ready-made symbols, rituals, and solidarities that can be accessed and appropriated by movement leaders' (Tarrow 1998: 112). Such religious actors are found in many different faiths and sects, yet share a key characteristic: a desire to change domestic arrangements so as to increase religion's influence. They adopt various tactics to try to achieve their goals. Some protest, lobby, or otherwise seek to encourage decision makers to adopt certain policies and others, often underpinned by involvement in civil society. Overall, numerous religious actors of various kinds seek to engage in current political, economic and social debates, in both domestic and international contexts. The forms these interventions take in relation to development outcomes in the developing world will be examined in forthcoming chapters.

Globalisation: challenges and opportunities for religion

The critical debate on globalization has been subdued since September 11. But the important issues it raises have not gone away, and need to remain at the core of national and international policy agendas. The tragic events of September 11 have surely widened public understanding and shaken the complacency that led many to behave as if developments in remote countries and societies could be safely ignored (Köhler 2002).

Processes of change and religious resurgence are often linked to the impact of globalisation, a topical, controversial and at times violent issue (Scholte 2005). In recent years, concerned by the perceived unfair and unjust socio-economic impact of transnational business corporations in particular and an increasingly globalised capitalism in general, anti-globalisation protesters – some of whom came from faith-based organisations – have periodically demonstrated – sometimes even fighting police – at regular Group of 7 (G7) summits (Held and McGrew 2002: 56–9).[4] In addition, the attacks on the World Trade Center in New York and the Pentagon in Washington on 11th September 2001, to which the head of the IMF, Horst Köhler refers in the previous quotation, also had profound global ramifications: religion was afforded 'a high place on the agendas of those concerned with globalization. Yet, the issues and the ways of responding are far from clear' (Society for the Scientific Study of Religion 2001).

The first problem is to agree as to what globalisation actually *is*. While there are numerous – sometimes competing – definitions, there is wide agreement that globalisation is a continuing means by which the world is more and more characterised by common activity. This emphasises how many highly important aspects of life – including wars, crime, trade and culture – are becoming now often globally inter-related. There is also acceptance that globalisation is also a matter of a change in consciousness: people from various spheres, including religion, business, sport, politics and many other activities, now think and act in a context characterised by an increasingly 'globalised' world (Haynes 2005a). A third point of concurrence is that 'territoriality' – a term signifying a close connection or limitation with reference to a particular geographic area or country – now has less significance than it once did. This suggests increasing interdependence, a process that captures both states and non-states, with what happens in one part of the world consistently affecting many others. Overall, globalisation reflects the fact that humankind is experiencing a 'historically unique *increase of scale* to a global interdependency among people and nations', characterised by (1) rapid integration of the world economy, (2) innovations and growth in international electronic communications, and (3) increasing 'political and cultural awareness of the global interdependency of humanity' (Warburg 2001).

In summary, globalisation is a wide-ranging phenomenon, often understood primarily in terms of its economic impact (Hirst and Thompson 2002). But this is by no means the whole story. To understand important current interactions between religion and globalisation, we need to take into account not only economic but also globalisation's technological, political, and cultural aspects. Consider the following:

> The various definitions of globalization in social science all converge on the notion that, as a result of technological and social change, human activities across regions and continents are increasingly being linked together (Keohane 2002: 31).

> Spatial reorganisation of production, the interpenetration of industries across borders, the spread of financial markets, the diffusion of identical consumer goods to distant countries, massive transfers of population within the South as well as from the South and the East to the West, resultant conflicts between immigrant and established communities in formerly tight-knit neighbourhoods, an emerging

worldwide preference for democracy. A rubric for varied phenomena, the concept of globalisation interrelates multiple levels of
analysis (Mittelman 1994: 429).

The term 'globalization' has come to be emotionally charged in
public discourse. For some, it implies the promise of an international civil society, conducive to a new era of peace and democratization. For others, it implies the threat of an American economic
and political hegemony, with its cultural consequence being a
homogenized world resembling a sort of metastasized Disneyland
(charmingly called a 'cultural Chernobyl' by a French government
official) (Berger 2003: 1).

These quotations collectively emphasise that globalisation is a controversial and multifaceted process underpinned by significant intensification
of global interconnectedness. They also point to the idea that globalisation implies diminution of the significance of territorial boundaries
and, theoretically, state-dominated structures and processes. A third
emphasis is that globalisation has different dimensions that heurist-
ically can be separated into economic, political, cultural and technological aspects that collectively influence how religions and other
actors behave (Baylis and Smith 2005; Thomas 2005). The combined
impact of these processes of globalisation is 'globalism', implying 'a
state of the world involving networks of interdependence at multi-
continental distances, linked through flows of capital and goods, information and ideas, people and force, as well as environmentally and
biologically relevant substances' (Keohane 2002: 31). Thus *globalism*
refers to the reality of being interconnected, while *globalisation* denotes
the speed at which these connections grow – or diminish. Overall, the
concept of globalism 'seeks to ... understand all the inter-connections
of the modern world – and to highlight patterns that underlie (and
explain) them' (Nye 2002).

Most observers and analysts interested in development issues would
probably agree that globalisation is an important phenomenon. But
there is little agreement regarding precisely *how* globalisation changes
our understanding of development – beyond the general idea that the
core of globalisation implies increasing interdependence between states
and peoples, with what happens in one part of the world affecting
what happens elsewhere. Instead, there are debates about globalisation
and its impact, and such exchanges are often polarised, sometimes
rather simplistically conducted along the lines of 'Is globalisation a

"good" or a "bad" thing?' For example, in reference to the latter interpretation, some see the term 'globalisation' as nothing more than a cover
for a thoroughly malign – and comprehensive – Westernising process.
In this view, globalisation is inherently undesirable, a process whereby
Western – especially American – capitalism and culture seek to dominate the world. As a result, it is believed, the Western world is kept rich
at the expense of the poverty of many non-Western parts of the world.
This is possible because, many contend, Western interests determine
trading terms, interest rates and dominance of highly mechanised
production, via its control of important international institutions, such
as the World Trade Organisation (WTO) (Held and McGrew 2002).

An alternative view of globalisation is to emphasise that it offers
enhanced opportunities for international cooperation in relation to
various issues, including social development and human rights, as well
as conflict resolution and peace-building. Globalisation is also seen to
enhance the chances of international cooperation to resolve a range of
economic, developmental, social, political, environmental, gender, and
human rights concerns and injustices. In particular, the end of the
Cold War was seen to offer an unprecedented opportunity for collective efforts involving both state and non-state actors to deal with a
range of global concerns. For many, progress would be enhanced by
bottom-up contributions from local groups and grassroots organisations around the world, including various religious organisations and
movements (Thomas 2005; Beyer 2006; Grey 2003).

Religious responses to globalisation

To deal with the opportunities and problems provided with globalisation requires both cooperation and the development of appropriate
institutions. What might be the basis of such cooperation? A basis of
shared principles and rules might provide a firm foundation to engage
both true commitment and support of many people around the world.
This underlines that both citizens and governments need to believe
not only that their voices will be taken into account but also that
their interests will be recognised. As the late Pope John Paul II said at a
gathering of religious leaders in Assisi, Italy, in 2002, listening to one
another 'serves to scatter the shadows of suspicion and misunderstand-
ing' (www.va/holy_father/john_paul_ii/speeches/2002/january/docu-
ments/hf_jp-ii_spe_20020124_discorso-assisi_en.html). Consequently,
it is important that all governments live up to their responsibilities
and take into account the effects of their actions on other governments and countries. Linked to this is the issue of international

decision-making, for example within the World Bank and the IMF, which should try harder to respect national and local responsibilities, religions, cultures, and traditions (Marshall and Keough 2004). In this context, faith-based organisations can be influential in building bridges of tolerance between the world's peoples and religions. This emphasises that as a principle, global action might usefully, as Köhler suggests, 'be built upon a foundation of inclusion, broad participation and local initiative'. And finally, a global economy also needs a more developed sense of global ethics, which reflect greater respect for human rights while also recognising the importance of both personal and social responsibility. In short, 'no matter what their religious convictions, people living together in local communities have always recognized and responded to common moral principles, such as sharing with those who have less, and protection of the vulnerable. As the world has become more integrated and interdependent, the scope for applying such fundamental values has widened' (Köhler 2002).

This might be termed the 'optimistic' version of what can happen when religions seek to work together. A more 'pessimistic' verdict might be that such strategies to try to deal with the 'downside' of globalisation are currently often more aspirational than rooted in reality. This is because the connection between economic and religious globalisation is a volatile mixture and as a result attempts to develop further development cooperation can be problematic. For example, religious 'fundamentalism' in the developing world often emerges and develops primarily as a reaction against modernisation and perceived imposition of democratisation processes that appear characteristic of western-style modernity, as well as against the globalised economy and the lecturing culture of the West. For its adherents religious 'fundamentalism' can provide a source of identity that, in alliance with conservative politics, strives for religious, cultural, political, and economic supremacy (Armstrong 2001). In short, it is important religion is not misused, to become 'a fig leaf in order to push through [unrestrained] economic globalisation on the western model' (Holenstein 2005: 32).

In summary, globalisation is a multifaceted process of change affecting states, communities and individuals. Faith-based organisations are not of course exempted from its influence and, as a result, like other social agents, they participate in and are affected by globalisation in various ways. Academic discussions of religion and globalisation – Roland Robertson (1995), Peter Beyer (1994, 2006) and James Spickard

(2001, 2003) are important voices – often highlight trends towards cultural pluralism as a result of globalisation, examining how various faith-based organisations respond. Some react positively, by accepting or even endorsing pluralism, such as 'some Christian ecumenical movements or the Baha'is. Other groups emphasise the differences and confront the non-believers in an attempt to preserve their particular values from being eroded by globalisation. So-called fundamentalist Christian, Muslim, and Jewish movements are well-known examples' (Warburg 2001).

Overall, the relationship between religion and globalisation is characterised on the one hand by tension between forces that lead to *integration* in globalisation and on the other hand by *resistance* to it. In this context 'integration' can refer to religious processes that both promote and follow from processes of globalisation. The concept of 'resistance' implies the opposite trend: explicit or implicit criticism of and mobilisation against some or all processes of global change manifested in globalisation. Both integration and resistance can be seen in relation to religious resources. Finally, the growing impact of religious discourses on development discourse and practice can be seen as a response to a world where many people believe that neither governments nor international organisations have legitimacy. And in this context, religion can function as an important source of 'soft power', linking individuals and groups across state boundaries in ways that encourage them to pursue their interests (Haynes 2007). 'It is therefore important to develop a more profound understanding of the basic assumption underlying the different religions and the ways in which people adhering to them see their interests. It would also be very useful to identify elements of communality between the major religions' (Reychler 1997). Emphasising the idea that religious organisations and movements often enjoy more legitimacy than some governments and international organisations, Juergensmeyer contends that in particular 'radical religious ideologies have become the vehicles for a variety of rebellions against authority that are linked with myriad social, cultural, and political grievances' (Juergensmeyer 2005).

In conclusion, thinking about the contributions that religions can make to achieving better outcomes in the context of globalisation, some religious individuals and faith-based organisations highlight the negative consequences of globalisation because it is said to lead to standardisation of cultures and greater focus on capitalist development that serves to challenge religious values in society.

Globalisation, religions and ethics

One of the key complaints made by religious figures is that globalisation encourages greater focus and concern with a consumer-dominated capitalist system, with monetary values often seeming far more important than values in respect of human beings (Parliament of the Worlds Religions 2004). In such a view, human beings are increasingly judged in the context of 'homo economicus' ('economic man'), while religious leaders believe that a greater focus on 'homo spiritualitus', implying a greater concern with transcendental and spiritual issues, is equally, if not more, important. The concern is that in an increasingly material world, apparently governed by interest rates and stock markets, people are rarely allowed the time to develop their spiritual self and moral values. In the context of development, exchanges between the North and the South are routinely unequal, creating or exacerbating poverty and frustration in the developing world (Hopkins 2001; Mayotte 1998; Serageldin and Barrett 1996).

To try to deal with globalisation's downsides, it is often suggested that religious organisations should urgently get together to develop an ethical/compassionate perspective to the debate on globalisation (Parliament of the Worlds Religions 2004). This implies that religion would *inevitably* be mixed with politics, but the goal is that faith-based organisations should try to ensure that politics contains clear ethical values. Is there common ground for religions to develop a common global ethic for good governance in the context of globalisation? It is widely accepted that better adhesion to good ethics – often informed by religious values – would help produce better governance (Barrow 2006). In other words, when politics is based on sincere respect of basic moral values the outcome is likely to be positive. What is the religious basis for such ethics? For Buddhism, the key is preservation and respect for all forms of life. Beyond this basic principle, the Buddha, the son of a king, established a list of qualities that any political leader should necessarily possess. 'He should be generous and giving, virtuous, gentle, self-controlled, non-confrontational; he should avoid falsehood and anger, irony or sarcasm'. In addition, Prince Gautama, the Buddha also established seven principles for good rule, including 'to meet in harmony, discuss and preserve harmony in spite of different opinions, abide by the rule of law, operate a balance between tradition and modernity, protect the womenfolk, respect elders, safeguard the practice of religion and be open to all religions and spiritual traditions in one's territory and abroad' (Al-Akwa'a 2005).

Hindu ethics are primarily related to reincarnation, a way of express-ing the need for reciprocity. Thus, *intention* is seen as very important. In Hinduism, selfless action for the benefit of others is an important concept, known as the doctrine of *karma yoga*. This aspect of service is combined with an understanding that someone else's unfortunate situ-ation, while of their own doing, is one's own situation since the soul within is the soul shared by all. Both kindness and hospitality are key Hindu values (Crawford 1989).

In Islam, there is a clear set of guidelines for good governance estab-lished in the Qur'an and in Islamic jurisprudence. Overall, Islam is a religion containing very precise rules for individuals and for the polit-ical and legal system as a whole. The Qur'an notes that a good leader always puts the interest of the people above his own interest. He con-sults his people regularly by different means – notably a Consultative Council (Arabic, *Majlis al Shura*) (Miles and Hashmi 2002).

Finally, for Christians, ethics is the reflection on moral experience and thinking about norms, values, ideas of the good, and stories of right conduct in the Christian tradition. Christian ethics are rooted in Scripture, the life of Jesus Christ, and the witness of the various Christian churches (Hill 2001).

Although the relationship between faith-based organisations and globalisation is often complex, we can note that ideas, experiences and practices – which are all significantly affected by globalisation – can encourage faith-based organisations to adopt new or renewed agendas to try to achieve objectives linked to human development. Many now look beyond local or national contexts towards regional and interna-tional contexts and fora for methods and means to accomplish this goal. In short, the context and circumstances of globalisation provide an important focus for the development activities of numerous faith-based organisations and religious individuals, many of which we shall examine in later chapters related to the MDGs

Overall, globalisation is characterised by a variety of socio-economic and human development concerns and issues. These include the eco-nomic range and clout of transnational corporations (TNCs) and the widely held perception – held by both religious and secular organisa-tions – that TNCs are taking economic power from governments and thus from citizens – and affecting efforts to control their own fates (Haynes 2005a). Many critics note a second downside to economic globalisation: apparent mass impoverishment of many already poor people especially in the developing world (Held and McGrew 2002; Scholte 2005). These circumstances lead numerous faith-based organisations and religious individuals – whether working alone or in tandem with governments and secular development agencies – to try to develop strategies to ameliorate various human development imbalances. Building from a shared concern with poverty, closer links have developed in recent years between various religious leaders and faith-based organisations, on the one hand, and secular development agencies, including the World Bank and the IMF, on the other (Marshall 2005a, 2005b). Cognisant of the polarising impact of economic globalisation, this common ground links them to what some see as an emerging global consensus underpinning the pursuit of the eight MDGs, identified in the Introduction chapter.

Yet while religious values can be an important resource for development, it does not mean that policy makers can simply add 'religion' to the range of policy instruments at their disposal, other than in rather exceptional cases. Instead, it suggests that governments and other key development actors – including secular development organisations – can in many cases usefully work closely with faith-based organisations in pursuit of shared development goals. Specifically, Ellis and ter Haar suggest various development areas in which religion *could* play a positive role in development. They include:

- Conflict prevention and peace-building;
- Wealth creation and production;
- Governance;
- Management of natural resources;
- Gender issues;
- Health and education (Ellis and ter Haar 2005: 4).

Later chapters examine such areas, with the intention of focusing upon the involvement of selected faith-based organisations in the developing world in relation to development outcomes.

Conclusion

Contemporary globalisation encompasses technological, political, economic and cultural dimensions. Their complexity is mirrored in the various ways that religions have responded to globalisation. On the one hand, religion can be used to justify violence while, on the other hand, various religious traditions have supported anti-violence social reform movements seeking to build a globalisation that is more equitable and fair than the currently existing order. Religious traditions are currently being used around the world, as vehicles for protest, especially in relation to what are perceived as the detrimental effects of globalisation. We shall see in Chapter 3 that another side of religion's involvement in current international relations in the wake of contemporary globalisation are various attempts to help end conflicts and bring greater harmony and cooperation.

Key questions are asked about how the major world religions can help build and sustain peaceful coexistence and better human development outcomes. This in circumstances where, encouraged by processes of globalisation, increasingly multi-faith societies must deal with a world suffering from what appears to many to be growing strife and economic disparity. How can religious individuals and faith-based organisations successfully advocate reconciliation and fairness in a world characterised by what often appears to be growing polarisation between rich and poor both within and between countries? A starting point is that because the world religions focused upon in this book – Buddhism, Christianity, Hinduism, and Islam – broadly share a set of theological and spiritual values that, theoretically, should facilitate efforts in this regard.

Principles and practice of 'good governance'[5]

> The fight against world poverty will only be successful if it is based on the political will and capacity of 'self help' – the efforts of poor countries to establish peace, the rule of law, and good governance at home and unlock the creative energies of their people (Köhler 2002).

How, why and when do faith-based organisations have a significant impact on public policy, including debates about good governance? The issue is particularly important in the context of deepening globalisation, because all governments – including those in the developing world – must take into account what happens beyond their individual country borders because many such developments affect domestic outcomes. For example, major donors and international financial institutions, such as the United States, Japan, the European Union, the World Bank and the IMF, base their aid and loan decisions on whether in their judgement putative recipients implement 'necessary' and 'appropriate' political, social and economic reforms, grouped together under the general rubric of 'good governance'. The World Bank, for example, has proclaimed that 'good governance' is a prerequisite for development. In short, most developing countries are highly dependent on external sources of developmental aid, and external aid donors now demand proof of the existence of 'good governance' before disbursing funds (http://www.worldbank.org/wbi/governance/).

The term 'governance' refers both to decision-making processes at the state level and the manner by which decisions are put into practice (or, in some cases not put into practice). Theoretically, whatever the precise nature of the political system within which they function, public institutions undertake three crucial functions: (1) conduct public affairs, (2) manage public resources, and (3) guarantee realisation of a range of development objectives (Cleary and McConville 2006). 'Good governance' occurs when these objectives are broadly delivered in a manner and context that is (largely) free of abuse and corruption, and with due regard for the rule of law. Although 'good governance' is seen as an ideal – difficult to achieve and implement in its totality – shared perceptions have recently developed in relation to what is desirable, an approach that may incorporate insights from both religious and secular thinking. There is wide agreement that irrespective of the precise nature of a political system, all governments should strive to achieve good governance, characterised by:

- Low and declining levels of corruption;
- Decision makers listen to and take into account minority views;
- Decision-making processes and structures take into consideration the views and opinions of all groups in society, including the weakest and the most vulnerable.

Principles and practices of good governance can be grouped into eight linked categories: (1) Participation, (2) Rule of law, (3) Transparency, (4) Responsiveness, (5) Consensus-orientated, (6) Equity and inclusiveness, (7) Effectiveness and efficiency, (8) Accountability.

Participation
- Participation by both women and men;
- Participation can either be direct or through legitimate intermediate institutions or representatives;
- Participation implies both the existence of a relatively unfragmented civil society as well as more general freedoms of association and expression.

Participation involves consultation in the development of policies and decision-making, elections and other democratic processes.

It gives governments access to important information about the needs and priorities of individuals, communities and private businesses. Governments that involve the public will be in a better position to make good decisions, and decisions will enjoy more support once taken. While there may not be direct links between participation and every aspect of good governance, accountability, transparency and participation are reinforced by developing fully democratic political systems. Given the very widespread influence of religions and faith-based organisations throughout the developing world, the participation within them of tens millions of people offers a major opportunity to increase significantly the overall level of societal involvement in governance.

Rule of Law

- Good governance requires fair legal frameworks that are impartially enforced;
- Human rights are given full protection, including those of religious and ethnic minorities;
- It is crucial to have both an independent judiciary and an impartial police force, with a minimal role for corruption.

The rule of law refers to the institutional process of setting, interpreting and implementing laws and other regulations. It means that decisions taken by the government must be founded in law and that private firms and individuals are protected from arbitrary decisions. For the rule of law to be present also requires a form of governance that is free from incentives that distort – through corruption, nepotism, patronage or capture by narrow private interest groups; guarantees property and personal rights; and achieves some sort of social stability. This provides a degree of reliability and predictability that is essential for firms and individuals to take good decisions.

The fight against corruption is a serious problem in many developing countries. Tanzania is no exception, and the problem of corruption and how to eliminate or at least reduce it is an important aspect of Norway's official development assistance, an integrated part of all supported projects and programmes. Like many other international participants in development, Norway is seeking to develop a joint anti-corruption strategy via dialogue not only with Tanzania's government but also by seeking to raise awareness through campaigns and cooperation with various faith-based organisations. In Tanzania, both Islam and the Catholic Church have broader networks than any other civil society organisations (http://www.norway.go.tz/Development/Governance/ Good+Governance.htm).

Transparency

- Accepted and implemented rules and regulations govern how decisions are taken, put into practice and enforced;
- Information is freely available to all, especially those who will be affected by such decisions and their enforcement.

Transparency is an important aspect of good governance. This is because transparent decision-making is critical for the development of a sense that what government does is rooted in the preferences of its citizens. Moreover, accountability and the rule of law require openness and good information so higher levels of administration, external reviewers and the general public – including those organised in religions and faith-based organisations – can verify performance and governmental compliance to the dictates of law.

Responsiveness

- Institutions and processes try to serve all stakeholders within a reasonable timeframe.

Good governance requires appropriate institutional mechanisms – that is, established procedures and organisations – to promote a good level of government responsiveness. This is done in various ways, including: *formal* political institutions – that is, permanent edifices of public life, such as, laws, organisations, public offices, elections, and so on. Second, there are various *informal* institutions, including the 'dynamics of interests and identities, domination and resistance, compromise and accommodation' (Bratton and van de Walle 1997: 276). It is the interaction of these various institutions that help determine the degree of good governance in a polity. The relative weight of these factors, as well as the factors themselves, will differ from country to country.

Consensus orientation, equity and inclusiveness

- Ensuring that all members of society feel that they have a stake in governance and that no one is excluded;
- All groups, especially the most vulnerable, have clear opportunities to try to maintain or improve their societal and developmental positions;

- Mediation of the different interests in society to reach a broad consensus in society regarding what is in the best interest of the whole community and how this can be achieved;
- Necessary to have a long-term perspective for sustainable human development and how to achieve it.

When a privileged elite minority is perceived to consume an inappropriate proportion of available resources then popular satisfaction with governance may fall or fail to develop satisfactorily. To avert this, it helps if governments preside over sustained economic growth and convinces the mass of people that it is shared among citizens with *relative* equity. Przeworski *et al.*'s (1996) comprehensive survey of evidence – covering 1950–90 – suggest that chances of good governance developing increase when a government: (1) manages to develop its country's economy in a sustained fashion; and (2) gradually, yet consistently, manages to reduce socio-economic inequalities via effective welfare policies. Przeworski (1988) claims that the maintenance of an adequate system of public welfare has a positive influence on good governance as it both reduces the inequalities among different social groups (a factor said to promote democratic collapse) and can help curb social unrest. As we shall see in later chapters, in many developing countries, faith-based organisations play an increasing role in various aspects of welfare provision, especially health and education.

In summary, chances of good governance appear to be linked to: (1) sustained economic growth, relatively equitably spread, even if it starts from a low base, and (2) state focus, via welfare policies, to ameliorate the plight of the poor and underprivileged and, as a result, develop a broad consensus in society regarding what is in the best interest of the whole community and how this can be achieved. Note, however, that it does not have to be state organisations that are in charge of improving welfare as an array of non-state, often faith-based organisations, now deliver a range of welfare benefits.

Effectiveness and efficiency

- Processes and institutions produce results that meet the needs of society while making the best use of resources at their disposal;
- Increasingly, it is related to sustainable use of natural resources and the protection of the environment.

Appropriate management of natural resources and a concern for the natural environment is regarded as crucial to the development prospects of the developing world. Mitchell and Tanner define the natural environment as including all the natural features of land, water, flora and fauna that supports human life and influence its development and character (Mitchell and Tanner 2002: 1). In recent years, religious networks have played a growing role with regard to the interaction of humans with nature. For example, each of the world religions focused upon in this book have developed an environmental outlook that draws on religious values: 'ecotheology' in Christianity, 'Islamic environmentalism' among Muslims, Vandana Shiva in the Hindu context, while Buddhism has also developed a focus on environmental concerns (Coward 2002).

Accountability

- Governmental institutions, as well as private sector and civil society organisations, must be accountable to the public and to their institutional stakeholders;
- In general organisations and institutions are accountable to those who will be affected by decisions or actions.

Accountability can be both an end in itself – representing democratic values – and a means towards the development of more efficient and effective organisations in the context of the development of good governance. Politicians and public servants are given enormous power through the laws and regulations they implement, resources they control and the organisations they manage. Accountability is a key way to ensure that this power is used appropriately and in accordance with the public interest. But accountability requires: (1) clarity about who is accountable to whom for what, and (2) a situation where civil servants, organisations and politicians are held accountable for their decisions and performance.

Accountability can be strengthened through formal reporting requirements and external scrutiny (such as an independent Audit Office, Ombudsmen, and so on). Democratic accountability, as represented by accountability of ministers to parliament and the parliament to voters, can be seen as an objective in itself, but it also strengthens accountability in general. Many countries are now seeking to strengthen accountability structures and processes through more focus on accountability for performance as opposed to limiting accountability to regularity of decisions (see Chapter 4).

Conclusion

Although comparative research is at an early stage, the following issues are central to an assessment of the role of faith-based organisations in developing good governance in the developing world. It is necessary to:

- Develop a better understanding of how faith-based organisations promote good governance, citizenship and rights, including, specific women's rights, by identifying their vision, strategies, how they operate, their structure and programmes, and how they mobilise public opinion and popular support to promote their agenda;
- Assess the potential of coordination between secular organisations and faith-based organisations on issues of governance, citizenship and rights;
- Consider the impact of faith-based organisations on individual countries' political situations, especially whether their activities contribute, actively or passively, to inter- or intra-religious tension.

It is hopefully clear from the preceding discussion that there are complex relations between the different aspects of good governance. For example, some factors can be seen as preconditions of others (for example, technical and managerial competence is one precondition of organisational capacity, and organisational capacity is one precondition of maintaining the rule of law). But there are also important effects in the other direction (for example, organisational capacity reinforces technical and managerial competence, accountability reinforces the rule of law). For these reasons, improving the quality of governance can often be highly problematic.

There is however evidence to suggest that despite problems a growing number of countries in the developing world are now trying to ensure improved governance across a range of public sector activities. On the other hand, politicians in many developing countries may still need further persuasion to try seriously to develop fully good governance principles and practices. There are various reasons for this, although two are particularly common. First, in periods of significant political and economic changes, which many developing countries are currently experiencing, ruling elites may perceive a primary need for an absence of turmoil in certain sectors so as to ensure the system's overall stability. For example, as the military and police may be called upon to ensure stability, they are sometimes made exempt from initial reforms. In addition, new politicians and administrators may lack both technical and managerial competences to tackle necessary reforms to usher in necessary reforms (Calvert and Calvert 2001; Pinkney 2005).

Faith-based organisations and 'good governance': problems and prospects

Many kinds of non-governmental organisations (NGOs) – both secular and faith-based – work to help deliver improved human development in the developing world, a goal that can best be delivered when conditions of good governance exist. Some NGOs provide various social services for those whom national governments cannot or will not assist, while others are more concerned with human rights, gender issues, democracy and governance. Overall, what can religious individuals and faith-based organisations do to help ensure achievement of good governance? It is widely noted that faith-based organisations are one of the driving forces working to effect improved development, political and social agendas – including improved development outcomes (Marshall 2005a, 2005b; Holenstein 2005; Alkire 2004). For example, some service-oriented faith-based organisations in both the Middle East and Africa enjoy annual budgets that in some cases can exceed that of the Ministries in charge of social welfare, while procedures for accessing their direct assistance and welfare services are more efficient and straightforward than those provided by the state in the public sector (Ellis and ter Haar 2005).

There is however limited research concerning what faith-based organisations in the developing world accomplish in relation to good governance objectives. Overall, there is a need for more systematic and ongoing qualitative and quantitative study at all levels, from national to regional. On the other hand, available evidence does suggest that faith-based organisations can play a role in promoting good governance by establishing linkages with political decision makers to influence policy. However, it is important to increase knowledge and understanding on how and why faith-based organisations have an impact on public policy, including development policy and practice. Important questions include:

- *Which* faith-based NGOs operate?
- To what *extent* do they integrate religion into their work?
- *How* do faith-based NGOs link to policy makers and how are their policy efforts relevant?

- *What* is the internal governance structure of such faith-based organisations?
- *What* is their own definition and perception of 'good governance'?

While an overall assessment of these issues will emerge following a focus in the remaining chapters of this book, because of its overall centrality to development outcomes, the issue of 'good governance' and faith-based organisations perceptions are examined now.

The first point to note is that various faith-based organisations are already centrally involved in some aspects of governance, including revenue collection. A failure to tax efficiently is one of the main problems facing many states in the developing world, especially in Africa. There governmental capacities are typically weak, while many regional states have serious budget deficits, with an unhealthy revenue reliance on dues derived from the import-export trade and/or on external sources of funding, especially foreign aid. This reliance derives from the fact that many states in the developing world have poor records of tax collection from their own citizens, leading to a fundamentally unhealthy situation where many states are highly dependent on foreign sources of finance (Burnell and Morrissey 2004). It is often noted that the nature of the relationship between a state and its domestic taxpayers is an important element in helping to develop both good governance and an authentic sense of citizenship (Pinkney 2005). Throughout the developing world, many religious networks manage to survive or thrive through donation of monies from their members. Contrasting with the endemic problems of citizenship in many developing countries, the ability of religious organisations to 'tax' their followers clearly indicates their skill in developing close bonds with their members and, in some cases, to show their accountability to them (Ellis and ter Haar 2005).

The question can be asked whether, in the many developing countries in Africa, Asia and Latin America where outside main population centers, state authority is often intermittent or fragmented and consequently where governments have little ability to tax their population, the extent to which religious networks can be expected to assume some government functions? The likely answer is that in the considerable number of weak or failed states in the developing world – that is, where the state fails to establish and develop efficient, centrally-controlled bureaucracies adequate to ensure a country's security, raise sufficient resources through taxation as to fund the reproduction of the state itself or ensure a minimum level of welfare for its citizens –

various non-state organisations – including faith-based organisations – are surely destined to play a much greater role in future. At the present time, indeed, many of the most effective non-state organisations have an explicitly religious focus, including running educational establishments or health services.

This should not however be taken to imply that the relation between governments, secular development agencies and faith-based organisations is always unproblematic. In principle however there is recognition that:

- Faith-based organisations are an important part of civil society whose engagement can help achieve increased tolerance, social cohesion and understanding;
- Faith-based organisations have a key role in providing education and achieving local and global justice, gender equality, and action for non-violent resolutions to conflict;
- The sharing of common values of all faiths can help promote and develop cultural understanding in many societies in the developing world.

On the other hand, not everyone shares this view. Some believe that religious issues are divisive, leading to complications and strife. In such views, serving humanity is most likely to be delivered through a focus on secular vehicles of social and economic development. The problems in this regard have surfaced during World Bank-led initiatives to build a bigger role for faith-based organisations in development policy in the developing world. In recent years many multilateral development banks and other official development institutions have actively sought, through various means, to engage in dialogue with a broad range of civil society institutions, including faith-based organisations. Yet results have been patchy and now questions are asked about the way forward, not only in relation to faith-based organisations but also in some cases to the governance and development roles of civil society more generally (Marshall 2006). In summary, faith-based organisations can face particular challenges not only in integrating their perspectives into the state-civil society dialogue but also into the operations of large aid organisations.

This point can be illustrated by a focus on problems encountered recently in trying to develop closer links between, on the one hand, governments, the World Bank, IMF and, on the other, faith-based organisations in relation to a joint World Bank/IMF initiative known as the Poverty Reduction Strategy Paper (PRSP). Introduced formally in 1999, the PRSP was a government-led approach to guide growth and poverty reduction within explicit strategic frameworks tailored for each client country. The purpose of a PRSP is to outline a comprehensive strategy to encourage growth and reduce poverty in a developing country, with overall the aim of bringing together different actors' priorities and analyses – collectively working under the general rubric of 'development' – with the intention of increasing chances of complementarity and coherence. In pursuit of this goal, various forms of consultation were held in each affected country with prominent figures and organisations. Overall PRSP consultations: (1) sought to adopt growth and development strategies that were economically rational, while (2) aiming to ensure that the policies and programmes that resulted were also compatible with what a country's people regarded as appropriate. Once consultation was concluded, a PRSP would be finalised. The World Bank and the IMF would assess its strengths as the basis for a country to receive loans and credits. Note that this means that the parameters of each PRSP were bound by what the World Bank and IMF believed was appropriate in relation to development policy and programmes (Levinsohn 2003).

Civil society's participation was seen as both essential and central in relation to PRSP design, and faith-based organisations were widely seen as an important aspect of the process of PRSP formulation. On the other hand, there was no coordinated strategy to engage faith-based organisations in PRSP processes, nor wide-ranging discussions to ascertain their views or evaluate experiences. The reason for this omission is that PRSP processes were primarily designed and led by state leaders and in many cases they were not active in seeking faith-based organisations' views, despite the fact that in each country, faith institutions were expected to be part of the overall participation process (World Faiths Development Dialogue 2003).

Problems surfaced when the WFDD, an organisation created by James Wolfensohn, then president of the World Bank, organised a four-day meeting in Canterbury, England, in July 2002. It involved individuals from 15 countries where PRSP consultations had already taken place, and from several different faith traditions. Michael Taylor, then director of the WFDD, led the consultation. World Bank representatives were among the observers; the IMF was invited to participate but no representative could be present. The meeting's main purpose was to gain an understanding of whether faith groups involved in framing PRSPs believed their voice had been taken into account (World Faiths Development Dialogue 2003).

Many faith participants not only emphasised that poverty is a complex phenomenon but also stressed that many people regard the importance of freedom and a satisfying life as a higher priority than simple gains in income or improvements in social indicators (Marshall and Keough 2004). For example, according to a Sri Lankan at the meeting, aspirations of Buddhist Sri Lankans differ from those of people living in countries tightly focused on economic growth, commenting that: 'The middle path, path to the human liberation in Buddhism, guides people for a simple, happy and content life' (Tyndale 2004). Two African participants highlighted that the importance of opportunities can rival wealth. A Tanzanian underlined the significance of rights in alleviating poverty, especially social well-being, as well as those related to security, justice, freedom, peace and law and order. In relation to Zambia, it was claimed that opposition parties were weak; consequently, 'only the [Catholic] church speaks out'. In addition, Catholic social teaching was said to serve as a source of inspiration for many Zambians, with its focus on human dignity particularly important in contrast to the government view that 'economic growth equals development' *tout court*. The Zambian participant also stressed that 'if growth does not benefit the human being, then it is not development at all' (Tyndale 2004).

A conclusion is that there are marked differences in perceptions of poverty between faith groups on the one hand and government and international development agencies on the other. That is, while governments and international development agencies almost invariably seem firmly oriented towards economic growth, faith groups have a range of viewpoints on poverty; most if not all consider it a more complex, less growth-oriented issue. The key practical question is *how* and *in what ways* can secular development agencies and governments constructively integrate religious perspectives into poverty reduction strategies? This is always going to be difficult to accomplish, however, because faith groups rarely view poverty reduction as the central question in the creation of more fulfilling, sustainable lifestyles.

A second conclusion is while paying lip service to the involvement of faith-based organisations in development, both governments and, to an extent, secular donor agencies either lack ability or are simply not interested in integrating alternative – including faith – perspectives into poverty reduction strategies. Over the years, this issue has often strained relationships and undermined confidence between government and civil society, with donor agencies' own biases adding a layer of complexity; and this has curtailed vigorous and constructive debate about poverty and how to reduce it.

Problems of interaction between faith-based organisations, on the one hand, and governments, on the other hand, had already surfaced prior to the Canterbury meeting. For example, in 2000, an initiative to bring faith-based organisations into development strategy decisions originally inspired by James Wolfensohn in 1998 ran aground following serious opposition from the World Bank's Executive Directors, that is, the 184 member countries' representatives. They brought up a number of fundamental objections to the Bank's faith dialogue that led to a decrease in the level of effort and changes in the form of engagement with faith institutions (Marshall 2005a)

Shortly after however the events of September 11, 2001, made it clear that religion's importance in global affairs, including those related to development issues, should not be underestimated. Nevertheless, fundamental objections raised by Bank member states regarding an enhanced role for faith-based organisations in development dialogues have continued significantly to inhibit not only development of the WFDD[6] but also more generally the involvement of faith-based organisations in development strategies in the developing world (Marshall 2005a). This is however not to imply that if a government chooses to engage with faith-based organisations in a specific country, then the World Bank and other secular development organisations would refuse to get involved. In addition, where faith-based organisations were already important elements in civil society forums, as in Zambia, then a continuation of their involvement was appropriate. Nevertheless, many questions remain concerning dialogue – as distinct from partnership involving joined action – beyond the country level. Three questions were especially prominent:

- Disquiet about the nature of politics when religion is involved;
- Apprehension about how some religious institutions viewed and affected Development; and
- Differing views as to whether a systematic dialogue with faith institutions was relevant or of priority importance for the World Bank (Marshall 2005a).

Overall conclusion

This chapter focused on three interlinked issues: widespread religious resurgence; impact of deepening globalisation on development outcomes and religious responses to it; and the role of religion in achieving 'good governance' in the developing world. In answer to the question: 'Why do many faith-based organisations now have a higher profile in relation to development issues compared to a few decades ago?', we can conclude that this is because, on the one hand, secular development policies and programmes have often led to disappointing outcomes. As a result, not only faith-based organisations themselves but also many ordinary people in the developing world now regard it as entirely correct that religion should be an influential voice in development strategies. On the other hand, many governments and some secular development agencies regard greater involvement of faith-based organisations in development with apprehension or suspicion, a perception often linked to what they see as problematic involvement of religions more generally in secular – political, social and economic – issues. Overall, the chapter stressed interconnections between religious resurgence, 'good governance', and processes of globalisation, that collectively stimulate increased cooperation, on the one hand, and competition and sometimes conflict, on the other, with variable outcomes for development outcomes.

2
Religion and Development: The Ambivalence of the Sacred[1]

We saw in the Introduction that the modern idea of the 'developing world' essentially dates to the post-1945 era. We also noted that, until recently, ideas about development usually overlooked or ignored religion – or even assumed that its influence on the develop-ment process and outcomes was inevitably baleful. Moreover it was widely assumed that religion's decline as a public actor was an essential aspect of modernisation: relegated to a matter of private belief in the developing world, just like it had been in the West (Ver Beek 2000; Van Geest 1998). Governments in the developing world, nearly all secularly orientated, would over time need to gain both strength and confidence and in this context religion was seen either as an irrelevance or as an obstacle to development that had to be overcome. Chapter 1 illustrated however that, far from disappearing from public salience, religion has maintained or even increased its public profile in many parts of the developing world. This is manifested in various ways: on the one hand, growing numbers of mosques, churches, temples and other religious sites and, on the other, in expansion of public religious rituals, includ-ing the spectacle of heads of state and other high-ranking politicians frequently making high profile public proclamations or gestures of their religious allegiance (Mayotte 1998; Thomas 2005). Reflecting religion's high public profile in this regard, Ellis and ter Haar aver that 'development in the twenty-first century will be shaped largely by religion. It is therefore important for any analysis or recommendations to take account of this' (Ellis and ter Haar 2005: 1).

We have also seen that an important facet of the growing public profile of religion in many parts of the developing world is widespread engagement with development issues. But how specifically does religion affect development processes and outcomes? There is no simple or single answer, no agreed view on the issue to be found in the current literature. This is partly because, as Tyndale notes, 'it is impossible to talk of religions in general without giving a false picture' (Tyndale 2004: 2). That is, among the world religions on which we focus in this book – Islam, Christianity, Hinduism and Buddhism – there is in practice little or no uniformity of beliefs, worldviews or social customs within any of them. And, even if we could clarify that we are not talking about abstract doctrinal beliefs or faith but about people or communities with different religious traditions seeking to put their beliefs into practice, when we try to isolate what these communities are doing for 'development', we get a mixed picture.

This chapter has two aims. First, it seeks to ascertain how religious beliefs relate to development issues in the developing world, by reference to ideas, practices and experiences. Second, it puts forward a simple typology of faith entities active in relation to development in the developing world. One general category of such actors operates at the international level, while another focuses primarily on development outcomes within countries. For heuristic reasons, the latter category is subdivided into 'pro-development' and 'anti-development' entities, although as we shall see such a simple dichotomy is problematic. This is because such labels are often applied in the (mostly secular) development literature, coming at the issue not from a religious perspective but from a secular viewpoint that understands development in conventional terms: increases or decreases in people's material well-being, such as: more and better education, welfare, health, clean water, and so on. On the other hand, religious people involved in development do not see development in a single-mindedly materialistic way. Instead, they highlight the human development aspects of 'development', underlining both religious and spiritual dimensions (Selinger 2004; Tyndale 2004; Alkire 2006).[2]

Rational choice, religion and development

Recent years have seen growing interest among development theorists and practitioners concerning the relationship of religion and development in relation to development outcomes in the developing world. Many would now accept that fundamental questions about human existence, including development and how to achieve it, cannot be answered only in modern secular 'scientific' terms (Ebaugh 2002). There is now a widespread urge to try to understand human motivations in relation to various areas of human endeavour, including development, which may not be sufficiently explainable in what Tickner calls 'instrumental rationalist terms'. This changed focus may be seen more generally as 'helpfully suggestive of ... ways in which we need to rethink contemporary knowledge production in order to better understand religious worldviews' (Tickner 2005: 20).

The focus on religious resurgence in many parts of the developing world underlines the notion that many people now feel an increased sense of religious fervour that can both infuse the faith-based organisations to which they belong and may even compensate for lack of material capabilities and comforts (Berger 1999; Thomas 2005). As Amartya Sen (1999) has noted, for many among the extremely poor in the developing world, regardless of specific religious tradition, religious faith is an extremely important facet of their identity. However, despite often extreme poverty, many such people, Sen avers, do not adopt what might be identified as a 'rational' line and, as a result, complain unremittingly about their perilous development position. Sen contends that instead many such people appear to reconcile themselves with their lot, and may even be grateful for small mercies. This is not to claim that this an acceptable substitute for an improved quality of life, only that it is one kind of coping mechanism. In other words, adherence to religious practices can complement other intrinsically valued aspects of human flourishing, such as: safety, health, knowledge, meaningful work and play, self-direction, culture and so on. A key value of religious faith in this context is that it can facilitate achievement of a degree of serenity, providing a meaning to life that would otherwise be absent or lessened. In this way, even when someone is very poor, lacking conventionally recognised development goods to a considerable extent, religion can comprise a hugely important – yet difficult to quantify – dimension of human well-that contributes significantly directly to a person's thriving and/or contentedness.

Several recent participatory and multidimensional developments have demonstrated the relevance of religion in aiding many among the poor in the developing world to cope with a lowly material position. For example, the recent Voices of the Poor study by the World Bank, which collected notions of well-being expressed by around 60,000 people in 60 countries, who considered themselves poor and were also judged to be poverty-stricken by their community, discovered that 'harmony' with transcendent matters (such as, a spiritual life and religious observance) was often judged to be a factor in well-being (Narayan *et al.* 2000). These views help to explain not only why so many poor people in developing countries believe it important to belong to a religion but also give an inkling of the importance that religion can play in development.

This does not imply, of course, that religious actors will necessarily always act in ways that all would agree are 'rational'. Instead, they may act in ways that appear – at least to many secular observers – as decidedly 'non-rational', albeit with a force that appears to be at odds with their material strength, thus confounding positivist expectations. This is because, as Kubálková notes, 'in contrast to the social science positivist understanding "the reality of God" surpasses human comprehension... God is not "out there", waiting to be discovered or observed by the processes of rational thought and scientific observation' (Kubálková 2006: 11). The veracity of this remark can be inferred from the fact that several of the world religions, including Judaism, Islam and Christianity, baulk at trying to describe the transcendent reality of God in normal conceptual language. Yet there would also be substantial agreement that the meaning ascribed to the reality of God is to a considerable degree fixed by social conventions and can, as a result, be expressed in everyday language. This representation of 'that which conventionally eludes representation' is important in providing believers with an appropriate map of reality, necessary to try to fix their identity in ontological terms. In this context, loss of identity would equate to loss of faith. The point is that religious and secular thought each start from different ontologies. How? Most obviously, *all* religions share a sense of distinction between mundane and transcendental reality. And religious thinkers see human experience as an important dimension of a multidimensional reality 'that is ordered by design but is not knowable to sensory perception ...A believer must follow the dictates of conscience that are beyond the realm of "rational choice"' (Kubálková 2003: 86–90). To approach human action through linguistic constructivism – that is, via a universe fashioned as a result of human action and involving meanings that humans give to their actions – is a methodological path by which we can seek to incorporate religion into studies of development. For Tickner, such linguistic constructivism is useful both for understanding religious worldviews and contemporary events. This is because the way we construct our world is crucial to how we act upon it. As a result, 'religious worldviews may be better understood using methodologies that are reflexive and dialogical not those based on instrumental rationality' (Tickner 2005: 3).

The conclusion is that trying to build theories covering religion's involvement in development, or politics for that matter, in relation to theories with epistemological foundations in secular rationalism will not necessarily help understand 'religious motivations or worldviews of those who express a deep hostility to modernity and secular thinking' (Tickner 2005: 3). Yet, it is not a simple task to try to integrate religiously-driven motivations with secular rationalism and arrive at an explanation of the roles that religion can play in development. It is necessary to recall that secular social sciences are endeavours that emerged out of the Enlightenment, tracing their intellectual foundations from non-religious rationalist thinking. Many religious believers have never accepted them. Unsurprisingly, then, both parties – religious and secular thinkers – attack each other for their perceived lack of realism. A topical and significant example was provided by 9/11 and its aftermath. Following the attack on the Twin Towers and the Pentagon, Muslim intellectuals and those interested in the world of Islam began a major search for the 'holy grail': a 'liberal' and 'moderate' Islam that could be identified, championed and disseminated in order to combat the religious extremism and terrorism that al-Qaeda's murderous escapades exemplified (Ramadan 2006). So far however such a religious ideology has not been found or, more accurately, various 'moderate' forms of Islam have been noted, but none has yet achieved hegemonic status among Muslims. In the next section, we examine more generally how religious ideas, experiences and practices play out in relation to development in the developing world.

Ideas

Most religions traditionally comprise ideas, beliefs and practices of a particular community. Thus religions have provided what Peter Berger (1969) calls a 'sacred canopy', enabling followers to make sense of their world. Beyer (2006) explains that there were once many individual and different societies around the world, each with its own set of practices, some of which today we would call religious. Often, religious ideas can be seen as 'the major organizing principles for explaining the world and defining ethical life' (Kurtz 1995: 3). Now, however, deepening globalisation dramatically undermines the notion that every member of a society must necessarily hold the same ideas in relation to religion. This is not only because globalisation encourages the idea that religion is a matter of individual choice but also that many religions now compete for individuals' attention, leading to what has been called a 'global marketplace of religion' (Bruce 2002). This spread of sometimes competing religious ideas leads to a situation where the once relatively autonomous sacred canopy is increasingly regarded as an artefact of the past. This process can be met with resistance, leading to 'the revival of more localised practices in the form of religious fundamentalist and other protest movements' (Kurtz 1995: 99).

Experiences

We saw in Chapter 1 that there is a dynamic and dialectic connection between globalisation and religion. Because of the impact of recent, deepening globalisation many religious individuals and groups undertake increased self-reflection, a result of the experiences they encounter following two simultaneous developments. On the one hand, cultural, religious and social differences between people sometimes appear increasingly visible as a result of globalisation. On the other hand, many people also experience direct or indirect pressure towards increased homogenisation and 'free' religious competition. This creates a field of tension where the value of religious belonging as identity-forming becomes more important while at the same time it is rapidly changing. This is because globalisation facilitates the transmission of both non-material – ideas, information and beliefs – factors, as well as material ones. Many religious actors seek to use any available opportunities to disseminate their religious ideas in various ways. Second, what religions do within a country is affected by social, political and economic experiences – and these in turn may well be affected by globalisation. As Berger notes, in some cases – for example, in relation to manifestations of Islamism (including 'Islamic fundamentalism') – this is a challenge that is seen to emanate from attempts to impose 'an emerging global culture, most of it of Western and indeed American provenance, penetrating the rest of the world on both elite and popular levels. The response from the target societies is then seen as occurring on a scale between acceptance and rejection, with in-between positions of coexistence and synthesis' (Berger 2003: 1).

Practices

Religious ideas and traditions are often connected intimately to specific cultures, but this is not to imply that they are static. On the contrary, religious traditions are generally dynamic, changing as they encounter each other. As a result, there are no 'pure', unadulterated religious traditions preserved intact over long periods of time until now (Kurtz 1995: 98). This implies that religious practices can differ – sometimes widely – even within what are ostensibly the same religious traditions. Thus there may be various – associated but different – versions of the same religious tradition encompassing different groups, for example, dissimilar social groups and classes (Haynes 1996a). Put another way, the 'sacred canopy' has generally not been uniform and religious practices vary from place to place and culture to culture, even among those ostensibly following the same religious tradition. As already noted in relation to ideas and experiences, the impact of globalisation is making religious practice even more diverse (Beyer 2006).

Examining the interaction of religion and development, religious ideas, experiences and practices are not only affected by globalisation but also, as we saw in Chapter 1, by demands, expressed both domestically and internationally, for good governance. This encourages religious individuals and faith-based organisations to adopt new or renewed agendas. This can lead to religions looking beyond local or national contexts to regional or international environments in relation to various development issues, including improved social and human rights. Religious individuals and faith-based organisations are often concerned with 'good governance', while international circumstances, including the impact of deepening globalisation, are often believed to be a significant factor in growing mass impoverishment of already poor people throughout the developing world (Held and McGrew 2002). Together, these concerns – the impact of deepening globalisation and the desire for 'good governance'– encourage religions to develop new foci of concern, expressed in anti-WTO protests and North/South economic justice efforts (Spickard 2001). 'Anti-capitalist', 'anti-debt' and 'anti-consumerist' movements and ideas collectively inform many different religious traditions at the present time, with notions of justice and equality often central as a source of ideas for philosophising about how to achieve development goals in the developing world. Overall, this contributes to ideas about an alternative world that many religious organisations are seeking to formulate in various interlinked issue areas, 'including human rights, environmental politics, global economic justice and equity between women and men' (Ezzat 2005: 44). In summary, religious responses to the twin imperatives of globalisation and good governance often focus squarely on development issues that collectively go well beyond the confines of what Christians would call 'church life'.

This is not to imply that the developing world's mainly secular governments and development professionals would all necessarily welcome increased religious involvement in development (Eade 2001). This is because most development programmes and policies are still primarily based on, the often implicit broad assumption that 'modernisation', in the Western and secular sense, is the ultimate goal of all societies, and *economic* development, not necessarily *human* development, the main goal and priority. As a result, 'religion' can still be regarded as a 'dirty' word, treated with suspicion and scorn, a significant impediment to progress, best removed from the public economic, political and development spheres. On the other hand, many aid practitioners and scholars now writing about development strategies concur that to try to exclude religion is likely to be counterproductive. In short, as already noted, there is growing recognition of religion's potential in achieving better development outcomes. As we shall note briefly below, before examining in following chapters at greater length in relation to achievement of the MDGs, many – perhaps most – development scholars and practitioners would now accept the need to see religion as an important dimension of development. This can extend to the notion that development – especially human development – is a partly religious or spiritual expression, the basis upon which many societies in the developing world develop, primarily through processes of self-renewal and growth while welcoming appropriate external material assistance. In short, there is wide agreement that religion is now a significant factor to be considered in any study or policy concerning social development (Wolters 2004).

According to Jos van Gennip, director of the Dutch development cooperation organisation Cordaid and deputy director general for development cooperation in the Dutch Ministry of Foreign Affairs, development professionals need to focus their attention on 'three levels: development at an individual, at a community and at a society level' (Quoted in Wolters 2004: 1). Regarding disappointment at development achievements in the developing world, especially among the poor, van Gennip highlights what he sees as one of the major problems: 'the empty space between the individual and the society. This empty space has become problematic in process of modernization and globalization. Religion can play an important role here' (Quoted in Wolters 2004: 1). Van Gennip is highlighting that for many religious people, development is more than materialistic growth alone, including reaching measurable development goals; a rounded sense of development accomplishment would also include the achievement of a range of goals linked to better holistic development in a human-centred sense. A starting point to achieve this goal would require that (secular) development agencies and local faith groups and communities work together, learning first to cooperate in reflecting on poverty, growth and development and, second, to construct new coalitions in development. The goal is to get the best from both worlds: 'functional rationality on the one hand and religion and spirituality on the other ... interrelated to get a concept of integrated (value based) development' (Tyndale 2004: 6). The aim would be to help fill the empty space between the individual and the society. To this end, development professionals should seek to undertake increased:

- *Academic reflection.* Study further the meaning of religion and spirituality for development, poverty reduction and the care for the environment;
- *Improved training.* Better training so Western development agencies and development workers 'develop an antenna' for the role of religion and spirituality in development;
- *Lobby and advocacy.* If successful, the results of this approach would need to be brought into public and political debates about development cooperation, identifying 'signposts' for alternative development policies (Wolters 2004: 1).

This should not be taken to imply that to improve the relationship between religion and spirituality,[3] on the one hand, and secular development thinking and practice, on the other, is necessarily an easy task. Each is coming at the problem from different starting points. For Holenstein,

> Religion and spirituality are sources of world views and views of life; they constitute creative political and social forces; they are forces for cohesion and for polarisation; they generate stimuli for social and development policies; they serve as instruments for political reference and legitimacy. Development co-operation cannot afford to ignore religion and spirituality (Holenstein 2005: 4).

In this list of mostly positive attributes, Holenstein also notes the potential for 'polarisation' in relation to religion. That is, we should not understand religion as a panacea that will right all development wrongs; some aspects can complement *and* motivate development, others can obstruct or undermine it. This is to emphasise the complexity one encounters when we focus upon the impact of religion on development activities in different faiths and regions of the developing world. As we shall in following chapters, religious people and faith-based organisations are notable as agents of advocacy, funding, innovation, empowerment, social movements, and service delivery. They can also incite or encourage violence, develop hierarchical leadership structures, or encourage women's subservience. In addition, analytic and conceptual complexity is further heightened by a highly subjective factor: what we personally believe about the relationship between religion and development.

This then is the issue at the heart of the conundrum about religion's role in development: its ambivalence. On the one hand, religion and spirituality can make essential contributions to human development to religious believers by (1) giving life metaphysical meaning and hope of well-being (2) helping mould individual and group behaviour in relation to culture, way of life, and work, and (3) facilitating development of positive social, developmental and political values that encourage community cohesion. In summary, religion and spirituality can be powerful, benign socio-cultural forces for motivation, inclusiveness, participation and sustainability. On the other hand, the spiritual and material resources of religion and spirituality can be misused and instrumentalised both from within and/or from without. Appleby explicitly refers to this ambivalence in the title of his book, *The Ambivalence of the Sacred: Religion, Violence and Reconciliation* (2000). He describes how both terrorists and peacemakers can emerge from the same community, and be followers of the same religion. One kills while the other strives for reconciliation. Appleby explains what religious terrorists and religious peacemakers share in common, what causes them to take different paths in fighting injustice, and how a deeper understanding of religious extremism can and must be integrated more effectively into our thinking about tribal, regional, and international conflict, the topic of Chapter 3. Overall, the ambivalence of the sacred encourages a dual view of religion in relation to development that can be judged, normatively, as follows:

- *Positive* role, when religion motivates civil engagement in pursuit of socially and developmentally constructive goals;
- *Negative* role, when religion (1) seeks to exclude others, (2) perhaps resorts to conflict and violence, and (3) overall seriously undermines achievement of socially and developmentally constructive goals.

To this point, this chapter has highlighted intersections of religion and development that can be examined and mapped from a variety of perspectives, which inevitably overlap to some degree. Re-establishing the role of religion in human development in the developing world necessarily implies challenging the modernist assumptions of secularism and positivist rationalism, social sciences based on European modernism, which in the religious view have proved to be inadequate to produce necessary answers and, as a result, need to be reformed and rethought (Ezzat 2005: 45). We have also noted that religious traditions and accompanying notions of justice and equality can become an important source of ideas for pondering on and trying to establish strategies to deal with the problem of how realistically to achieve development goals in the developing world. Many religious entities now seek to think and work in the context of such goals, in relation to, *inter alia*, conflict resolution and peacemaking; eradication of extreme poverty and hunger; better health; environmental sustainability; and improved educational opportunities. These topics are looked at in detail in Chapters 3–7.

Religion and development: international, national and local initiatives

In this section, we identify and examine religious entities that operate at the international/regional and national/local levels. Significantly motivated by religious concerns, such actors are normatively identified as 'pro-development' or 'anti-development'. After introducing and discussing the categories in this chapter, in the following chapters we will examine faith-based entities in Africa, Asia and Latin America, with a focus on Christian, Islamic, Buddhist and Hindu bodies.

International/regional faith-based entities

The first question is: How do international agents 'talk' across the secular-religious divide and find common ground on the way forward in terms of development strategy and outcomes? To try to answer this question, it is useful to refer again to the MDGs. While seven MDGs refer primarily to action seen as needed *within* developing countries, the eighth refers to the need to 'develop a global partnership for development', implying the need for both developing and developed countries to work together to resolve development concerns. One dimension of such a partnership is increased interaction between secular development agencies and faith-based organisations, to cooperate with each other to work out strategies to achieve agreed development objectives. During the late 1990s and early 2000s there were a number of such initiatives, focusing on interactive partnerships that, first, sought to bring together interested parties to discuss strategy and, second, to work out practical solutions to identify pressing developmental problems. We have already noted an important initiative in this regard, dating from 1998: the WFDD.[4] Jointly inaugurated by

James Wolfensohn, then president of the World Bank, and George Carey, at the time Archbishop of Canterbury and head of the Anglican Church,[5] the initiative sought to promote a development dialogue between several religious faiths, the World Bank and the IMF. Over the next seven years, until Wolfehnson's retirement from the World Bank in mid-2005, the WFDD sponsored case studies and organised publications and workshops with faith leaders and development professionals on various themes, including: World Development Reports, PRSPs and, more generally, the MDGs themselves.[6] At around this time, other international initiatives also emerged, including: an IDB initiative ('Social Capital, Ethics, and Development'; details at: http://www1. worldbank.org/prem/poverty/scapital/) and a series of 'World Council of Churches Dialogues' with various secular development organisations, including: the ILO, the IMF, and the World Bank (Alkire 2006). In addition, the United Nations Population Fund also began a continuing dialogue with faith leaders (Working from Within 2004). Overall, such initiatives can be seen as part of a wider process of bringing together secular and faith-inspired views on development which also found expression in contemporaneous international campaigns that, drawing on religious principles and teachings, were often notable for their dynamism, energy, and ethical and moral foci.

Jubilee 2000 was one such initiative. It was founded in 1996 as an ecumenical initiative, primarily involving Christian organisations, but with support from representatives of other faiths, including Islam. The Jubilee concept drew on the biblical idea of the year of Jubilee, the 50th year, as referred to in Leviticus (25: 10): 'And you shall hallow the fiftieth year and you shall proclaim liberty throughout the land to all its inhabitants'. The Christian foundation for the campaign had its roots in the belief that God hears the cries of suffering people and inspires Christians to work for a better world, calling on them to acts of justice, mercy and reconciliation. Many churches and faith-based organisations more generally backed the claim that these teachings religiously compelled Christians to advocate for public policies and laws based on justice and compassion, including international debt relief for the poorest countries (http://www.jubileedebtcampaign. org.uk/?lid=282). The overall focus of the campaign was cancellation of unpayable international debts in the world's poorest countries by the end of the year 2000.[7] By January 2000, Jubilee 2000 had collected more than 18 million petition signatures from 120 countries, and established campaigning groups in over 60 countries worldwide.

Jubilee 2000 identified the 52 poorest countries in the world that were collectively in urgent need of debt cancellation. Three-quarters of these countries (37) are in sub-Saharan Africa; collectively they owe US$376 billion. The impact of the Jubilee 2000 campaign was demonstrated when the international community – in effect, the world's richest countries – agreed to the Heavily Indebted Poor Countries (HIPC) initiative. Results were generally encouraging: by September 2006, 'Nominal debt service relief under HIPC to the 20 completion point countries has been estimated to amount to US$44 billion' (World Bank 2006). But to put this into perspective, Jubilee 2000 has assessed that it would actually cost 'only' US$71 billion to cancel all the debts owed by 52 of the poorest countries. This is only *one third of one percent* of the annual income of the richest OECD countries! (Soka Gakkai International 2000)

It was always intended that Jubilee 2000 would disband at the end of 2000 and this it did. However, offshoots were formed following the closure of Jubilee 2000, focusing efforts on campaigning to try to ensure that governments made good on their promises. Jubilee Research at the New Economics Foundation, located in London, took over from Jubilee 2000 in 2001, providing expert analysis and data on developing countries' indebtedness. In addition, the Jubilee Debt Campaign (JDC), also based in Britain, was the campaigning successor to Jubilee 2000, collecting together many of the leading lights of Britain's original Jubilee 2000 membership. JDC calls for total debt cancellation of the world's poorest countries' unpayable debt. In the USA, in addition, Jubilee USA also focuses on the issue of countries' unpayable debts in the developing world, while the Faith Action for People-Centered Development Policy[8] represented a group of US-based Protestant and Catholic churches and faith-based organisations that campaign for US and global policies that promote justice, reconciliation, and the poverty reduction worldwide. In addition, the international debt issue was one of the targets of the Make Poverty History Campaign in 2005.

The ecumenical nature of the Jubilee 2000 campaign was emphasised by support for the initiative from Sahib Mustaqim Bleher, General Secretary of the Islamic Party of Britain. In support of the campaign, Bleher stated that 'the Qur'an encourages debt cancellation whenever a debtor is unable, due to his particular circumstances, to repay the debt: "and if (the debtor) is in difficulty, then (there should be) postponement until (he is) at ease, but that you should give it as charity is (even) better for you, if you knew" (2: 280)'. Bleher's comments highlight that Islam is a religion that counts obligatory regular charity as one of its 'five pillars'. It also emphasises that Islam cannot properly be practised without due regard to its social dimension, nor without reference to economic justice. The main emphasis in the Qur'an, however, is put upon prevention of the very situation that made the Jubilee campaign necessary. In line with the Qur'anic demand that 'wealth should not only circulate between the rich amongst you' (59: 7), Islam categorically forbids the taking of interest to prevent the accumulation of large capital sums. In addition, to tolerate wrong doing, or oppression, is also considered by Muslims to be unacceptable (Jubilee USA Network 2001).

A second category of religious entities that operate at the international/regional includes transnational faith-based organisations, many of which are concerned with development issues. For example, some are significant purveyors of education, service delivery and other non-market goods. Examples are common within the Christian and Islamic worlds. For example, the International Islamic Relief Organisation (IIRO) is one of the most active Islamic transnational NGOs in Africa, operating in several countries including Uganda and Kenya. The IIRO was established in 1978 as a humanitarian NGO to provide assistance to victims of natural disasters and wars all over the world, because some 80% of refugees and victims, it claims, are Muslims. The IIRO claims that its relief programmes are directed solely towards the provision of medical, educational and social support for those in desperate need. It also aims to encourage local entrepreneurs by sponsoring viable economic projects and small businesses that can help victims find employment and earn a living. To fulfil these objectives, the IIRO has established a wide network of national and international contacts with various Islamic and non-Islamic relief organisations, institutions and individuals, operating in several countries in Europe, Asia and Africa. The major part of IIRO's financial contributions comes from private donations in Saudi Arabia, and an endowment fund (Sanabil Al-Khair) was established to generate a stable income to finance IIRO's various activities. The IIRO has several departments, including: Urgent Relief and Refugees; Health Care; Orphans and Social Welfare; Education; Agricultural Affairs; Architectural and Engineering Consultancy; and the 'Our Children project' (www.islamic-knowledge.com/Organizations.htm). Transnational Christian development agencies include: Catholic Relief Services and World Vision International, an organisation in control of significant economic resources. World Vision International is among the largest and best studied of such transnational NGOs, with a budget of $1.97 billion in 2005 (http://www.wvi.org/wvi/pdf/WVI2005AnnualReport.pdf).

In conclusion, various liaisons between secular development agencies and faith-based organisations noted in this section collectively highlight that in recent years various international and interactive initiatives have developed. Many were inspired by the same concerns represented in the MDGs and how to achieve them by 2015. For example, unpayable debts, development inequalities and perceived deleterious effects of economic globalisation feature prominently in many of the initiatives noted above. What they also had in common was a shared goal to try to achieve better development outcomes in the developing world by bringing together international secular and faith-based entities to work on the problems.

National and local initiatives

Various faith based initiatives within developing countries, at both national and local levels, have emerged and developed over the years. Many have achieved prominence in the context of civil society support for development priorities (Haynes 1999; Thomas 2005: 219–45). However, as Ezzat notes, for long periods 'the religious factor was ... excluded (or rather expelled) from the semantic field and marginalised in academic debates' (Ezzat 2005: 44). As we noted above, revising the assumptions of modernist social theory on religion's role in development – and politics more generally – hinges on a reclassification of the idea of civility that does not depend on its secularity. Active involvement of various religious actors in civil societies worldwide is widely noted, especially in the developing world and former communist countries of Eastern Europe, a development that led to renewed focus on the de-secularisation of civility (Weigel 2003; Ramet 1998). In addition, many secular social movements also draw heavily on religious notions of justice and equality; and different faiths – including Roman Catholicism, Judaism and Buddhism – are often inspiring sources of generic liberation theologies sharing a common focus on often ideologically radical democratic conceptions (Klicksberg 2003; Gutierrez 1973; Sulak Sivaraksa and Ginsburg 1992).

As Ezzat notes, 'There is no way we can understand the logic, strategies and dynamics of civil society anywhere in the Third World unless we bring the transcendental dimension back into our analysis. Religious devotion is a fundamental motive for many social movements in the South, from Latin America to Africa and South Asia' (Ezzat 2005: 45). In addition, some religions deliver a range of services to consumers, including religious schools paid for and directed by churches, mosques and temples, while government-funded and directed programmes can also be faith-based. (We examine examples of such programmes in the following chapters). Together these examples reflect the widespread fact in the developing world that there is often much less of a division between the secular and the religious, especially when compared to nearly all Western countries. We have already noted that involvement of faith-based organisations in development has led to scrutiny, with some pointing to what is widely perceived as the 'ambivalence of the sacred'. But, at the risk of oversimplifying what is widely agreed to be a complex issue, we can dichotomise such concerns: religious entities are either normatively 'pro-development' or normatively 'anti-development'. The obvious problem with this dichotomy is that each category is often derived normatively from assumptions rather than objective evidence. For example, 'religious fundamentalists' are routinely labelled as 'anti-development' while religious campaigners, such as those linked to Jubilee 2000, are more likely to be judged to be 'pro-development'. It may be however that *both* groups want 'development' but a development that each concep-tualises very differently, although both might highlight the impor-tance of *human* development over *material* development.

Take the example of the Sarvodaya Shramadana Movement (SSM) in Sri Lanka, founded by a 26-year-old teacher A.T. Ariyaratne in 1958. Inspired by Mohandas 'Mahatma' Gandhi and the Buddha, Ariyaratne sought to awaken members to their 'inner person', urging them then to change outer structures by common activities such as volunteer work camps – with the slogan: 'We build the road and the road builds us' (www.sarvodaya.org/). Overall, SSM aims to help people to help themselves; its philosophy is embodied in its name which means, the 'awakening of all by voluntarily sharing people's resources, especially their time, thoughts and efforts' (Fisher 1993: 146). SSM sees develop-ment as a means, not an end, as 'Material wellbeing is no more than the vehicle necessary for spiritual awakening' (Lean 1996). Since the late 1950s, SSM has worked in one-third – c.8,000 – of Sri Lanka's 23,000 villages, home to more than three million people – and has grown over the years to be Sri Lanka's most important national devel-opment organisation, employing about 7,000 people. Over 30,000 trained village youths work in their local communities. SSM's areas of interest include nutrition, health, education, housing, water supply and sanitation, agriculture, savings and credit, rural industries and marketing. In short, as Ariyaratne puts it, millions of rural people in

Sri Lanka 'are participant-beneficiaries of an integrated rural awakening programme' (quoted in Ekins 1992: 101). Regarding the potential for 'ambivalence' in the activities of SSM, it is important to note that the organisation employs language derived from several sources (including, Buddhism, Hinduism, and the Indian nationalist leader, Mohandas 'Mahatma' Gandhi) – emphasising a rather generic moral focus of great significance for both policy and better governance agendas. SSM has been successful in creating 'ideas that carry a sense of morality in policy debates' without alienating 'those who do not share their religious derivation'. More generally, Hutanuwatr and Rasbach suggest that Buddhist values provide an alternative to modernising development agendas, 'offering a conceptual basis on which self-reliant, non-violent communities can form' (Hutanuwatr and Rasbach 2004: 4).

An example of an ideologically different kind of faith-based development network compared to SSM is the tens of thousands of Basic Christian Communities (BCCs) in Latin America. Since their foundation in the 1960s, BCCs have engendered a large literature (Levine 1984; Medhurst 1989; Casanova 1994; Sabia 1997). First emerging in Brazil, BCCs spread throughout the region, focusing on community development through the application of group effort, drawing on Christian principles. An essentially biblical radicalism, often melded with facets of Marxism-Leninism, the tenets of liberation theology stimulated numerous Roman Catholic priests in Latin America to champion the concerns of the poor. The contemporaneous development of liberation theology focused attention on socio-political divisions and associated political struggles in Latin America. Liberation theology is an intensely political concept, essentially a radical religious response to poor socio-economic conditions. Central to the idea is the notion of dependence and underdevelopment; the use of a class struggle perspective to explain social conflict and justify political action; and the exercise of a political role to achieve both religious and political goals. In the 1960s, the Church in Latin America was radicalised by influential theologians and religious thinkers – such as Gustavo Gutierrez and Paulo Freire – whose ideas were put into effect by mainly younger priests, serving to help develop a socially progressive Catholicism. BCCs were the most concrete sign of the spread of liberation theology concerns in Latin America. The political effects of liberation theology in Latin America are widely believed to have contributed to the democratisation of the region from the 1970s (Haynes 1993: 95–109).

Because of the nature of Latin America's extant political arrangements in the 1960s and 1970s – throughout the region, a period of
military rule – it is unsurprising that many BCCs became highly politicised. The most dynamic period in BCC existence was often during
the years of military rule, that is, from the 1960s to the 1980s. In
El Salvador, for example, BCCs began as non-political development
vehicles that later evolved into politicised organisations with the tacit
blessing of the Catholic hierarchy (Cardenal 1990: 245). In Colombia,
on the other hand, local conservative bishops vigorously attacked
liberation theology – the ideology of many BCCs (Levine 1990: 26).
Socialist Nicaragua was also the home of numerous BCCs during the
1980s, the period of Sandinista socialist rule. The Sandinistas saw the
BCCs as political allies and, as a result, encouraged them (Serra 1985:
151–74; Sabia 1997).

However, BCCs were often regarded as communist front groups by
conservative military governments. In Chile, for example, where leftist
political parties were banned after the military takeover in 1973, BCCs
became a haven for left-wing radicals incensed by what they saw as a
series of politically repressive and economically stringent measures –
whose net effect was seriously to disadvantage the poor. During the
rule of General Pinochet (1973–90), it was not uncommon for BCCs,
especially in the capital, Santiago, to incur the wrath of the regime.
Verbal attacks began to appear in the government-controlled media by
1977, charging that the Chilean BCCs' umbrella group, the Vicaria de
la Solidaridad (the Vicariate of Solidarity), harboured communist
sympathisers and received foreign money to support political dissi-
dents. As a result, many local BCC members were harassed. Foreign
priests were also frequently perceived as politically undesirable and in
the second half of the 1970s, around 400 foreign priests were expelled
from Chile, precipitating a net decline of over 10% in the total clergy
(Smith 1982: 343).

Over time, however, military governments in Latin America were
gradually forced onto the defensive by a combination of domestic and
international pressure for democracy. BCCs were often important in
this regard because, by helping to establish and develop a sense of
community empowerment, they were leading factors in the growth
and significance of civil society in many Latin American countries
(Mainwaring and Viola 1984; Hewitt 1990). By actively seeking to
ameliorate poor development positions – for example, by pressing
for infrastructural improvements, such as sewers, streetlights, and electricity – BCC activists learnt that the best way to achieve development

goals was not necessarily by appealing as individuals to powerful figures and bureaucratic authorities, but instead to coordinate the community in pursuit of better development – that is, to achieve improvements by a collective focus on shared goals.

The overall point, however, is that unlike the SSM which achieved development successes through application of a philosophy that went out of its way not to alienate or dichotomise, the BCC approach was often overtly political and confrontational. This highlights another sense of the ambivalence of faith-focused development entities: the extent to which they alienate or attract religious and political constituencies during campaigns for improved development.

A third focus in this section is religious fundamentalist entities, often said to represent a key form of 'anti-development', especially perhaps when the observer's chosen development visions are linked to a process of secular modernisation. Most contemporary religious fundamentalisms are reactive against perceived unwelcome manifestations of modernisation, especially declining moral values and/or perceived undermining of the family as a social institution (Haynes 2002). To many religious fundamentalists God was in danger of being superseded by a gospel of technical progress accompanying sweeping socio-economic changes. Around the world, the pace of socio-economic change, especially since World War II, everywhere strongly challenged traditional habits, beliefs and cultures, and societies were under considerable and constant pressure to adapt to modernisation. Not least, in an increasingly materialist world one's individual worth was increasingly measured according to secular standards of wealth and status; religion seemed ignored, belittled or threatened. Thus to many religious fundamentalists unwelcome social, cultural and economic changes were the root cause of what they saw as a toxic cocktail of religious, moral and social decline.

Drawing on data compiled from studies of numerous religious fundamentalist groups from several religious traditions in different parts of the world, Marty and Scott Appleby arrive at the following definition of those who adhere to religious fundamentalism. They are people who hold a 'set of strategies, by which beleaguered believers attempt to preserve their distinctive identity as a people or group'. They see themselves acting in response to a real or imagined attack from those who, they believe, want to draw them into a 'syncretistic, areligious, or irreligious cultural milieu' (Marty and Appleby 1993: 3). Following an initial sense of defensiveness as a result of perception of attack from unwelcome, alien forces, fundamentalists may well go on to develop an offensive strategy aimed at altering radically prevailing socio-political realities in order to 'bring back' religious concerns into public centrality.

Finally, religion can also be seen as anti-development when understood as a practical development and social problem: that is, when religious leaders or institutions appear to obstruct development, or when religious rhetoric is used to try to conceal other, more mundane, motives. For example, there are value conflicts within many religions that focus upon family planning methods, including contraception and abortion. There is also much controversy about how to prevent HIV/AIDS and educate communities about the disease, as the issue invariably includes a focus on both sexual morality and women's role in society more generally empowerment. As noted above, organisations such as the United Nations Population Fund now undertake respectful and temperate dialogue with faith leaders and various religious institutions, including the Roman Catholic Church. The overall point is that such dialogue, as well as religious cooperation with aid donating countries, needs to engage and work with religious values, values that might be ambivalent about, for example, the societal and religious status of women and girls. One current example in this regard is the ABC (Abstinence, Being Faithful, Condoms) approach to HIV/AIDS prevention that, championed by the US government, threatens US funding for condoms in the developing world (Sinding 2005). In addition, many Western development professionals and analysts would regard patriarchy as engrained in the cultural forms of many world religions, a viewpoint that inform much writing and debate on the topic of females, religion and development (Rai 2005). Many topics in this category do not actually relate centrally to development *per se* but to sexuality, prayer, family life, violence, and so on. There is however active engagement between many faith-based organisations and agendas informed by 'gender and development' issues, including: women's empowerment, reproductive health, education, and personal security.

Finally, religion's involvement in conflict, conflict resolution and peace-building is another source of ambivalence in the development literature and accompanying dialogues. As we shall in the next chapter, there is a burgeoning literature on religion's contributions to conflict and violence. Accounts often focus on various parts of the developing world – including Sri Lanka, Kashmir, Sudan, Iraq, Afghanistan, and Chechnya – where armed groups claiming religious motivations for their endeavours are commonly found. Such conflicts not only cause and intensify poverty but also more generally significantly disrupt – if not curtail altogether – various development programmes (Alkire 2006; Ellis and ter Haar 2005; Bock 2001; Haynes 2007). But this is only one side of the story. In Chapter 3, we also examine religious initiatives in relation to conflict resolution and peace-building, projects that have become increasingly important in recent years in many parts of the developing world.

Conclusion

This chapter has argued that it is essential to integrate religion into thinking about development. However, this is not to imply that this will be a panacea for generally better development outcomes in the developing world. In other words, the argument is *not* that applying religious or spiritual resources will result in a major breakthrough in development in the developing world. Moreover, appreciating that religion can be a resource for development does not mean that policy-makers – whether in the developed or developing world – can merely add religion to their inventory of policy instruments without trying to integrate more fully religious insights into development programmes and policies.

Better development outcomes can result, however, if some basic changes are made – not necessarily in relation to specific sectors or by identifying new policy instruments – in the ways in which both development and its implementation are considered. This chapter has suggested that better development outcomes can occur when the concept of human development is placed centrally in development priorities and agendas. This would imply however a sea change from the current approach adopted by most if not all secular development agencies that implicitly or explicitly are most concerned with improving material outcomes. To improve human development implies bringing into the development equation both religious and spiritual ideas – not as an adjunct to economic development but as a crucial component of a wider, more inclusive understanding of development. In some cases, for example, 'failed' states in various parts of the developing world (such as, Somalia, Sierra Leone, Liberia, Sudan, and Afghanistan) the very notion of state-led policy implementation might usefully be rethought as the necessary instruments to put into effect – operative, rational bureaucracies no longer exist (Haynes 2005a: 236–43). As a result, policy in the conventional sense cannot be applied at all – and the activities of faith-based organisations could well be crucial in delivering even minimal development goals.

We have also noted in this chapter that it is possible to distinguish specific sectors – education, poverty reduction, health, environmental sustainability, perhaps improved gender equity – where religion can and often does play a developmentally constructive role. The following chapters examine the role of faith-based organisations in relation to various topics. In addition, we examine key questions in relation to how Islam, Christianity, Hinduism and Buddhism and can help build and sustain peaceful coexistence, as well as enhanced social and human development in circumstances where, encouraged by globalisation, increasingly multi-faith societies must deal with a world suffering from what appears to many to be growing strife and economic disparity between rich and poor, both within and between countries. How can religious individuals and faith-based organisations successfully advocate greater reconciliation in relation to conflict and more fairness regarding development? The answer may include the understanding that religious individuals and faith-based actors are most effective when they seek to use their resources systematically to emphasise peace, avoidance of the use of force and the necessity of secular, inter- and intra-faith collusion to achieve development objectives. This would build on what we identified in the first chapter: the world religions broadly sharing a set of values rooted in theological and spiritual beliefs could facilitate efforts.

3
Conflict, Conflict Resolution and Peace-building

In recent years, religion has made a remarkable return to prominence in Western development circles. Confounding the expectations of secularists, religion has a strong – perhaps growing – significance as a strong source of identity for millions of people in the developing world. Consequently, religious individuals and faith-based organisations, as carriers of religious ideas, play an important role in many societies, both as a source of conflict and as a tool for conflict resolution and peace-building. Religious hatreds and differences are central to many recent and current conflicts in the developing world. There is also evidence that religious forces can also play a constructive role in helping resolve them and build peace, via early warnings of conflict, good offices once conflict has erupted, as well as advocacy, mediation, and reconciliation. This chapter highlights how religion can (1) both encourage conflict and peace in the developing world, and (2) offers examples – from Mozambique, Nigeria and Cambodia – of religious peacemakers who are significant in attempts to reconcile previously warring communities and achieve social cohesion, crucial foundations of progress in human development.

By now, it is hopefully clear that the main task addressed in this book – to explain and account for religion's often-ambivalent involvement in human development in the developing world – is not straightforward. In part, this is because there is no single, elegant theoretical model enabling us to deal adequately with all relevant cases of religious involvement in human development. On the other hand, we have noted that the influence of religion is increasing in relation to what we identified as 'good governance' issues in the developing world, an issue often affected by the multiple impacts of globalisation. Recent and current globalisation – characterised in the developing

75

world by its often destabilising economic, political, cultural and technological effects – can also affect religions by undermining associated traditional value systems. A consequence is that, in many developing countries many people are said to feel both disorientated and troubled and in response (re)turn to religion to try to deal with associated existential angst (Norris and Inglehart 2004). Such people may find in religion a source of comfort, serenity, stability, and spiritual uplifting. Some may experience new or renewed feelings of identity that not only help provide believers' lives with meaning and purpose but also can in some cases contribute to inter-religious competition and conflict (Carlson and Owens 2003).

Globalisation leads to greatly increased interaction between people and communities. As a result, encounters between different religious traditions are increasingly common but although not always harmonious, which can lead to what Kurtz labels 'culture wars' (Kurtz 1995: 168). The reason, he contends, is because various religious worldviews encourage different allegiances and standards in relation to various areas, including the family, law, education and politics. Increasingly, it appears, conflicts between people, ethnic groups, classes, and nations are framed in religious terms. Such religious conflicts seem often to 'take on "larger-than-life" proportions as the struggle of good against evil' (Kurtz 1995: 170). Such conflicts can seriously affect a country's chance of development. According to Hans Kung, an eminent Roman Catholic theologian,

> the most fanatical, the cruelest political struggles are those that have been colored, inspired, and legitimized by religion. To say this is not to reduce all political conflicts to religious ones, but to take seriously the fact that religions share in the responsibility for bringing peace to our torn and warring world' (Hans Kung, quoted in Smock 2004).

In summary, conflicts can have religious roots, whereby religious differences drive accompanying hatred and violence. The implication is that 'religions and faith communities' can be effective as 'angels of peace' as well as 'warmongers'. The *ambivalence* of the religious factor is linked to the fact that the relationship of the world religions to violence is ambiguous. 'All great God-narratives are familiar with traditions that legitimise force in certain circumstances, claim victims in the battle for their own beliefs and demonise people of other religions. However, at the same time there are sources that proclaim the incompatibility of violence with religion, demand sacrifices for peace and insist on respect for people of other religions. If we are to assume that, for the foreseeable future, the religions of the world will continue to be a factor in political conflicts, then it is high time that we strengthened the "civilising" side of the sacred and made it more difficult for it cynically to be taken over by political interests. What is said here about the relationship of world religions to violence can be considered generally valid for religions overall'. (Holenstein 2005: 10).

This ambivalence becomes clear when we focus upon current religious involvement in large-scale conflicts. For example, large-scale violence in Africa, Asia and other parts of the developing world is increasingly associated with serious social conflicts, some of which involve religious tensions. Focusing upon Commonwealth countries, many of which are also developing countries, Barringer notes that religious tensions are very often linked to other issues. These include: 'ethnicity, culture, class, power and wealth, played out both within' countries, for example, Nigeria, Fiji, Cyprus, Sri Lanka, and between them, for example, India and Pakistan (Barringer 2008: 2). Turning to the Middle East, we can easily understand that stability and prosperity are key goals, central to achievement of peace and the elimination of poverty among constituent states. However, the region is widely identified as one that has a number of religious conflicts – between, Israel and, on the one hand, the (mostly Sunni Muslim) Palestinians and, on the other, Lebanon's Shia Hisbullah guerrillas. They are also conflicts within Iraq between Shia and Sunni Muslims and between Shia Iran and Sunni Saudi Arabia. Such conflicts draw our attention to the fact that the Middle East is the emblematic birthplace of the three monotheistic world religions (Christianity, Islam, and Judaism). As a result, there is a legacy not only of shared religious wisdom but also of sometimes intense societal conflicts. This implies a complex relationship that not only impacts on all regional countries, but also on some far away from the region, including, the Philippines (which has seen growing numbers of Islamic extremist groups in recent years), as well as various Western countries, including the United States, the United Kingdom and Spain, all of which have experienced Islamist bombing outrages in recent years.

A key to eventual peace in the region may well be achievement of significant collaborative efforts among different religious bodies, which along with religious and secular organisations from outside the region, including both Europe and the United States, may through collaborative efforts work eventually to develop a new model of peace and cooperation to enable the Middle East to escape from what often seems an endless cycle of religion and culture-based conflict. It is important to note that this emphasises that in the Middle East religion is intimately connected *both* to promulgation and prolongation of conflicts *as well as* attempts at their reconciliation. This implies that religion's contribution to conflicts in the Middle East is ambivalent: it can play a significant, even a fundamental, role contributing to conflicts in various ways, including how they are intensified, channelled or reconciled. On the other hand, it can play an important role in seeking to resolve conflicts and build peace. This dualistic role of religion is not of course limited to the Middle East but also present in conflicts in Asia (notably Sri Lanka, and India/Pakistan), Africa (for example, Sudan, Nigeria and Algeria) and elsewhere in the developing world.

These introductory comments point to the fact that religion is by no means invariably associated with conflict, as it can play a significant role in attempts to resolve inter- and intra-group clashes and help build peace. Bartoli (2005: 5–6) notes that 'all religious traditions contain references in the form of didactical stories, teaching or even direct recommendation as to how the faithful should act in order to achieve harmony and peace within him/herself in the first place'. Appleby (2006) points out that, more than a decade after the publication of a seminal text on this topic, Douglas Johnston and Cynthia Sampson's *Religion, the Missing Dimension of Statecraft* (1994), numerous relevant books and journal articles have appeared, collectively focusing on how religious actors can play a role in ending conflicts and building peace (sources). Summarising an initial set of findings regarding religious peace-building and faith-based diplomacy, Appleby notes the follows:

- Religious leaders are uniquely positioned to foster non-violent conflict transformation through the building of constructive, collaborative relationships within and across ethnic and religious groups for the common good of the entire population of a country or region;
- In many conflict settings around the world, the social location and cultural power of religious leaders make them potentially critical players in any effort to build a sustainable peace;
- The multigenerational local or regional communities they oversee are repositories of local knowledge and wisdom, custodians of culture, and privileged sites of moral, psychological and spiritual formation;
- Symbolically charged sources of personal as well as collective identity, these communities typically establish and maintain essential educational and welfare institutions, some of which serve people who are not members of the religious community (Appleby 2006: 1).

Before turning to the issue of religious involvement in conflict resolution and peace-building, we focus on religious involvement in conflict in the developing world.

Religion and conflict

Although religious believers would normally regard their chosen religious expressions as both benevolent and inspiring, sometimes religious faiths are linked to violence and conflict both between and within religious groups (or at least entities with a religious veneer). We can note the ramifications of September 11, 2001, in this regard. In the half decade since then, a massive literature has appeared on religious contributions to conflict and violence (For a major bibliography, see National Commission on Terrorist Attacks 2004). We can also take into account the fact that various armed groups claim religious support for their activities in various parts of the developing world.

It is however hardly surprising that religion is often implicated in both domestic and international conflicts, because religious conviction contains within it various sources of related danger:

- *Religion is focused on the absolute and unconditional and as a result can adopt totalitarian characteristics.* The monotheistic religions – Christianity, Islam and Judaism – may have especial difficulty trying to distinguish between, on the one hand, claims of the absolutely divine and, on the other, the traditions and history of human existence;
- *When claiming both absolute and exclusive validity, religious conviction can lead to intolerance, over-zealous proselytisation and religious fragmentation.* Religious exclusiveness is also typically hostile to both pluralism and liberal democracy;
- *Religion can increase aggressiveness and the willingness to use violence.* Added symbolic value can be an aspect of religious conviction, deriving from profane motivation and aims that become 'holy' objectives;
- *Leaders within faith-based organisations may seek to legitimise abuses of power and violation of human rights in the name of religious zeal.* Because such leaders are nearly always men, there can also in addition be specific gender issues and women's human rights concerns.

According to Holenstein, religious power interests may try to make use of the following susceptibilities:

- Domination strategies of identity politics may seek to harness real or perceived 'ethnic-cultural' and 'cultural-religious' differences;

- Misused religious motivation informs some recent and current terrorist activities;
- Leaders of religious fundamentalist movements 'lay claim to a single and absolutist religious interpretation at the cost of all others, and they link their interpretation to political power objectives' (Holenstein 2005: 11).

Holenstein's last point relates to what Kurtz has called 'exclusive accounts of the nature of reality', that is, that followers only accept religious beliefs that they regard as *true* beliefs (Kurtz 1995: 238). Examples include the 'religions of the book' – Judaism, Christianity and Islam – because each faith claims authority that emanates principally from sacred texts, actually, similar texts. Such exclusivist truth claims can be a serious challenge to religious toleration and diversity, essential to our co-existence in a globalised world, and make conflict more likely. On the other hand, many religious traditions have within them beliefs that can help develop a peaceful, multicultural world. For example, from within Christianity comes the idea of non-violence, a key attribute of Jesus, the religion's founder, who insisted that all people are children of God, and that the test of one's relationship with God is whether one loves one's enemies and brings good news to the poor. As St Paul said, 'There is no Jew or Greek, servant or free, male or female: because you are all one in Jesus Christ' (Galatians 3: 28).

In terms of contemporary conflicts, three forms involving religion are worth noting: religious fundamentalisms; 'religious terrorism' and how it thrives in 'failed' states; and controversies surrounding 'the clash of civilisations' thesis (Huntington 1996; Gopin 2000; Appleby 2000; Juergensmeyer 2000, 2005).

First, some religious 'fundamentalisms' are associated with religious and political conflicts in some developing countries (Marty and Appleby 1993). Although often individually distinctive, many religious fundamentalisms share a common characteristic: believing themselves to be under threat, followers adopt a 'set of strategies, by which [these] beleaguered believers attempt to preserve their distinctive identity as a people or group' in response to real or imagined attacks from non-believers who, they believe, are trying to draw them into a 'syncretistic, areligious, or irreligious cultural milieu' (Marty and Appleby 1993: 3). In such a context, fundamentalists' 'defence of religion' can develop into social or political offensives with domestic and/or international ramifications.

Second, 'failed' states may provide the circumstances that encourage conflicts linked to religious terrorism (Juergensmeyer 2005). Examples of recent and current failed states in the developing world include: Cambodia, Iraq, Somalia, and Afghanistan (Haynes 2005a: 224–43). Such states are very unstable environments lacking effective central government, circumstances that are often conducive to the development of secular or religious terrorism. Circumstances prevailing in failed states may encourage people to turn to religion as a result of a feeling that their existential security is threatened. In addition, absence of effective central government provides circumstances conducive for international religious terrorist groups, such as al-Qaeda, to thrive; in some cases, failed states – including Afghanistan, Iraq, and Somalia – have all become 'safe havens' in recent years for al-Qaeda, a launching pad for their attacks (Burke 2004, 2006). For example, Gunaratna avers that al-Qaeda has cells in up to 60 countries worldwide, dispensing money and logistical support and training to radical Islamist groups in numerous countries, many of which are geographically distant from the failed state, including the Philippines and Indonesia (Gunaratna 2004; Haynes 2005a: 224–43; Howard and Sawyer 2004).

Third, the US academic, Samuel Huntington, first presented his 'clash of civilisations' in an article published in 1993, followed by a book in 1996. His main argument was that, following the end of the Cold War, a new, global clash was under way that, replacing the four decades long conflict between liberal democracy/capitalism and communism, was a new fight between the (Christian) 'West' and the (mostly Muslim, mostly Arab) 'East'. The core of Huntington's argument was that after the Cold War the 'Christian', democratic West found itself in conflict especially with radical Islam, a political movement concerned with changes in the political order, united by antipathy to the West, and inspired by anti-democratic religious and cultural dogma encapsulated in the term, 'Islamic fundamentalism', a key threat to international stability. Christianity, on the other hand, was said by Huntington to be conducive to the spread of liberal democracy. In evidence, he notes the collapse of dictatorships in southern Europe and Latin America in the 1970s and 1980s, followed by the development of liberal democratic political norms (rule of law, free elections, civic rights). These events were regarded by Huntington as conclusive proof of the synergy between Christianity and liberal democracy, both key foundations of a normatively desirable global order built on liberal values. Others have also alleged that Islam is inherently undemocratic or even anti-democratic. For example, Fukuyama (1992: 236) suggests that Islamic 'fundamentalism' has a 'more than superficial resemblance to European fascism'.

However, it is one thing to argue that various brands of political Islam have qualitatively different perspectives on liberal democracy that some forms of Christianity, but quite another to claim that Muslims *en masse* are poised to enter into a period of conflict with the West. That is, there are actually many 'Islams' and only the malevolent or misinformed would associate the terrorist attacks with an apparently representative quality of a single idea of Islam. Moreover, the September 11 atrocities – as well as subsequent bomb outrages, do not appear to have been carried out by a state or group of states or at their behest, but by al-Qaeda, an international terrorist organisation. Despite energetic US attempts, no definitive proof was found to link the regime of Saddam Hussein in Iraq with either Osama bin Laden or al-Qaeda.

In addition, the idea of religious or civilisational conflict is problematic because it is actually very difficult to identify clear territorial boundaries to civilisations, and even more difficult to perceive them as acting as coherent units. It has been suggested that Huntington's image of 'clashing civilisations' focuses too closely on an essentially undifferentiated category – 'a civilisation' – and as a result places insufficient emphasis on various trends, conflicts and disagreement that take place within all cultural traditions, whether Islam, Christianity, or Judaism. The wider point is that cultures are not usefully seen as closed systems of essentialist values, while it is implausible to understand the world to comprise a strictly limited number of cultures, each with their own unique core sets of beliefs. The influence of globalisation in this regard is to be noted as it leads to an expansion of channels, pressures and agents via which various norms are diffused and interact.

Finally, the image of 'clashing civilisations' ignores the very important sense in which radical Islamist revolt and al-Qaeda terrorism is aimed primarily *internally* at many governments within the Islamic world that are accused of becoming both corrupt and un-Islamic. Since the 1970s, a general rise of Islamist groups across the swathe of Arab countries and elsewhere is much more a consequence of the failure of modernisation to deliver its promises than the result of bin Laden's influence. That is, the contemporary Islamist resurgence – of which al-Qaeda is integral part – carries within it both popular disillusionment at slow progress as well as growing disgust with corrupt and unrepresentative governments in the Muslim world that have refused to open up political systems to become more representative. Confronted by state power that seeks to destroy or control its communitarian structures and replace them with an idea of a national citizenry based on the link between state and individual, Islamist groups have widely appeared as vehicles of popular political aspirations.

But it is difficult or impossible to be sure regarding the actual level of support for bin Laden and al-Qaeda in the Muslim world, although there is almost certainly a high degree of anti-US resentment and a general belief that the West is opposed to Islam. Such a perception is fuelled by the US move back towards rather uncritical support for Israel's Sharon government, the invasion of Iraq and subsequent inability to rebuild a viable administration in the country. At the same time, in the US there are voices that appear to play up the notion of civilisational conflict. For example, Congressman Tom Lantos has stated that

> unfortunately we have no option but to take on barbarism which is hell bent on destroying civilization ... You don't compromise with these people. This is not a bridge game. International terrorists have put themselves outside the bonds of protocols.[1]

Such remarks appear to reflect a deep-rooted tradition in western international thought that believes it is appropriate to set aside normal rules of international relations in certain circumstances, for example, 'certain kinds of conflict or in struggles with certain kinds of states or groups' (Hurrell 2002: 195). During the centuries of western imperialism, there were frequent debates about what rights non-Christian and non-European peoples should enjoy. In the centuries of competition and sometimes conflict between Christianity and Islam, there arose the notion of holy war – that is, a special kind of conflict undertaken outside 'any framework of shared rules and norms' – as well as that of 'just war' waged for 'the vindication of rights' within a shared framework of values. In addition, there is a further strand of conservative western thought that 'asserts that certain kinds of states and systems cannot be dealt with on normal terms, that the normal rules that govern international relations have to be set aside'. For example, during 1980s the Reagan government in the USA averred that there was a basic lack of give-and-take available when dealing with communist governments, which meant that it was appropriate that some basic notions of international law could be set aside in such contexts. This conservative tradition is also manifested in the remarks of Congressman Lantos noted above,[2] and suggests that available options are restricted to the choice of 'contain or to crusade'. It also indicates that 'such positions clearly continue to resonate within and around the current US administration' (Hurrell 2002: 193–5).

In summary, various contemporary conflicts in the developing and developed worlds have religious components. What they also have in common is a close link between religion and identity politics.

Religion and identity politics in the developing world

While the notion of 'identity' is normally applied to individuals, it can also be a collective concept, extending to groups, communities and even countries in relation to their various ethnic, religious and cultural entities. As a result, individuals may feel personally injured when they perceive that others – who they believe share their identity – are being ill-treated. The kinds of conflicts that can result are known as identity clashes – involving self-identified, often polarised, groups, within or between countries. Malek notes that 'for an "identity" or inter-group conflict to occur, the opponents must assign an identity to themselves and their adversaries, each side believing the fight is between "us" and "them." Conflicts where the antagonists seem to be fighting about their identities are called "identity-based conflicts" or "inter-group conflicts"' (Malek 2004).

What are the key sources of identity? Many identities are based on shared values, beliefs, or concerns that not only include religion but also extend to political ideologies, ethnicity, nationality, or culture (Gopin 2000, 2005). This does not necessarily imply that such people's identities are monolithic entities – because in fact *everyone's* self-conception is a unique combination of many identities, such as: community, religion, ethnicity, nationalism, gender, class, family, gender, and so on. Their relative importance and compatibility differs at various times and circumstances. This implies that individual and collective identities are constructed from a number of available traits and experiences, all of which are subject to interpretation. For example, race and religion are important sources of identity in some societies, while in others political ideologies and nationalism are judged to be of more significance. In addition, some analysts speak of various sources of identity, such as religion or ethnicity, as ancient, unchanging phenomena. Others stress that *all* identity are socially constructed: that is, people choose their history and ancestry and, as a result, may *create*, as much as *discover*, differences from others (Gopin 2000; Malek 2004).

A sense of identity is by no means necessarily a bad thing. But when a sense of identity helps to create or encourage intense, destructive conflicts, then analysts refer to what they call 'destructive' identities (Rosen 2005). That is, if a source of identity, such as religion, ethnicity or nationality, is heavily reinforced or underpinned *and* is highly significant to someone, then (real or imagined) threats to that sense of identity can be difficult to ignore, and conflict can result. This is because in groups cultural patterns can create conflict, as they may inherently include a tendency to mistrust other groups or to belittle them. When ideologies polarise groups the result can be conflict between them. For example, a group with a belief that their religion is *inherently* superior to all others would regard others with different religious beliefs as essentially inferior. If such a group believed that it was going to be the victim of attack from another group, they would likely seek to defend themselves. Fearing physical attack, the group may act pre-emptively to prevent the feared attack, thus threatening the other side. The result of threat and counter-threat can be a self-perpetuating destructive struggle, of the kind that has tragically occurred between Israel and Palestinians (Rosen 2005). Such a situation can be exacerbated by the actions of political leaders – individuals who may seek to benefit personally from construction of exclusivist identities – who may gain power as a result of arousing the emotions and enmity of members of their group against others. Identity is often created by past interactions.

Kamrava avers that 'it is their sense of identity which largely determines how people behave politically and in turn view their own political environment' (Kamrava 1993: 164). It is widely accepted that stresses and strains associated with both modernisation and globalisation contribute to manifestations of religious and ethnic identity in the developing world (Juergensmeyer 2005; Gopin 2005; Appleby 2006). However, these factors do not impose themselves inexorably on an otherwise blank or uniform cultural and political situation; rather, struggles to develop modern political institutions and a developed economy have often conflicted with pre-modern social norms and traditions; and in some cases a sense of religious and/or ethnic separateness have resulted in inter- or intra-group conflict. On the other hand, it is impossible accurately to predict where such conflict will occur by the use of a simple fragmentation model, as we shall see below. In recent years, serious societal conflicts have erupt in a religiously and ethnically homogeneous country, such as Somalia, although not in Tanzania, a country with pronounced religious and ethnic fragmentation. This suggests that governmental skill in achieving social solidarity which can transcend potential ethnic or religious schisms may be an important factor in explaining whether inter- or intra-group conflict occurs within a country or not. In short, in some cases religious and/or ethnic fragmentation leads to competition and conflict although not in others (Haynes 1995b).

It is plausible to hypothesise that political stability will normally be low and chances for inter-group conflict high in a country with extensive religious and/or ethnic schisms. Many developing countries have religious fragmentation and in some cases ethnic cleavages as well (Lane and Ersson 1994: 133). Table 3.1 indicates which developing countries have high levels of ethnic *and* religious fragmentation – thus making them potentially very unstable indeed. Eleven African states (Angola, Cameroon, Chad, Côte d'Ivoire, Kenya, Liberia, Mali, Nigeria, Tanzania, Uganda, and Democratic Republic of Congo) score very high, that is, 0.8 or more, on the ethnic fragmentation index, as does India. Religious divisions are also pronounced in a number of African countries (Cameroon, Central African Republic, Chad, Côte d'Ivoire, Kenya, Liberia, Malawi, Mozambique, Rwanda, Tanzania, Togo and Uganda), as well as the Caribbean island of Trinidad and Tobago. Eighteen African countries, plus Indonesia and Malaysia, have to accommodate serious religious *and* ethnic cleavages. However, the data in Table 3.1 do not allow us to give a straightforward answer to the following question: Does religious and/or ethnic fragmentation in a developing country lead to violent conflict between groups that regard themselves as separate? The answer is: sometimes. Of the 20 countries in Table 3.1 which score high on *both* religious and ethnic fragmentation indices, six (31.5%), all in Africa: Angola, Chad, Ethiopia, Liberia, Mozambique, and Uganda, have experienced recent serious civil conflict. During the 1990s there was also serious civil conflict in Burundi, Rwanda, and Somalia: in the first two countries the main cause was ethnic rivalry – Hutu versus Tutsi – while in Somalia it was a result of inter-clan[3] discord, not ethnic or religious contest *per se*. Yet, none of these three countries appears in Table 3.1 in relation to the ethnicity criterion and only Rwanda is notable for 'religious fragmentation'. In short, developing countries with apparently most serious ethnic and religious divisions are *not necessarily those that experience serious civil conflict*. Its likelihood may be linked to whether governments manage to deal with effects of widespread, rapid, destabilising social and economic changes that affect both local power structures and societal, including religious groups.

For example, the post-colonial Indian republic inherited a Western-style democratic political system following independence in 1947.

Table 3.1 Ethnic and religious fragmentation in Africa, Asia and Latin America

Region	Country	Ethnic fragmentation[a]	Religious fragmentation[b]
Africa	Angola	0.80	0.49
	Benin	0.75	0.53
	Botswana	0.51	0.54
	Burkina Faso	0.72	0.59
	Cameroon	0.86	0.73
	Central African Republic	0.74	0.63
	Chad	0.80	0.70
	Côte d'Ivoire	0.87	0.67
	Ethiopia	0.70	0.61
	Kenya	0.86	0.69
	Liberia	0.86	0.64
	Malawi	0.65	0.73
	Mozambique	0.73	0.62
	Rwanda	low	0.64
	Sierra Leone	0.78	0.57
	South Africa	0.68	0.48
	Tanzania	0.95	0.73
	Togo	0.72	0.64
	Uganda	0.92	0.66
Asia	Indonesia	0.77	0.59
	Laos	0.61	low
	Malaysia	0.71	0.55
	Philippines	0.79	low
	India	0.90	low
	Nepal	0.69	low
	Pakistan	0.63	low
Latin America	Bolivia	0.70	low
	Ecuador	0.60	low
	Guatemala	0.58	low
	Peru	0.63	low
	Uruguay	low	0.49
	Venezuela	0.54	low

[a] Ethnic fragmentation index over 0.55 signifies a high level of ethnic fragmentation
[b] Religious fragmentation index over 0.45 signifies a high level of ethnic fragmentation

Source: Adapted from data in Lane and Ersson (1994: 134–5).

Post-colonial Indian governments have sought rapidly to develop the country's economy via a process of industrialisation. The country is notable for its religious diversity – including, Islam, Hinduism, Sikhism, Christianity, Jainism and Buddhism – as well as ethnicity and caste factors. Yet, despite occasional outbreaks of sometimes serious inter-religious conflict between either Hindus and Sikhs, or Hindus and Muslims, governments in India have for the six decades of independence managed to keep the country intact, democratic and recently developing quickly (Varshney 2003). What seems to be significant here is the degree of governmental skill in dealing with factors that are theoretically conducive to social conflict (Needham and Rajan 2007).

In religiously and ethnically diverse East Africa, on the other hand, there was a different outcome. There, late 19th century-European colonialism interacted with Arab and Islamic influences that had predated it by some 800 years. The forms of government that the colonialists left were, like India's, invariably based on Western models, but the level of governmental skill in dealing with implicit or explicit societal divisions appears to have been much less. Very few states in East Africa were, until recently, democratic, while serious societal conflicts do occur: in Somalia civil war broke out in the early 1990s while in October 1995 ethnic riots left five Kenyans dead (Barrow 1995; Haynes 2005c).

Regarding South-east Asia, another region of religious and ethnic fragmentation, after independence from colonial rule ancient religious and cultural determinants – notably Buddhism and Confucianism – were juxtaposed with the Western idea of statehood and its accompanying institutions of centralised government, monopoly of the means of force, and a comprehensive administrative structure. These factors towards social homogeneity were not necessarily sufficient, however, to eliminate ethnic and religious challenges to governments in several regional countries, including Myanmar, Indonesia and Thailand. Finally, as already noted, in relatively religious and ethnically homogeneous Latin America, several countries, including Nicaragua, Peru, Bolivia and Mexico – have important ethnic minorities whose influence on national-level politics is significant.

Finally, in relation to Latin America, Tokatlian (2006) identifies in several Latin American countries – including Colombia, Bolivia, Peru, Ecuador, and even Brazil, Argentina and Venezuela – growing signs of ethnic fragmentation and associated conflicts. In no regional cases, however, is religious fragmentation a source of societal conflict.

In conclusion, the above examples illustrate that religious identity – especially in contexts of societal fragmentation – can be important sources of conflict in the developing world.

Conflict resolution and peace-building

Religious individuals and faith-based organisations from a variety of religious traditions are actively involved in attempts to end conflicts and to foster post-conflict reconciliation between warring parties in the developing world (Bouta *et al.* 2005). This is not an entirely new phenomenon as religious individuals and/or representatives of various faith-based organisations have for several decades carried out mediations. Examples include: mediation undertaken by the Quakers and financed by the Ford foundation in the Nigerian Civil War, 1967–70; the work of the WCC and the All Africa Conference of Churches in mediating a cessation to the Sudan conflict in 1972; efforts made by John Paul Lederach (Professor of International Peace-building at the University of Notre Dame) in Nicaragua in the 1980s; and the recent work of the Imam of Timbuktu in mediating various West African conflicts (Conflict and Resolution Forum 2001). Smock (2004) contends that to focus single-mindedly on conflicts within and between religions not only oversimplifies causal interconnections between religion and conflict, in particular by disregarding important alternate variables, but also leads to an underestimation of attempts emerging from various religious traditions to help resolve conflicts and build peace. When successful, religion's role in helping resolve conflicts and build peace is a crucial component in helping achieve human development more generally.

'Religious peacemakers' are religious individuals or representatives of faith-based organisations that attempt to help resolve inter-group conflicts and build peace (Appleby, 2000, 2006; Gopin 2000, 2005; ter Haar 2005). According to Appleby, religious peacemakers are most likely to be successful when they: (1) have an international or transnational reach, (2) consistently emphasise peace and avoidance of the use of force in resolving conflict, and (3) have good relations between different religions in a conflict situation, as this will be the key to a positive input from them (Appleby 2006: 1–2). As we saw in Introduction, the world religions focused upon in this book share a broadly similar set of theological and spiritual values and views and this potentially underpins their ability to provide positive contributions to conflict resolution and peace-building. Practical effects in this regard have increased in recent years, with growing numbers and types of religious peacemakers working to try to build peaceful coexistence in multi-faith societies, while advocating reconciliation and fairness in a world that often seems characterised by social and political strife and economic disparity (Bartoli 2005).

Religious peacemakers' conflict resolution focus is said to be increasing and in some cases becoming more effective, focused in the following areas:

- Faith-based organisations are increasingly active and increasingly effective in attempts at peace-building;
- Faith-based organisations have a special role to play in zones of religious conflict, but their peace-building programmes do not need to be confined to addressing religious conflict only;
- Although in some cases peace-building projects of faith-based organisations resemble very closely peace-building by secular NGOs, the various religious orientations of these faith-based organisations typically shape the peace-building they undertake;
- These organisations' peace-building agendas are diverse, ranging from high-level mediation to training and peace-building-through-development at the grassroots;
- Peace can be often promoted most efficiently by introducing peace-building components into more traditional relief and development activities (Smock 2001: 1; Smock 2006).

Bouta *et al.* agree that faith-based peace-building initiatives 'have contributed positively to peace-building', exemplified in four main ways. They can provide: (1) 'emotional and spiritual support to war-affected communities', (2) effective mobilisation for 'their communities and others for peace', (3) mediation 'between conflicting parties', and (4) a conduit in pursuit of 'reconciliation, dialogue, and disarmament, demobilization and reintegration' (Bouta *et al.* 2005: ix). Appleby's conclusion is to note the promise that religious peacemakers offer while also noting two problems: (1) 'there is often a failure of religious leaders to understand and/or enact their potential peace-building roles within the local community', and (2) many religious leaders lack the ability to 'exploit their strategic capacity as transnational actors' (Appleby 2006: 2).

Overall, it is clear that there are many faith-based organisations from various religious traditions engaged in peacemaking activities in relation to specific contexts and conflicts, in various parts of the developing world, including Africa and Asia. In some cases, however, their full potential may not be realised because of problems relating to geographical focus of their attentions, as well as an occasional reluctance to be involved in a peacemaking role (Bouta *et al.* 2005; Appleby 2006; Smock, 2001, 2004, 2006).

Conflict resolution and peace-building in action: Mozambique, Nigeria and Cambodia

Religious peacemakers seek to help rebuild good community relations and encourage development of peaceful and constructive relations between previously warring communities. In this section, we examine examples of religious peacemakers in Africa and Asia, regions of the developing world where such activities are common. First, we look at the work of the Catholic lay organisation Sant'Egidio in Mozambique, which was instrumental in bringing that country's civil war to an end in 1992. Second, we examine the individual efforts of two religious individuals – Islamic and Christian peacemakers – in Nigeria. Finally, we switch focus to Asia, highlighting efforts of Buddhist individuals and groups to help resolve conflict and build peace in Cambodia. Overall, the examples indicate that religious peacemakers can make a difference: left to their own devices, it is very likely that conflicting groups would have failed to reach a *modus vivendi* and perhaps lapse back into conflict – with potentially destabilising effects on regional and international stability and peace. As Mozambique's president Joaquim Chissano reminds us: 'Conflicts, particularly violent conflicts between and within states in other parts of Africa, and in the world in general, are also a danger to our peace and tranquillity. Helping other peoples keep and maintain peace is also a way of defending our own peace' (Harsch 2003: 16).

Mozambique: Sant'Egidio, conflict resolution and peace-building

Increased interest and activity in faith-based peacemaking is connected to the increasing role of NGOs, civil society actors, and religious groups that have recently and collectively increased their peacemaking efforts. For example, a peace deal in North Uganda between the Lords Resistance Army and Government of Uganda in 2006 was mediated over the preceding years by a Christian NGO, Pax Christi (Simonse 1998). More generally, large-scale violence in many African countries is often associated with social conflicts, with religion and/or ethnicity characteristics. Numerous regional countries – including, Liberia, Sierra

Leone, the Democratic Republic of Congo, Côte d'Ivoire, Nigeria, Burundi, Rwanda, Angola, Sudan and Mozambique – have been beset by serious political violence, with a proliferation of armed conflicts and numerous deaths of local people, most of whom were civilian non-combatants. In addition, as Harsch notes, millions more 'succumbed to war-related epidemics and starvation' (Harsch 2003: 1). In all such cases, conflicts were informed by a variety of issues, including religious and/or ethnicity factors.

Many traditional – that is, non-religious – conflict resolution and peace-building missions were established to monitor peace agreements between established armies holding separate territories. But they discovered success hard to find, not least because they were not necessarily well suited to deal with such conflicts. Many recent conflicts in Africa have been civil wars or insurgencies, with multiple armed factions and with grievances rooted in various factors, including: poverty, inequality and other development issues. Moreover, even when peace accords were successfully negotiated, it was not always the case that all political and military leaders were able or willing fully to control their followers. In some countries, such as Sierra Leone and Liberia local fighters, who profited from the chaos of war, saw more advantage in continuing to fight than to lay down their arms (Harsch 2003: 14).

Would faith-based organisations have more success than non-religious entities in helping to resolve conflicts and put peace back on the agenda? While the evidence is mixed in this regard (Appleby 2006), it is the case that in some African conflicts faith-based organisations have met with success. Perhaps the most illustrative case of this type of peacemaking was the mediation by the Catholic organisation Sant'Egidio, credited with playing a key role in ending the civil war in Mozambique in 1992.

Sant'Egidio is a prominent example of a religious group active in faith-based peacemaking. It is an international Catholic NGO that takes part in attempts at peacemaking in various conflicts in many parts of the world. Originally, its principal focus was to serve the needs of the urban poor in Italy. (Bouta *et al.* 2005: 71). Founded in 1968 in Italy, Sant'Egidio has grown and now has approximately 50,000 members in 70 countries. Sant'Egidio is a Church public lay association, formally recognised by the Catholic Church but with an autonomous statute. This means that its membership is 'lay' – that is, not professionally religious – although its adherents have a clear religious motivation, an important part of its negotiation activities. Appleby explains that Sant'Egidio began its activities with charity, humanitarian action and development cooperation uppermost in its thinking, concerns moulded by spirituality and shared principles, including prayer, communicating the gospel, solidarity with the poor and dialogue with other religions (Appleby 2006: 10). However, despite its avowedly religious orientation, Sant'Egidio's conflict resolution and peace-building activities have focused more on 'non-religious' conflicts than on 'religious' conflicts, and more on the international level than on the national or local level.

During the early 1980s Sant'Egidio became engaged in various international dialogues. The aim was to try to prevent or reduce tension between conflicting groups and to seek to mediate between them. Since then Sant'Egidio has played an active peace-building role in several African countries beset by civil war, including: Algeria, Burundi, Democratic Republic of Congo, Côte d'Ivoire, Mozambique and Sierra Leone. It has also been active elsewhere, including: Colombia, Guatemala, and Kosovo. In each case, the country was beset by serious conflict between polarised groups; in some cases, conditions were exacerbated by the fact that the effectiveness of central government to administer had diminished significantly (Smock 2004).

One of the clearest success stories of Sant'Egidio's peacemaking efforts occurred between 1989 and 1992 when the organisation was extremely influential in resolving the civil war that had ravaged Mozambique since the mid-1970s. The Catholic Archbishop of Beira, Don Jaime Goncalves, was familiar with Sant'Egidio and its work from the time years before he had spent in Rome. Following well intentioned but eventually unsuccessful efforts to end the war emanating from the international community, Archbishop Goncalves thought Sant'Egidio might succeed in bringing the government together to talk peace with the rebels of the Mozambican National Resistance (RENAMO) insurgents. He was right: The effort took months but eventually Sant'Egidio not only contacted the RENAMO leadership but also encouraged Mozambican government officials to agree to meet with them (Bouta *et al.* 2005: 71–2).

Sant'Egidio was successful in its efforts because both RENAMO and the government perceived Sant'Egidio as an organisation characterised both by a welcome neutrality and a compassionate outlook, with but one interest in Mozambique: to end the civil war and promote peace. That is, Sant'Egidio was understood to have no political or economic agenda; throughout the negotiations this perception was bolstered as the organisation demonstrated a position of both even-handedness and neutrality (Smock 2004). As far as the Mozambique government was concerned, as an NGO, Sant'Egidio could set up a meeting between RENAMO and the government without it meaning that the RENAMO rebels would be regarded as an entity with the same status as the ruling regime. But Sant'Egidio also had a second important asset: 'humble awareness of its own shortcomings in orchestrating international diplomacy, which caused it to seek out the special expertise of governments and international organizations' (Smock 2004: 1). The nucleus of Sant'Egidio's mediation team was the Archbishop of Beira, Don Jaime Goncalves, an Italian socialist parliamentarian and former diplomat, and two key leaders of Sant'Egidio. These efforts were complemented not only by the United Nations but also by ten national governments, including those of the United States, Italy, Zimbabwe and Kenya. Once peace negotiations were successfully completed in 1992, the United Nations assumed responsibility for the implementation of the peace agreement. Over the last 15 years, Mozambique has been peaceful. There have been several national level elections, won by the ruling FRELIMO party. RENAMO has served as the main political opposition to the government (Appleby 2006).

In conclusion, the mediation work of Sant'Egidio in Mozambique illustrates how faith-based organisations with relevant skills can offer a unique ability to mediate between previously warring factions. They do this by building on a reputation for neutrality and compassion and by utilising not only their own skills but also those of other – not necessarily – institutions, in an initiative which, in the case of Mozambique, brought the battling parties together and brought the civil war to a close (Bouta *et al.* 2005: 72–3).

Nigeria: seeking accommodation between warring religious communities

Nigeria has a population of more than 100 million people divided between Muslims, Christians and followers of traditional African religions. There are around 45–50 million Muslims (c.50% of the population), 35–40 million Christians (c.35–40%), and about 10–15 million followers of traditional religions (c.15%). However these figures are necessarily speculative because the only census since 1963 (that of 1991) failed to ask respondents about religious affiliation. Religious competition between Muslim and Christians is now perhaps the single most significant political issue in the country (Korieh 2005). Since the 1960s, religion has been prominent in Nigerian civil conflict where missionaries and religious partisans see themselves in a zero-sum game to win souls, sometimes entering into deadly conflict.

Antipathy between them flared in the 1980s, when many Christians believed that the predominantly Muslim north of the country enjoyed a disproportionate portion of both political power and economic resources (Ibrahim 1991: 135). Tensions were raised by the government's secret decision in 1986 to join the 45-member Organisation of the Islamic Conference (OIC), within which Saudi Arabia and Iran – with their contending visions of the appropriate Islamic society – strive for diplomatic and political prominence. The Nigerian government's motivation for seeking to join the OIC was probably primarily financial. Economic aid would have been expected from oil-rich OIC member states – yet many Christians feared that Nigeria's membership of the OIC would jeopardise the country's status as a secular state and reduce the status and position of Christians (Korieh 2005). Muslim supporters of the membership bid countered that Nigeria was a member of the Commonwealth, a 'Christian' organisation, led by the British monarch who, legally, must be a Protestant Christian (Kukah and Falola 1995). The issue was not settled before a further religious controversy erupted in 1987. Now the point of contention was whether a *Shari'ah* court of appeal would be allowed in the democratic regime which was scheduled (as it turned out, abortively) to accede to power in late 1992. Muslim members of the Constituent Assembly wanted *Shari'ah* law in the Nigerian constitution, while Christians would not countenance such a move. Negotiations on the issue broke down (and were to an extent superseded by other controversies), whilst President Babangida was forced to affirm in October 1988 that Nigeria would remain a secular state despite membership of the OIC.

Tensions between the two communities had already escalated into political violence. In early 1987, and again in May and October 1991, anti-Christian riots broke out in parts of northern Nigeria (Maier 1991). In total, over 3,000 people were killed in Christian-Muslim clashes between 1987 and 1993. The death toll included about 1,000 killed in a series of pitched battles in May 1992 when Christian Katafs fought Muslim Hausa and Fulani. Churches were destroyed and both Christians and Muslims killed and injured. The political context of this religious violence was the continuation of the military government, a regime that sought not to encourage public political debates (Maier 2001). As a result, with political parties banned and with no legislature, public anger and frustration among Muslims was channelled into religious issues. In effect, many ordinary Muslims were turned into 'fundamentalists' in the sense that they began to perceive their Christian countrymen and women as their chief foes, while many

Christians, fearing what appeared to them to be a growing threat from Islam, retaliated.

From the early 1990s, inter-religious violence became a common feature of life in Nigeria, primarily involving Muslim and Christian communities. One of the worst-hit regions was the northern state of Kaduna. Generally, Nigeria has a high level of religious violence that claimed more than 10,000 lives during the 1990s, and Kaduna was the main area of the deaths (Haynes 1996b: 213–21). This led in 1995 to the founding of the Muslim-Christian Dialogue Forum (MCDF), a charity to foster Christian-Muslim dialogue. It was the result of the combined efforts of two former enemies – a Christian pastor, James Movel Wuye, and a Muslim imam, Muhammed Nurayn Ashafa, both esteemed members of their religious communities. They served as joint national coordinators of MCDF, based in Kaduna. Both made the decision to turn away from similar paths of violence and militancy. Instead, they embraced non-violence, reconciliation, and the advocacy of peaceful relations between their communities, and sought to encourage others to join them in this goal (Moix n/d).

Three years earlier – in 1992 – relations between the two men were very different: each tried to have the other killed in a clash in Zangon Kataf, Kaduna state. Christian killers murdered Ashafa's uncle, believing that the latter was Ashafa himself; Muslim assassins hacked off Wuye's arm and left him for dead. Discovering their mistakes, both men saw the events as a signal from God and henceforward they started to work together as peacemakers. They founded MCDF and in 1999 co-authored a book, *The Pastor and the Imam: Responding to Conflict*, which describes their experiences and illustrates the Bible's and the Qu'ran's commitments to peace. A few years later, in 2003, both were enrolled as students at the School for International Training (SIT), participants in the peace-building institute held every June at SIT's Vermont campus (Wuye and Ashafa 2005).

Ashafa and Wuye wrote in their book that,

> Religion today, instead of serving as a source of healing sickness, hunger, and poverty, and stimulating tranquility and peaceful co-existence among human beings, is used to cause sadness. It is bringing pain instead of relief, hatred instead of love, division instead of unity, sadness instead of joy, discrimination and destruction instead of accommodation and development. This is especially true between some adherents of Islam and Christianity. Nigeria has its own share of this negative phenomenon. Its ethnic-religious

conflict has become a matter so serious and devastating that it can now be seen as a harbinger of the danger of a crisis such as those that have engulfed the former Yugoslavia, Rwanda and Liberia (Ashafa and Wuye 1999: 1).

To seek to help address these issues, in March 2003, the MCDF and the US Institute of Peace jointly promoted a five-day dialogue workshop in Kaduna. Participants came from the Christian and Muslim communities, with one youth leader from both faiths chosen to take part from 30 of Nigeria's states. The reason to focus on the youth at this event was taken in recognition that both Muslims and Christians from this age group have been responsible for much of the religious violence in Nigeria in recent years. More generally, the forum sought to add to the work of the Nigerian Inter-Religious Council, a body comprising older, senior religious leaders that has consistently condemned Nigeria's religious violence (www.usip.org/religionpeace/programs.html). Following the Kaduna forum, plans were made to organise further inter-faith gatherings in other parts of Nigeria.

When the workshop started, each side was adamant that the other was to blame for religious violence in Nigeria. When it concluded, participants agreed on a 17-point consensual declaration containing various recommendations, including that:

- Both Christians and Muslims should love each other unconditionally as brothers and sisters;
- Both communities should show good will to each other at all times;
- It was important better to inform members of each religious community about the beliefs and tenets of the 'other' faith; and
- It was necessary to cooperate with government in order to hand over for justice those people who continue to use religious violence contravention of the law (Crawley 2003).

In summary, this Nigerian case shows that when interfaith dialogue is skilfully organised it can encourage religious enemies, including those who have engaged in religious warfare, to work together towards peaceful accommodation.

Cambodia: conflict resolution and the legacy of Khmer Rouge rule

Buddhism had to contend with serious attempts in Cambodia to eradicate it in the 1970s. During five years of rule by the communist Khmer Rouge, the regime tried energetically to exterminate religion in the country – including Buddhism, the major faith – while killing millions of Cambodians as a central facet of state policy (Poethig 2002). A Vietnamese invasion ousted the Khmer Rouge in 1979 following an international outcry. After the demise of the Khmer Rouge, the country experienced a lengthy period of political instability. More than $1.75 billion was spent on the work of the United Nations (UN) Transnational Authority in Cambodia alone. Over time, an initially hesitant state began to acknowledge the continued cultural, social and religious salience of Buddhism to millions of Cambodians, recognising its popular appeal and allowing Buddhism a growing voice in national affairs.

Following the demise of the Khmer Rouge in the late 1970s and the social and political instability that followed, Cambodia was a major focus of concentrated peace-building activities from the early 1990s. This was focused at several levels, including the popular level, where an initiative known as the 'Dhammayietra walks', whose central tenet was compassion and non-violence, inspired people throughout Cambodia. Its message of the hope of peace to rebuild the war-torn country was in stark contrast to what had gone before, representing an important initiative drawing on core Buddhist norms and values (Bartoli 2005: 4).

The Dhammayietra walks had their origins in the UN-monitored repatriation of Cambodians from border camps in Thailand in 1992. It is said to be an important contribution towards the revival of Buddhism in Cambodia after the Khmer Rouge and consequent political instability. The concept of the Dhammayietra walks draws upon discourses and practices revealed in the context of a 'socially engaged Buddhism' that has gained visibility not only in Cambodia and Thailand but also in other Asian countries where Buddhism is a significant religious tradition since the early 1980s. The notion of an 'engaged' interpretation of Buddhist doctrine represents a significant revival of Buddhism in post-Khmer Rouge Cambodia that Poethig (2002) argues was only possible because of its transnational and inter-faith formation. She points to the fact that socially- engaged Buddhism in Cambodia is often linked to the return of Cambodian Buddhist exiles from Thailand and other regional countries. This development required two simultaneous moves in order to maintain its usefulness. On the one hand, it is represented as an exemplary Khmer Buddhist response to Cambodia's entrenched conflicts, as it forges its discursive identity within the 'local' space of the nation. On the other hand, this local space is also 'mobile' – and this is where the Dhammayietra walks acquire both religious and peace-building significance. The leading figure behind the walks – a Cambodian called Maha Ghosananda – instructed the walkers to move 'step by step' towards peace. The aim was symbolically to reverse what Maha Ghosananda identified as examples of 'dangerous mobility' – including, massive internal and external relocations and refugee flights of the Khmer Rouge era that affected millions of Cambodian, as well as the still serious danger of treading on landmines in many parts of the country – which turns the act of walking itself into a mindful act. As Poethig notes, 'it is this discursive move that loosens the Dhammayietra's ties to the nation allowing it to slip across political and religious borders and ally itself with a broad and diverse network of interfaith peace groups that are its transnational public forum' (Poethig 2002: 28).

Conclusion

In this chapter we examined the role of religion in conflicts, conflict resolution and peace-building. Regarding conflict, we saw that inter-religion tensions and competition were often implicated in the 'politics of identity'. In the second half of the chapter we turned to the role of religious individuals and faith-based organisations in conflict resolution and peace-building in three countries: Mozambique, Nigeria and Cambodia, involving respectively a Roman Catholic NGO (Mozambique), Protestant and Muslim religious and community leaders (Nigeria) and the efforts of a Buddhist monk, Maha Ghosananda, in Cambodia. While the contexts, issues, and religious faiths and actors differed from country to country, the common factor in each case was that while religious causes of conflict receive much public attention, religious peacemakers' efforts in conflict resolution and peace-building tends to get much less attention and publicity (Smock 2004; Appleby 2006). Research indicates, and this chapter would underline, that religious faiths typically encourage members to work towards resolving conflicts and develop peace (Bouta *et al.* 2005). This is reflected in the fact that growing numbers of religious organisations seem to be looking for opportunities to promote peace, including in circumstances where religion itself is seen to contribute to conflict, such as in Nigeria and Cambodia (United States Institute for Peace 2003).

Overall, the hope is that, as a result of increased public recognition and support and development of more effective peacemaking strategies, the conflict resolution and peacemaking skills of faith-based organisations and religious individuals would develop further in order to achieve undoubted potential. Peacemaking ability is likely to develop in this way when, acting under the auspices of a religious group, individuals and groups are seen as reflective of a high moral standing, credibility, and stature, to the extent that they can be regarded by all apolitical or neutral in conflict situations. However, peacemaking should not only be about short-term building of peace, but should in addition aim to develop restorative justice and/or the establishment of what are considered 'right relationships' between formerly conflicting groups through acknowledgement of each other's position and accountability of those acting on behalf of religious communities. In some cases, faith-based organisations may enter a conflict situation and focus primarily on trying to resolve its immediate manifestations while not looking as closely at the structural problems that underlie the conflict and trying to work towards addressing important background issues that make conflict more likely.

Finally, there is the question of how to *prevent* conflicts developing in the first case. While there are some organisations involved in conflict prevention, there is generally insufficient attention paid to this crucial factor. There is a relatively ineffective United Nations' early warning and prevention programme in existence. Overall, faith-based organisations have not yet been that successful in conflict prevention. More effort needs to be made in studying ways to improve attempts to defuse conflict before it breaks out.

4
Economic Growth, Poverty and Hunger

We have the opportunity in the coming decade to cut world poverty by half. Billions more people could enjoy the fruits of the global economy. Tens of millions of lives can be saved. The practical solutions exist. The political framework is established. And for the first time, the cost is utterly affordable. Whatever one's motivation for attacking the crisis of extreme poverty – human rights, religious values, security, fiscal prudence, ideology – the solutions are the same. All that is needed is action (UN Millennium Project 2005).

The fight against world poverty will only be successful if it is based on the political will and capacity of 'self help' – the efforts of poor countries to establish peace, the rule of law, and good governance at home and unlock the creative energies of their people. It requires investment, not least in human capital and healthy integration into the global marketplace (Horst Köhler, IMF managing director, address to a conference of US and Canadian Catholic Bishops, Washington, DC, USA, 29 January 2002).

Governments, United Nations (UN) IFIs, including the World Bank and the IMF, and secular development agencies have worked on the issue of poverty alleviation over the years. Yet the fact remains that at least one in six of the world's people are still living in abject poverty. Over time, it has become clear that whether on their own or collectively these entities do not have all the answers to achieve desired poverty reductions and associated improvements in living standards in the developing world.

The quotations above reflect both a growing desire to build up partnerships involving the private sector, NGOs and the religious world as well as realisation that achievement of the MDG centring on eradication of extreme poverty and hunger by 2015 will be highly problematic. A starting point is to ascertain what is meant when talking about 'poverty eradication'. While the claim of all development policies is to seek to reduce and eliminate poverty in the medium and long term, when discussing what poverty actually means, different ideas often arise as to its meaning. This is because poverty is a complex, multi-dimensional phenomenon with diverse characteristics.

Defining poverty and measuring it are controversial issues. In the development literature, poverty was for many years defined primarily in terms of a lack of income (in money or in kind) necessary to ensure access to a set of basic needs (source). Over time, the concept of poverty was extended to include not only a lack of income, but also absence of access to health, education and other services. More recently, the definition of poverty has expanded further, to include various factors, including powerlessness, isolation, vulnerability, and social exclusion (source). The result is that poverty is now a multi-dimensional phenomenon. It can be defined as the 'inability of individuals to ensure for themselves and their dependants a set of basic minimum conditions for their subsistence and well-being in accordance with the norms of society' (PARPA 2001: 11).

This chapter focuses on the MDG of eradication of extreme poverty and hunger. It highlights that these have been goals of a variety of development agencies for decades but success has proved to be elusive. It argues that to achieve these goals it would be necessary to undertake reforms at both international and domestic levels. Third, there is a great need for coordinated relationships between secular development agencies and faith-based organisations active in this area; working together there is more likelihood of success that working apart. Finally, we examine the work of faith-based organisations from the Christian, Buddhist and Muslim traditions, active respectively in India, Cambodia, and parts of Asia and Africa. The overall conclusion is that there is untapped potential in working towards eradication of extreme poverty and hunger in the developing world, but it would be a grave mistake to expect that faith-based organisations on their own can effect needed changes. What is required are more robust and effective partnerships between secular development agencies and faith-based organisations to have a greater likelihood of success.

Announced in 2000, the eradication of 'extreme poverty and hunger' was the first of the eight MDGs announced. It was hoped that they would be achieved by 2015. Yet, when governments met in early November 2006 in order to assess the extent of progress made in achieving the goal of a 50% cut in food hunger by 2015, there was a serious lack of progress to report. Data released contemporaneously by the UN's Food and Agriculture Organisation (FAO) indicated that there had not been a reduction as planned – but in fact an increase of more than 25 million chronically undernourished people during 1996–2006 (www.fao.org/). As a result, there were 850 million such people, more than 13% of the global population of 6.5 billion. According to Mulvany and Madeley (2006), this was 'testament to how current global policies, far from working, are consigning the hungry to stay hungry'. Failure to achieve progress on this issue, according to an NGO, World Forum for Food Sovereignty, was not due to a *lack of* but too much political will. The Forum pointed to 'advances of trade liberalisation, industrial agriculture, genetic engineering and military dominance', claiming them to be the chief causes of the growing problem of hunger and poverty in the developing world ('Final Declaration of the World Forum on Food Sovereignty' 2001).

According to a recent report, there are four main factors to blame for this situation: (1) growing power of transnational corporations, (2) diminishing land and water resources, (3) climate change and deforestation, and (4) the impact of free market, neo-liberal economic policies (Pimbert *et al.* 2005).

First, the report points out that in recent years small numbers of multinational corporations have acquired control over the world's food system. These TNCs control not only seed, livestock and agrochemical industries but also transport, processing and retailing; and in the process they take a large and growing share of the price paid by consumers. The result is that farmers around the world – including the developing world – are compelled to accept falling farm gate prices. Some, as a result, face bankruptcy (Pimbert *et al.* 2005: 2).

Second, diminishing land and water resources around the world exacerbate both hunger and poverty. The situation is made worse by the apparently uncontrolled appetite for industrially produced livestock, typically fed on grains and starchy vegetables, a process that uses millions of hectares of land that could be used for food production for humans. In addition, huge areas of land in developing countries – employed for intensive farming in the post-1960s 'green revolution' are now poisoned by pesticides; and some are also salinised by poor irrigation. The consequence is that yields are stagnating or falling, while pressure mounts to convert land to produce biofuels for the affluent (Pimbert *et al.* 2005: 15, 34).

Third, environmental catastrophes – including climate change and deforestation – are the main causes of both lower rainfall and drought in many parts of the developing world. These factors can fundamentally affect the ability of small farmers in the developing world to produce sufficiently for their own needs. This has become a major problem for food production. The problem is caused by less frequent yet inordinately heavy rainstorms, with declining numbers of trees causing erosion, reducing soil quality and producing meagre harvests (Pimbert *et al.* 2005: 21).

Finally, Mulvany and Madeley (2006) state that 'free market, neo-liberal economic policy has encouraged and justified the elimination of small-scale food producers' in the developing world. Often, the FAO claims, such 'farmers and indigenous peoples are seen as "residues" of history – people whose disappearance is inevitable. Throughout the world, small farmers, pastoralists, fisherfolk and indigenous peoples are increasingly being displaced'.

In summary, efforts to decrease hunger in the developing world seem to be fighting a losing battle against increasingly powerful MNCs, falling amounts of land and water resources, climate change and deforestation, and the impact of free market, neo-liberal economic policies.

Secular development and faith-based organisations

Long marginalised or ignored, issues of spirituality and religion have had a hard time trying to influence development theory and practice. For a long time after World War II, secular worldviews were the foundation of conventional development understandings and policy. Over time, however, it became clear that there was no evidence to support the view that religion would wither away as a result of modernisation and economic development and that a novel rationality would everywhere conquer 'primitive' superstition and backward religious worldviews.

Yet we have already noted that religious beliefs are central to the lives of most people in developing countries. While religious teaching and practice have diminished in significance in the North, they continue to influence the worldview of those living in the poverty-stricken nations of the South. It is thus important to consider the ways in which religion can help as well as poverty alleviation for poor people in the developing world.

To what extent can faith-based organisations play a meaningful role in helping achieve eradication of extreme poverty and hunger? On the one hand, religion is increasingly recognised as a potentially or actually important factor when thinking about how to improve development outcomes in the developing world – and there is no reason to presume that a potential role in poverty alleviation would not form part of its concerns. On the other hand, however, it is not realistic to expect that faith-based organisations on their own could deal with serious development shortfalls, including the problem of poverty and hunger. To achieve this, what is required are basic policy changes – not so much in specific sectors or in the identification of new policy instruments – as in the way in which both development and its implementation are considered. In particular, most religious individuals and faith-based organisations would probably contend, the concept of *human* development should be placed at the top of the development agenda, rather than being considered, as often appears to be the case now, as an add-on to the 'really important' task of economic development. This would require in many developing countries where state faculties are often weak or even non-existent for some people, a rethinking of the very notion of policy implementation via the state and secular development agencies. In extreme cases, that of state weakness or collapse, it is impossible to apply development policy in the conventional sense. There is a growing number of 'failing' or 'failed' states in the developing world, including such countries as Afghanistan, Iraq, Somalia, Liberia and the Democratic Republic of Congo (Thürer 1999). Such polities cannot realistically be revived by the techniques currently being used; instead they require new thinking about poverty alleviation and development more generally. External powers – for example, British troops in Sierra Leone, instrumental in rebuilding the state after that country's civil war ended in 2002 – can play a vital role in facilitating state strengthening. Yet the task of political, social and developmental reconstruction should primarily be internal projects, involving local people and their representative organisations – including religious entities – rather than being planned and implemented by external personnel.

Of course, not all states by any means in the developing world are failed or even failing states. Yet, in numerous countries in the developing countries power is now fundamentally fragmented, often finding its main expression in social networks, including those expressing various religious ideas. The consequence is that in some developing countries, development issues, including poverty and hunger alleviation strategies, can usefully be considered in relation to *social networks* rather than via formal – usually state – bureaucracies alone. It is important to stress however that policy-makers should not regard societal networks as development panaceas; they are *not* simple substitutes for effective bureaucracies and should in some cases be seen as *potentially* capable of carrying some developmental responsibilities. This is because they are *not* professional state or development agency bureaucracies but *networks* motivated by different criteria, with different norms, beliefs and values, derived from religious origins and foundations. *If* it was a question of simply approaching leading figures in religious networks with a developed, non-negotiable policy plan, complete with budget, then ineffective implementation would be a likely outcome. This might be because of the potentially corrupting influence of external injections of funds, perhaps serving to undermine a previously functioning network based on other values. Instead, external secular development experts and their fund holders need to carefully build relationships over time with network members, moving forward consensually to focus on shared development concerns, including poverty alleviation and eradication. In this way, ideas, plans and programmes could emerge consensually over time, with their foundations in a high degree of social trust among those taking part. The task could be facilitated in regard to developing partnerships focusing on poverty alleviation in the developing world because the topic is of central concern to the world religions we focus upon in this book: Islam, Christianity, Hinduism and Buddhism.

Unfortunately, however, international development bureaucracies tend to have at least three major characteristics working against such an outcome.[1] First, development agency personnel, like other officeholders, may regard the size of the budgets they administer as linked to their overall prestige. As a result, such people may prefer to administer larger budgets – which may run into millions of dollars – compared to those that 'only' runs to the thousands. In other words, an administrator with a smaller budget is likely to derive correspondingly less prestige from the task at hand. Yet, in many developing countries relatively small amounts of money are often preferable to bigger sums – not least because smaller sums may be easier to administer and actually achieve better results compared to large sums that can induce wastage or corruption. This is because in the developing world, societies have different textures to Western ones and, as a result, are not amenable to the same manner or using the same techniques (CGAP 2004).

The second problem is that desk officers or unit directors based in Western capitals (or even in major population centres in developing countries) may not have much time or desire to spend lengthy periods of time getting to know key members of local religious networks, necessary to develop the high levels of mutual trust from which comes the collective ability to develop crucial ideas (Gervais 2004). Until recently, on their own admission, IFIs such as the World Bank and the IMF had remarkably little contact with the worlds of faith and with the people who worked in that world, whether globally, nationally or locally. But if we are serious about improving development outcomes in the developing world, starting with poverty alleviation, it is necessary for Western officials to change quite fundamentally their *modus operandi*. To achieve better development outcomes, including poverty alleviation, they need to develop *genuine* long-term partnerships with relevant religious figures in their networks. The starting point in what is necessarily a time consuming and fraught process of trust-building, is that of representation, with secular and religious actors working together as equal partners, reflecting the developmental importance of the latter. Throughout the developing world various religious entities own land, provide services such as healthcare and education, help poor people in need, care for orphans and disabled people and support income generating activities by farmers, fisherfolk and slum dwellers (Olsson and Wohlgemuth 2003: 157–8).

It remains the case, however, that governments in many developing countries are unwilling to work closely with religious entities in pursuit of development goals – despite the fact that they often make significant – if unsung – contributions towards, for example, provision of health and education services. Explaining this state of affairs necessitates a focus on various political factors. For example, governments may prefer in some cases to operate with one religious tradition in preference to others or, alternatively, to adopt a secular agenda that rules out the possibility of working with faith groups at all (WFDD 2004). The issue is complicated further by the fact that while many religious organisations claim to be politically neutral, this may not be true in practice – often because of sometimes complex relationships between faith-based groups and government, including religious groups that may act as significant sources of political opposition to incumbent regimes. In addition, while religions have many positive insights to contribute, they may at times cause people to hold worldviews that are inimical to 'standard' – that is, secular – ideas of what is appropriate for social and economic development (Thomas 2005).

The overall consequence is that faith-based organisations' development work, including poverty alleviation, has long been 'invisible' to IFIs' development teams on the ground. Faith-based entities are rarely featured in project analysis and documentation, general institutional vocabulary, research agendas, dialogue with countries, speeches, and internal staff training. Even today, with the partial exception of the World Bank with its WFDD initiative, it is unusual to find faith issues mentioned consistently or prominently in development agency literature or websites. It would be incorrect to claim however that secular development agencies always ignored the developmental work of religious entities. But it would be more accurate to say that interactions typically involved specific individuals and were often both irregular and transient; as a result, they were not institutionalised. Neglect was a result either of a lack of familiarity about what faith-based organisations do, of preconceptions about the differing roles of the latter compared to secular development agencies or a consequence of specific suspicions and assumptions that faith-based organisations' goals were fundamentally different to those of secular agencies' development objectives. In short, regular, meaningful consultation with faith-based groups in the developing world was not easy for IFIs and secular development agencies more generally.

This is not to imply that alone or together faith groups have the ultimate solutions to poverty and hunger eradication. But it is to suggest that 'structures of belief, practice and institutional organisation that exist in the name of religion are perhaps some of the least appreciated variables in the development process' (Pawlikowski 2004: 17).

Spiritual capital and development: problems and prospects

A further issue that often separates international development bureaucracies and religious development networks is the issue of what development is *for*. The former will think primarily of development in terms of *economic* development, necessary to meet material needs, measured perhaps through growth in the Gross National Product (GNP). The latter will ask: Is that all there is to development? Can economic growth capture the concept adequately? While most religious traditions would accept that development should conceptually include only material progress, they would also council that this should not be at the expense of its social and cultural dimensions. Dahl offers the example of conventionally developed societies that invariably have an effective legal system developed over a long period as a result of legislative action and judicial elucidation. But this is rarely judged by economists to be 'a capital asset and included in national accounts, despite a very high human investment and replacement cost. Because development has such social dimensions, each society must define development in its own terms to reflect its underlying culture, values and goals' (Dahl 1998).

This is where the issue of 'spiritual capital' comes in – when thinking about what development *is*. Lillard and Ogaki characterise spiritual capital 'as a set of intangible objects in the form of rules for interacting with people, nature, and spiritual beings (God, gods, buddhas, angels, evil spirits as believed to exist by individuals and in different religions) and believed knowledge about tangible and spiritual worlds'. The result is a body of rules and knowledge that is used to administer and direct behaviour between, on the one hand, individuals and, on the other, between a person and the natural world. This definition highlights how 'spiritual capital is conceptually distinct from physical, human, or social capital because the payoff to spiritual capital includes returns that accrue in both the near term and in the long term – possibly even after death' (Lillard and Ogaki 2005: 1).

This makes it clear that in most if not all religious worldviews, the concept of development is more than a perception of the desirability of using a series of 'rational' economic, political, and social actions to achieve material progress. It is also fundamentally about a concern with redemptive hopes and expectations. As Peter Berger points out in *Pyramids of Sacrifice* (1975), development is also a 'religious category'. This suggests that even for those unfortunate people living most precariously, with a serious lack of expectation of improving their material quality of life, the concept of 'development' is not bounded *only* by a desire to achieve better material conditions in the here and now. Instead, for such people, most of who will be religious in the developing world 'development' involves a clear vision of *redemptive transformation*. This sense of spiritual capital is founded on an understanding that *all* resources are entrusted to people. As a result, both individuals and groups are called upon to preserve and develop a wealth of resources for which they are accountable here and later and which endowments must be managed. Thus, spiritual capital is about this entrustment of responsibility and a care for the creation it exhibits. 'Within various religious traditions, creative obedience or norms in economic activities are one primary way for adherents to acknowledge and demonstrate faith' (Malloch 2006).

From the context of this frame of reference, economic development is part of a wider process by which individuals and groups work together, galvanised by a concern to care for and use wisely resources necessary to sustain and enhance life – that is, 'development'. In such a view, 'economic development' is centrally concerned with how gifted resources are managed creatively by custodians whose activities are guided by faith commitments. The result is that desirable and authentic economic growth is bounded and informed by various factors. Derived from religious worldviews, these involve the application of normative rules and principled habits and practices that unavoidably take into consideration peoples' preservation needs – that is, physical, mental, social, cultural and spiritual demands – but not at the cost of unacceptable environmental degradation. This conception of spiritual capital is regarded as of such importance to religious worldviews that it has been called 'the third or missing leg in the stool which includes its better known relatives, namely: human and social capital' (Berger and Hefner 2003).

In summary, it is clear that there is not one set of religious principles that regulate any given economic polity. On the other hand, all religious peoples, regardless of to which faith they adhere, make individual and collective choices whereby personal faith is a highly important factor. The implication is that spiritual capital is a useful concept and an important idea within the wider context of economic development. It has however often been overlooked in modern theories of development. In addition, as they live close to the poor, faith-based organisations in the developing world are often in a good position to offer practical advice in relation to the interaction of social capital with wider development concerns. As a result, they can positively influence the substance of development. For example, a faith-based approach towards the provision of social services can emphasise human dignity, involving a wider focus on policies and practices that involve compassion, solidarity, participation and self-confidence. The inference is that for faith communities development must essentially include not only the material and economic but also spiritual and social dimensions of life. 'A relationship with the divine, that has consequences for individual as well as communal life, is of central importance to many people living in developing countries and influences how people choose to live their lives. Religion is not confined to the church or the mosque but spills over into all areas of life from family relationships to employment choices' (World Faiths Development Dialogue 2004: 1).

International development policies: lack of concern with spiritual issues

Many faith groups would contend that secular economic development programmes are not developmentally plausible, even within their own 'rational' terms of reference. To improve things, they would need to incorporate other important – spiritual, cultural, political, social and environmental – dimensions of life (Tyndale 2004: 3–4). Given this concern, it will come as no surprise to learn that for faith-based organisations the MDGs, including poverty and hunger eradication, are necessarily part of a broader context. Faith-based organisations will have important questions: How is poverty defined? When we think about development, what *kind* of development do we have in mind? Can development in the developing world come about without sustained international actions? The late pope, John Paul II, was well aware that the problem of poverty alleviation could not be solved by activities within developing countries alone; they would also require fundamental international commitments. Pope John Paul II's encyclical, *Sollicitudo Rei Socialis*, pointed to what he regarded as necessary international reforms – covering world trade, monetary and financial systems – that would be crucial steps in a wide campaign of poverty alleviation. In addition to the Pope, other influential religious leaders such as the Dalai Lama and the former Archbishop of Canterbury, Dr George Carey – have also added their voices to demands for change.

Many faith-based organisations are said to regard the World Bank, the IMF and other secular development entities as 'large, difficult to understand, arrogant, driven above all by an agenda to create, and even concentrate, wealth, and removed from daily issues' (Marshall 2005a). Perhaps even worse, they are also often seen as centrally contributing to serious social and economic problems in the developing world. Such concerns can lead to problematic relationships, with specific issues leading to a deepening sense of tension, including: advice to governments in Africa, Asia and Latin America on managing their overall finances, especially the issue of growing international indebtedness; financial crisis management; and how to deal with often larges, relatively unproductive and often poorly managed public sectors. In recent years, both the World Bank and the IMF are seen as inextricably linked to state policies that reduced subsidies to the poor, brought in or effected sometimes onerous taxation regimes, leading to: deep cuts in social programmes, reductions in state employment often through selling of state-owned enterprises, cut the money available for welfare, including health and education, projects, privatisation of service provision, especially water, and, finally, undermined or did away with barriers erected to protect local farming and industry from 'unfair' external competition and subsidies (Haynes 2005b).

Such IFI-endorsed development programmes contributed to

> a growing sense of awareness that while the global move towards free trade, market economies and modern technologies has brought rapid economic growth and many benefits, it has also been responsible for sowing the seeds of economic, technological and social imbalance [the] world over. Redressing this imbalance will require radical changes in our present mind-set and policy frameworks. The state and all other sections of civil society must engender a new paradigm of values, which will ensure an ethos of greater sharing and co-operation (Kurien 1996: 2).

Kurien is referring here to what is generally agreed among secular development analysts and religious leaders to be a generally disappointing outcome to internationally devised development programmes applied in the developing world from the 1970s. During this time dozens of developing countries adopted economic liberalisation policies due to serious economic problems they were experiencing. These included: balance of payments crises; instability or collapse of national currencies; high or very high rates of inflation; insupportable fiscal deficits; and intolerable levels of international indebtedness. These developments were typically preceded by periods of economic stagnation and/or declining rates of economic growth, leading to growing unemployment, worsening poverty and, in many cases, political instability.

Such policies were primarily focused in what were known as SAPs, following pressure from Western governments, the IMF and the World Bank (known as 'the Washington consensus'). Economic liberalisation and reducing the state's economic – and hence developmental – role became a uniform condition for the receipt of continued or new external economic assistance. Policies had several aims. Collectively they sought to encourage at home improved fiscal and monetary discipline, lower inflation, and reforms leading towards market economies and, internationally, free(er) trade, improved capital flows and better economic cooperation between developing countries. Measures adopted included: national currency devaluation, interest rates rises, decreasing the availability of credit and cutting government spending. In summary, to achieve these goals, the following key steps were judged to be necessary:

- Cut government spending, including health and welfare expenditures;
- Slash wage levels and severely constrain wage rises in order to reduce inflation and make exports more competitive;
- Expand the role of the private sector through privatisation of state assets;
- Liberalise foreign trade;
- Loosen control of capital, capital movement, and money markets, including the lifting of restrictions on foreign investment;
- Agricultural and industrial production shifted from food staples and basic goods for domestic use to commodities for export;
- Protect weaker sectors of society by strengthening social safety nets (Brecher and Costello 1994: 56–7).

These adjustment prescriptions were primarily designed by the IFIs, encouraged by rich Western countries and implemented by debtor governments – typically without popular debate or civil society participation. Yet associated reforms often had profound consequences for people, especially poor people, in the developing world. Stories from around the developing world highlight a consistent theme: conditions for many people living in poverty and suffering under injustice and discrimination became worse as a consequence of these measures (Religious Working Group on World Bank and IMF 1997). Recent research backs up such impressionists conclusions, with agreement that in most cases, SAPs led to (1) more, not less poverty in many developing countries, (2) economic 'progress' for some; but this occurred in a numerically small number of countries (typically with large populations and unusual appeal for foreign investors, such as China and India). But even in the 'successful' cases, most people were not actually better off and indeed many were actually poorer than before (Haynes 2005b).

In summary, enforcement of cutbacks, privatisation, and liberalisation of capital were uniform conditions imposed to receive continued foreign aid. Yet the precise ways adopted to protect weak and vulnerable sectors of society were often left rather vague, and rarely enforced to an extent that would permit them to offset growing inequalities. In summary, SAPs were externally-imposed, yet seriously flawed development strategies that often undermined the already weak developmental position of many poor people. As a result, there were widespread calls to reform SAPs, tame financial markets, 'upsize' the state, and 'downsize' the single global market (Held and McGrew 2002; Pettifor 2003).

Case studies: The National Forum of Fishworkers (India), Santi Sena (Cambodia), and the Aga Khan Development Network (Pakistan and Kenya)

Faith-based organisations in the developing world run a variety of poverty-related programmes. In recent years, numbers of such programmes have increased, partly in response to what are widely seen as increased inequalities and injustices stemming from the international policies described in the previous section. While their focus is wide, they may include: primary healthcare and education, rural savings and credit, natural resource management, development of physical and productive infrastructure, increased agricultural productivity and development of human skills. What they also have in common, at least rhetorically is a significant concern for community-level participation and decision-making. Such programmes also claim to want to encourage people in participating communities to increase their confidence and competence. They also want to promote the idea of informed choices for participants, giving them the confidence to choose from a range of appropriate and available options for sustainable, equitable development so as to be able to influence their own development futures. Our case studies – drawn from Christian, Buddhist and Islamic examples from Asia and Africa – suggest that the most effective way to organise communities in a sustainable manner is around *economic* activities. This is because they respond best to poor people's most pronounced and immediate priority: improvement in economic and developmental position. Such initiatives can also provide a constant stream of benefits that encourage people to remain organised and contribute towards the provision of services, crucial to health and education improvements. In addition, the case studies highlight what can be regarded as common religious precepts that inform what these groups do, almost irrespective of the religious tradition from which they emanate. Finally, while such faith-based poverty alleviation strategies can be important they are in no way a substitute for state-led and funded programmes and policies.

The National Forum of Fishworkers, India

The National Forum of Fishworkers (NFF) was founded in the South-western state of Kerala in the early 1970s. Its inspiration was drawn from Christian ideas of liberation, which initially gave vision, energy and hope to the organisation's members. Over time, however, the NFF expanded its membership to welcome Muslims and Hindus. It became a secular organisation, open to people of any religion or none. As a result, the NFF exhibited what might be called a 'secular spirituality', going beyond any particular religious faith, which provided the subsequent driving force behind the NFF's development. Over time, the NFF has made a significant contribution to development for fisher communities in Kerala. It did this by acting as a medium for the formation of a secular movement of fisher people that led to some important material improvements.

More than 80% of India's billion people are Hindu. Kerala has an old Christian tradition dating from the arrival of Jesus's apostle, St Thomas, in the 1st century CE. Although only 2.5% of India's total population is Christian, in Kerala the proportion is nearly five times as high: 12% of Keralans are Christian, and in the fishing villages of the state's southern tip Christianity – especially Catholicism – is the dominant faith (Embassy of India n/d).[2]

There was a great deal of debate within the Catholic world in the early 1960s which eventually led to the Second Vatican Council ('Vatican II'; 1962–65) that called for Christians to become more socially and politically aware and active. In some sectors of the Church this led to the adoption of what was known as a 'preferential option for the poor'. Bernard Pereira, then Bishop of the Latin Catholic Church in Trivandrum, Kerala, was inspired by this debate. He was especially concerned with the poverty of the fishing communities in his diocese. He responded with an innovative project in 1961: founding a model fishing village, called Marianad, 25km north of Trivandrum on an unoccupied expanse of land. 'Low cost housing was constructed and little by little the poorest families of the area started to arrive' (Tyndale n/d: 3). Once the village was established, foreign Christian volunteers were invited by the Bishop to work on the project. The aim was to develop the village community according to clear principles founded in the belief that grassroots participation was crucial for its health. As a result, all adult village inhabitants had the opportunity to participate in decision-making (Abraham 1996). It is important to note however that not all welcomed this innovative model of village democracy. In particular, 'the increasing confidence of the fisher people was not always appreciated by the more conservative clergy of the diocese' (Tyndale n/d: 3). This suggests that NFF views about liberation and empowerment were not uniformly adopted among Kerala's Christians for two main reasons: first, there were diverse political opinions that had little to do with religion *per se*. Second, it was also a question of how different Christians understood and put into practice their Christian faiths.

Over time, the specifically Christian liberation theology foundations of the NFF were augmented by the introduction of members from other religious traditions. There was, however, a continued understanding that to accomplish overall societal development it was necessary to liberate poor and oppressed people from structural relationships of domination and subservience that combined to perpetuate their poverty and their oppression. As the Bible puts it: 'The exaltation of the humble and the meek may be concerned with putting mighty individuals down from their seat' (Luke 1: 52). Supporters of this interpretation of Christ's gospel have faith in the power of God, working through the medium of ordinary people, to transform the world into a place in which none is excluded but where everyone from the highways and byways is invited to the feast (Luke 14: 12–24). Believing in this interpretation of Christ's gospel it would be inconsistent to accept the inevitability, still less the desirability, of economic policies and outcomes that work to accumulate both wealth and power in the hands of a few. In short, the ideas of Christian liberation theology that underpinned formation of the NFF over three decades ago developed over time to become a principle shared by all members regardless of whatever religious tradition they came from. This led to the view that it was important 'to try to change the way the world is ordered in the interests of the powerful as a whole' (Tyndale n/d: 9).

In conclusion, our brief focus on the NFF in Kerala highlights the importance of Christian liberation theology, especially the significance of giving power to those who are powerless. The key issue is the belief that for poverty reduction strategies to be effective it is necessary to enable people, as far as possible, to make their own choices about matters that affect their lives. Both the overall aims of the NFF and the way that the organisation worked were significantly affected by these principles. There was a pronounced emphasis on training, although money was in short supply, while there were consistent efforts to encourage women to achieve and retain decision-making positions (Abraham 1996).

Finally, people of other religions or of course none may well share many of the values highlighted above as characteristic of Christian liberation theology and as such of importance for development strategy including poverty alleviation. NFF members from other religious traditions, including Hindus and Muslims, would necessarily identify with the view that 'development' is centrally concerned with, first, making possible that people have the wherewithal to sustain or increase their livelihoods by working collectively with other people and, second, being concerned with the environmental impact of what they do to acquire their living, in this case, fishing. In addition, given that both Hinduism and Islam have strong traditions of sharing with the poor, then it is unsurprising that they would share spiritual motivation in this regard that more generally highlights the inspiration and power to be found in all three religions: Christianity, Islam and Hinduism.

Santi Sena, Cambodia

Like the NFF in Kerala, Santi Sena[3] is a faith-inspired NGO. Whereas the NFF draws on liberation theology with roots in a particular interpretation of Christianity, working in Cambodia, a primarily Buddhist country, Santi Sena draws on Buddhist norms, beliefs and values to engage in socio-economic work that aims to alleviate poverty and increase popular well-being. A senior Buddhist monk, the Venerable Nhem Kim Teng, head of the Prey Chlak Pagoda in Svay Rieng province, established Santi Sena there in April 1994. Santi Sena was founded in two problematic contexts: first, Cambodia's attempt to recover from a situation of disorder and horrible social anarchy when, encouraged by UNTAC (the United Nations Transitional Authority in Cambodia) the government sought to improve human rights and, second, the associated necessity of trying to deal with a worsening problem of widespread poverty as a result of earlier political and economic developments.

Much of Svay Rieng province borders Vietnam. Comprising nearly 700 villages it is a poverty-stricken and economically weak area, with most local people involved in rice farming but only managing to collect one annual harvest. As a result, farms tend to be poor, with each hectare capable of producing an average of only about 800kgs. Lacking access to much in the way of natural resources, most local people do not have alternative or additional sources of income to augment their earnings. Consequently, many people travel to surrounding population centres, where some find work as poorly paid wage labourers, while others beg for food in neighbouring Vietnam

(Venerable Nhem Kim Teng n/d)). Svay Rieng province drew the attentions of Santi Sena as a poverty-stricken part of the country that might benefit from a Buddhist approach to poverty alleviation. Seeking to solve these problems in an effective and sustainable way, it became clear to the Venerable Nhem Kim Teng that outsiders could not effectively resolve Cambodia's developmental shortfalls. Rather, it was imperative to seek to enable and empower local people so they could identify, prioritise and solve their own problems. The plan was that they would seek to accomplish this by better use of existing resources and by employing underused potential in pursuit of development activities through use of self-help methods inspired by Buddhist principles and practice. While this approach had undoubtedly been influential in the past in Cambodia, the disruption of the Khmer Rouge period and its aftermath in the 1970s and 1980s had significantly undermined its potential for development-orientated activity capacity, including poverty alleviation (Venerable Nhem Kim Teng n/d).

Santi Sena's philosophy has its origins in the Buddhist belief that 'development' is invariably 'human development' whose target is necessarily and primarily poorer people. To assist such people to provide opportunities for themselves and their communities, Santi Sena believed that the long-term goal of being independent from outside support was a priority task. To formulate a plan to achieve these objectives, the Venerable Nhem Kim Teng had long discussions with other, less senior, Buddhist monks and novices about what they should do for their supporters and how they should do it (in Buddhism, monks advise ordinary people and the latter should in turn resolutely support the former).

Four principles emerged from the talks. The first was *Sate Sappa Aharati Thika*. That is, as every person needs to survive they must have access to basic needs (food, life security, shelter and society). Second was the principle of *Attahe Attano Neath* or 'self-reliance' (no one will help us other than ourselves; God will help you only if you have helped yourself first). Third, there was *Rajadhamma* or the ten ethical principles by which people with the means should help poorer people. Finally, *Sanga Kich* encompassed the main tasks of monks: learning Buddhist scriptures, advising people on how to survive in the appropriate way according to Buddhist beliefs, not damaging the environment, constructing a peaceful society, increasing security for those people who need it and conserving traditional cultural values (USAID 2005).

Santi Sena's development vision emerged from this discussion. Fundamental to its concerns was the idea that Cambodian people deserved to be able to 'live in peace, justice, social well-being and dignity', in accordance with the Buddhist precept *Sate Sappa Aharati Thika* noted above (source). To realise its vision of poverty alleviation, Santi Sena sought to act as interlocutor between state development entities and local populations in Svay Rieng province in order to help develop community initiatives. In particular, it sought to focus on vulnerable and marginalised people, of which there were several groups: female-headed households, homeless people, children, youth, disabled people, and poor farmers. Monks sought to disseminate Santi Sena's vision through community outreach.

In conclusion, Santi Sena is an example of a Buddhist-inspired development approach, whose main aim is poverty alleviation among the poorest and most deprived members of society. It aims to increase people's awareness of the issues, motivate their interest in helping resolve them, encourage their willingness to work collectively, and seeks overall to assist the poor *(question)* to assist themselves. Its philosophy has firm foundations in traditional social values and Buddhist tenets, that are not only especially important in Cambodia since more than 95% of population are Buddhist but also because during the years of Khmer Rouge misrule Buddhism was marginalised to the extent that some feared for its survival in the country (Kamm 1998).

The Aga Khan Development Network (Pakistan and Kenya)

Unlike the NFF, active in Kerala state, India, and Santi Sena, which operates in Svay Rieng province, Cambodia, the Aga Khan Development Network (AKDN) is a transnational development organisation that operates in more than 20 countries.[4] The AKDN is closely linked to the Ismaili Imamat, a branch of the Islamic Shia sect.[5] Bringing together a number of initiatives developed over the last four decades, it aims to 'realise the social conscience of Islam through institutional action'. Its main focus is poverty alleviation, working to improve the living conditions of and opportunities for poor people by helping improve levels of knowledge while reducing ignorance and disease. It comprises ten separate organisations, including: the Aga Khan Foundation, Aga Khan Health Services, Aga Khan Fund for Economic Development, Aga Khan Rural Support Programme and Focus Humanitarian Assistance (http://www.akdn.org/). The AKDN is unusual among Muslim development initiatives in that it stems from a tiny sect within Islam. It is, on the other hand, also representative of related Muslim initiatives more generally. Many are transnationally oriented, focus on numerous countries, especially in Asia and Africa, and derive their sources of funding both from rich individuals and from religiously-based contributions from Muslims around the world.

The AKDN's main objective is to reduce rural poverty, particularly in resource-poor, degraded or remote environments, of which there are many in both Asia and Africa. It concentrates its energies and resources on a relatively small number of programmes of significant scale. It has worked to develop a model of participatory rural development that brings together a set of common development principles, coupled with the flexibility to respond to specific contexts and needs (SIPA 2006).

As with the other faith-based NGOs that we have examined in this chapter, the AKDN operates on a secular basis, that is, it is not concerned about the faith, origin or gender of people it seeks to assist. However, AKDN's values and ethics come from a specific religious tradition, Islam. It is motivated by: (1) a strong sense of compassion for the vulnerable in society, (2) the need for restraint in how the rich and powerful act, and (3) their duty to contribute to improve the quality of life for the unfortunate in society. Underpinning this focus is a more general concern with human dignity and respect and support for what Islam regards as God's greatest creation, people. The inference is that the most pious Muslims are those people who are socially conscious and who accept that they must use part of their wealth, whether in terms of personal talent or material riches, to try to improve the lives of the impoverished, deprived and marginalised. In other words, those at the margins of existence have a moral and religious right to receive society's compassion. However, the Muslim ethic seeks to discourage dependency as it is believed that it leads to a reduction in an individual's dignity. Rooted in Muslim belief from the time of the Prophet Mohammed, there is a great emphasis in Islam on the importance of key charitable impulse: help the needy to help themselves (Nasr 1967, 1975, 1996).

In Islam, the key to a dignified life is an enlightened mind. This is symbolised in the Qu'ran's metaphor of creation that includes the individual, as an object of rational quest. A relevant prayer in the Qur'an is: 'My Lord! Increase me in knowledge' (Qu'ran 20: 114). Good health is also regarded in Islam as a necessary component of a life of dignity. This is because the body is understood to be the resting place of 'the divine spark'. This spark is not only gifts to people's individuality and true nobility but also helps to bond individuals within a common humanity. The Qu'ran says: 'O mankind! We created you from a single soul, male and female, and made you into nations and tribes, so that you may come to know one another. Truly, the most honoured of you in Allah's sight is the most righteous of you. Allah is All-Knowing, All-Aware' (Qu'ran 49: 13). This invites people to strive for goodness.

The notion of common humanity is expressed in the AKDN's programmes via its focus on rural savings and credit, natural resource management, productive infrastructure development, increased agricultural productivity and human skills development. The context of all these initiatives is a central concern with community-level participation and decision-making. The overall objective is to make possible that community members can make informed choices from a range of appropriate options, all of which facilitate both sustainable and equitable development. To achieve this, the AKDN adopts as its central strategy an institutional structure at the village level. This is the medium by which local people can help determine what are their priority needs, as well as to make decisions concerning how best to manage common resources for the benefit of all. In addition, these village organisations aim to act for the community, becoming the interlocutor not only with government but also with other development partners, including NGOs and the private sector. The approach is said to be helpful in developing the necessary social capital to provide a necessarily supportive environment for improving a community's material assets and, in order to engender income growth in an equitable and sustainable manner, to harness and direct individual self-interest.

To build community assets, the AKDN not only works to improve community management of natural resources – including, forestry, soil conservation, water storage and irrigation infrastructure – but also building or developing basic economic needs, including infrastructural improvements, such as rural roads and agricultural storage facilities. To promote income growth, AKDN encourages improvements in agricultural productivity by introducing and developing management reforms, better and more productive farming methods, improved input supplies, marketing, land development, augmentation of off-farm incomes and general support of community enterprise development.

To see whether the AKDN's principles are put into operation in the field, we conclude this section with a brief look at specific poverty alleviation programmes, one in Kenya and the other in northern Pakistan.

The Coastal Rural Support Programme (CRSP) was established in Kwale district, on the Kenyan coast, in 1997. It was established here because the Aga Khan Foundation understood that shortage of water, insufficient and inadequate food and low incomes were combining to undermine its already established primary healthcare projects. Seeking to draw on knowledge derived from other AKDN programmes, especially the creation or strengthening of local community structures, CRSP seeks to double over a decade incomes of the poorest 60% of families who live in the catchment area. Overall, CRSP is a participatory rural development project with an overall community development strategy. It features several initiatives, including: rural savings and credit, management of natural resources, development of communications infrastructures, improving farming productivity and development of human capacity. Responding to a community request, in 2004 the initiative was expanded further to include a strategy to improve early childhood development (Canadian International Development Agency 2006).

AKDN is also active in poverty alleviation in northern Pakistan, where 300,000 Ismailis live. Through the Aga Khan Rural Support Programme (AKRSP), it supports irrigation and rural development in the area (Nasser n/d). In recent years, the AKRSP has installed more than 180 micro-hydro power units in Chitral District, North-West Frontier Province. They provide electricity to about 175,000 people, who use it not only to improve the quality of lighting sources but also to power radio, television and various appliances, including electric butter churners. The value of the initiative is particularly clear when it is taken into account that this is a very remote and fragmented area of Pakistan, the Hindu Kush mountains, whose communities are far removed from conventional electricity supplies. Until the initiative, they were compelled to use smoky and unreliable pinewood torches or expensive kerosene lamps for their lighting needs. Although the region is short of many natural resources, it does have numerous fast-flowing rivers that are well suited for electricity generation via small-scale hydroelectric power rather than intrusive large dams that local communities would not necessarily have found appropriate for their needs (The Ashden Awards for Sustainable Energy 2006).

In conclusion, AKDN training programmes aim to support village-level institutions by improving their effectiveness and sustainability. The organisation's philosophy is to try to encourage improvements in both management and technical skills, believed to be a crucial factor in the successful implementation and maintenance of local development activities. Second, the AKDN seems well aware of the need to build and develop its knowledge base and expertise through interaction with and learning from rural communities' development experiences. This is an approach to rural development that, drawing on religious precepts, believes that goals can best be realised through learning, analysing and disseminating lessons learned from field experience.

Overall conclusion

The aim of this chapter was to highlight the MDG of eradication of extreme poverty and hunger and examine the role of faith-based organisations in this regard. We noted that numerous secular development agencies have been ostensible working towards these goals for decades but without conspicuous success. It is clear that a necessary starting point to achieve these goals is the undertaking of fundamental reforms, both internationally and domestically. It would also likely improve outcomes if there was greater coordination between secular development agencies and faith-based organisations active in this area; working together there is more likelihood of success than working apart. Finally, we examined the work of three specific faith-based organisations: The NFF (India), Santi Sena (Cambodia) and the AKDN (Pakistan and Kenya).

Working from Christian, Buddhist and Muslim traditions, we saw that each of these organisations has a similar *modus operandi*, with local communities centrally involved in drawing up development projects and in their execution. It suggests that there is untapped potential in working towards eradication of extreme poverty and hunger in the developing world, but it would be a grave mistake to expect that faith-based organisations on their own can effect needed changes. What is required are more robust and effective partnerships between secular development agencies and faith-based organisations to have the best chance of success.

5
Environmental Sustainability

Concern for the natural environment, including appropriate management of natural resources, is rightly regarded as crucial to the development prospects of the developing world. 'Ensure environmental sustainability' is one of the MDGs, announced in 2000. For Mitchell and Tanner, the natural environment is defined as including all natural features of land, water, flora and fauna that support human life and influence its development and character (Mitchell and Tanner 2002: 1). In recent years, religious networks have played a growing role with regard to the interaction of humans with nature and the environmental issues that inevitably arise (Coward and Maguire 2000, 2002). Each of the world religions focused upon in this book has recently developed their environmental positions. For example there is 'ecotheology' in Christianity and 'Islamic environmentalism' while, in addition, both Hinduism and Buddhism have recently articulated religiously-based critiques of environmental damage and how to improve environmental sustainability (Ammar 1995; Narayanan 2000). One result is the growth in the numbers of religiously-based environmental NGOs in the developing world. In summary, these developments have made both nature and the environment new, cutting-edge topics in many religious worldviews.

Gary Gardner (2002), research director at the Worldwatch Institute, a US-based environmental research organisation, claims that around the world 'religious institutions ... are going green and providing a push to the [secular] environmental movement'. As a result, he avers, many secular environmental organisations, such as the Alliance of Religions and Conservation, now work closely with a variety of religious entities on a variety of environmental issues (Tucker and Grim 2001). Gardner documents that these novel alliances are increasing in both frequency and significance, concerned with, *inter alia*, tree planting in Kenya, deforestation in Thailand, and conservation in northern Pakistan (see below). According to Gardner:

> This collaboration could change the world ... These groups have different but complementary strengths. [Secular] environmentalists have a strong grounding in science. Religious institutions enjoy moral authority and a grassroots presence that shape the worldviews and lifestyles of billions of people. It's a powerful combination that until recently remained virtually unexplored (Gardner 2002: 5).

This chapter examines efforts to build an environmentally sustainable world through the actions of religiously-based people and faith-based organisations in the developing world. In some cases, as we have already noted, there are liaisons between, on one hand, secular environmentalists and advocates of sustainable development and, on the other, such religious entities. But to achieve the goal of better environmental protection requires that distrust between both groups is overcome. Secular environmentalists are often concerned about what they sometimes regard as the worrying characteristics of religious involvement in societal affairs, while religious individuals and faith-based organisations may have views – for example, on the role of women, the nature of truth, and the moral place of human beings in the natural order – that are often different from what environmentalists believe. Yet both share important interests that may well be complementary. For example, each looks at the world from a moral perspective, views nature as having value that surpasses economics and opposes excessive consumption. Consequently, 'religious institutions, as organizational wings of religion with their perceived strength and inherent dimension of natural resources management, hold a [considerable] promise for involvement in mainstream environmental management' (Ajit 2004).

From Stockholm to Kyoto and beyond

In this chapter we are concerned with various environmental issues of major importance in the developing world, including: climate change, pollution, animal species protection, and deforestation and desertification. Environmental issues first emerged as a contentious global issue in the 1970s, becoming a focus of societal concerns in many countries, as well as internationally. The United Nations Conference on the Human Environment held in Stockholm in 1972 is regarded as the first important international manifestation of concern about the environment (Vogler 2001: 192). Representatives of 113 countries attended. They agreed to what was known as the '26 Principles' that called upon governments to cooperate in protecting and improving the natural environment. Following the Stockholm conference, a series of events and developments reinforced the message that environmental protection was an essential step to protect humankind's well-being. These included the 1984 Bhopal (India) disaster, when an explosion at a factory producing toxic chemicals killed more than 4,000 people; a near-meltdown of the nuclear reactor at Chernobyl, Ukraine, in 1986; degradation of European forests due to acid rain; an expanding hole in the ozone layer and consequential skin cancers; pollution of the seas and overfishing and, most recently, unmistakeable signs global warming that threatened the very existence of many low-lying countries and islands, including in the developing world.

Consequently, the relationship between people's social and economic demands and the natural environment began, for the first time, to be discussed in a serious and scientific way. Following Stockholm a second major international conference took place in 1992: The United Nations-sponsored 'Earth Summit' held in Rio de Janeiro, Brazil, a tangible sign of growing global concern. More than 100 heads of state and 30,000 bureaucrats and representatives of NGOs attended. They discussed 24 *million* pages of preparatory documents and sought to make wide-ranging decisions regarding the future of the global environment. The Earth Summit was called specifically to confront two pressing problems: environmental degradation and poverty and underdevelopment, interlinked issues affecting millions of people especially in the developing world. The outcome was 'Agenda 21', trumpeted as 'a plan of action to save the planet', endorsed by representatives of all countries present. However, Agenda 21 was a compromise between, on the one hand, most Western states (which claimed to protect the environment) and, on the other, many developing countries (often advocates of a growth first strategy, that often appear to observers to reflect relatively little concern with environmental protection) (Haynes 2002: 215–43).

Critics argued that Agenda 21 was an inadequate, merely aspirational response to public concern, lacking teeth to ensure necessary progress in relation to environmental protection in the developing world (Tucker and Grim 2001). However, despite failure to produce an agreement on tropical rainforest destruction (one of Rio's main concerns), the Earth Summit did give rise to a Framework Convention on Climate

Change. This was significant because, as Vogler notes, it 'marked the beginnings of a systematic international attempt to grapple with the problem of "global warming"', one of the most significant threats with which the human race has had to deal (Vogler 2001: 193). At the end of 1997, measures were agreed to control emissions of the greenhouse gases held responsible for global warming. In July 2001, despite the withdrawal of the United States from the protocol, 185 countries agreed in principle limited but concrete measures to try to deal with the problem (Brown 2001). In late 2006, the Stern Report on Climate Change gave additional focus to the issue of climate change – although this did not imply that there was consensus on how to deal with the problem.

Developing environmental crises in the developing world

The exploding issue of climate change was but one of the issues high-lighted in the context of environmental sustainability in the early 2000s. Like many other environmental concerns, it drew attention to the increasing desirability and plausibility of partnerships involving both secular and religious in relation to the environmental crisis threatening the long-term viability of current development policies in many developing countries (McFague 1993). Economic globalisation in particular was seen as a development that not only widened further the already vast gulf between rich and poor but also placed further pressures on the natural environment as developing countries sought to catch up with their developed counterparts via industrialisation strategies (Loy 2000). Apart from climate change, three further important environmental problems affect many developing countries: (1) economic development with scant concern for environmental protection, (2) desertification and deforestation, and (3) skewed land use patterns that deepen poverty among the poor. In many developing countries, religious environmental NGOs seek to focus attention on the problems, although as our case studies below indicate, results are mixed.

Climate change

The Earth is the Lord's and the fullness thereof (Psalms 24: 1).

Mischief has appeared on land and sea because of what the hands of men have earned. That (Allah) may give them a taste of some of their deeds: in order that they may turn back from Evil (Qur'an 30: 41).

By 2006, the international scientific community had reached consensus on the causes and potential consequences of climate change. The Intergovernmental Panel on Climate Change (IPCC) referred to 'discernible human influence on global climate', reporting that the current atmospheric concentration of carbon dioxide, the main human-made greenhouse gas affected by human activity, has not been exceeded in at least the last 400,000 years (Houghton 1992: 23). In addition, a United States National Academy of Sciences (NAS) report published in 2001 pointed out that:

> Climate change simulations for the period of 1990 to 2100 based on the IPCC emissions scenarios yield a globally-averaged surface temperature increase by the end of the century of 1.4 to 5.8 C (2.5 to 10.4F) relative to 1990.... Even in the more conservative scenarios, the models project temperatures and sea levels that continue to increase well beyond the end of this century (National Religious Partnership for the Environment n/d: 3).

It is now agreed by all serious scientists that consequences of even relatively modest climate change will include: increasingly common heat waves, severe droughts, torrential rains often followed by floods, rises in global sea levels of up to one metre, tropical diseases in regions that are currently temperate and momentous biodiversity reductions. Collectively, their impact would be profound, seriously affecting health and well-being of people everywhere, although it is anticipated that climate change would fall disproportionately both upon developing countries and on poor people who live there. Effects would include exacerbation of existing health inequities and disparities in access to adequate food, clean water, and other resources.

The chief cause of climate change and associated environmental destruction is undoubtedly human action. As a result, the issue is not limited to scientific and policy issues alone but also includes moral and ethical concerns which for many people are significantly influenced by religious convictions. The quotations at the beginning of this section emphasise that in both Islamic and Christian scriptures, all creation is judged to be God's/Allah's handicraft; as a result, it is 'good', available for the benefit of all. God/Allah creates a covenant with people to act as his 'stewards of life'. As a result, it is widely agreed in many religious worldviews people everywhere – especially in the developed world where most climate change inducing gases are generated – must care about the state of the earth and make much greater efforts to safeguard and improve the needs of the most vulnerable as well as those of future generations. While religion and science do not necessarily agree on the sources of these ideas, the principles they encapsulate – such as, stewardship, justice, protection of the weak, inter-generational duty, and prudence – are clearly common, even universal, values emphasising the urgent moral challenge to humankind that global warming poses.

In December 2005, an important United Nations climate change conference was held in Montreal, Canada. Hundreds of representatives from faith-based organisations attended and took the opportunity to deliver a statement, 'A Spiritual Declaration on Climate Change', that proclaimed:

- 'We hear the call of the Earth;
- We believe that caring for life on Earth is a spiritual commitment;
- People and other species have the right to life unthreatened by human greed and destructiveness;
- Pollution, particularly from the energy-intensive wealthy industrialised countries, is warming the atmosphere. A warmer atmosphere is leading to major climate changes. The poor and vulnerable in the world and future generations will suffer the most;
- We commit ourselves to help reduce the threat of climate change through actions in our own lives, pressure on governments and industries and standing in solidarity with those most affected by climate change;
- We pray for spiritual support in responding to the call of the Earth' (World Council of Churches 2005).

This ringing endorsement of shared faith principles relating to climate change in particular and environmental protection more generally was not an isolated example of religious concern. In addition, various religious entities now lobby for action at local, national and international levels. For example, in the United States, leaders of 86 Evangelical churches presented an 'Evangelical Climate Initiative' (http://www.christiansandclimate.org/), while in the United Kingdom, a church-based climate change campaign – entitled 'Operation Noah' – has sought to put pressure on the British government to encourage the latter to take a leading role in international climate negotiations (http://www.christian-ecology.org.uk/noah/). Overall, however, such statements rarely call for *specific* actions to combat climate change. Instead, they tend to emphasise that more than enough evidence now exists to make serious action an essential next step and that necessary actions would accord with religious principles.

Desertification and deforestation: impact on the developing world

In addition to climate change, desertification and deforestation are also highly significant environmental problems in many parts of the developing world. 'Desertification' refers either to invasion of arable land by sand or to irreversible damage to vegetative cover. The United Nations Environmental Programme (UNEP) estimates that more than 1.2 billion hectares – about 10% of the earth's vegetated surface – has undergone moderate or severe soil degradation since 1945. UNEP calculates that an area the combined size of North and Latin America is imminently threatened by desertification. Large swathes of the Middle East, Africa, Asia and Latin America, where rainfall is low are at particular risk (Coward and Maguire 2000).

Two theories compete to explain desertification. The first blames so-called 'primitive' farming measures – that is, smallholder agriculture and nomadic pastoralism – and population pressures which combine to produce both famine and hunger. However, evidence suggests that neither smallholder agriculture nor nomadic pastoralism leads to desertification *providing* there is sufficient land available for all. This is because conventions typically exist which means that land has sufficient time to recover before farming resumes (Harrison 1987). A second theory contends that the main problem is modern, capitalist agricultural enterprises farming practices involving intensive mechanised agriculture and large-scale raising of cows, sheep and other animals. While the real reason for desertification probably lies in a combination of the two areas of concern, it seems clear that it is often due to several social and economic factors, including changing land use and industrial-scale farming.

'Deforestation' refers to massive, often irreversible, destruction of forests. Globally, tropical moist forests ('rain' forests) are the 'richest ecosystems in biomass and biodiversity on land'. They cover an area of 1.5 billion hectares, with about 65% found in Latin America, and the rest divided between Africa and East and South East Asia. During the 1990s and early 2000s, more than 20 million hectares were destroyed *each year* and, at current rates of destruction, *no* rainforests will be left in 50 years time (Thomas 1994: 62).

Rainforest is destroyed for a variety of reasons, including farming and timber extraction. For example, more than 150 million cubic metres (mm^3) of rainforest were destroyed in Brazil each year in the

1980s and 1990s. Over 75% of forest loss was the consequence of slash and burn farming, undertaken by poor, landless people desperate for arable land. Less than 1% of the timber was exported. In Malaysia, on the other hand, the proportions of timber exported and burnt for farming was reversed: 80% of timber is exported. The Malaysian government argues that it has a perfect right to exploit and export timber because 'economic growth is needed first, to generate the ability to clean up the environment later' (Eccleston 1996: 134).

Whether for farming, as in Brazil, or for export, as in Malaysia, deforestation leads to negative local, regional and global consequences. Locally, it threatens or destroys lifestyles of people who depend upon the forest for a living; regionally, it leads to leaching and erosion of soils, flash floods and desertification; globally, it results in reduced biomass stocks and species diversity, changing patterns of rainfall, and encourages climate change.

Skewed land use patterns

Environmentally destructive effects of desertification and deforestation are exacerbated by development patterns and programmes that take natural resources away from the poor, who tend to use them sustainably, and put them in the hands of others who may exploit them less sustainably. Lack of secure control over resources, swift population growth, inequity and sometimes-misguided government policies form a common context of poverty leading to environmental deterioration of both agricultural and non-agricultural land. Over 350 million of the 800 million poorest people in the developing world now live on marginal or fragile lands and consequent serious environmental degradation is virtually certain. However, whether poor people are displaced by influential individuals who use their land for cash-cropping, plantations or ranches or whether it occurs by state policy – for example, the Brazilian government's plan to populate the Amazon basin – results tend to be similar: When displaced people are forced to seek livelihoods on marginal or unsuitable land, struggles for survival will result in significant environmental damage (Peluso 1993: 46–70).

Poverty drives environmental deterioration when desperate people overexploit their resource base, sacrificing the future to try to salvage the present. Often the logic of short-term needs encourages poor, landless families to burn sections of rainforest or to farm hardly viable land – such as mountain slopes. Unsurprisingly, the most impoverished, most overcrowded regions suffer worst ecological damage. For example, in parts of South Asia, including northern Pakistan, Nepal and Bangladesh, millions of poor people inhabit environmentally degraded regions, for example, crowded hill country on the margins of the Himalayas. In China, many impoverished people live on the Loess Plateau, where soil is swiftly eroding. In the Philippines, northeast Thailand, Brazil's Amazon basin, and several West African countries in the Congo basin, impoverished farmers try to eke out precarious livings on plots reclaimed from the forest. In parts of East and southern Africa, on the other hand, poor people try to exist on already defor-ested land that inexorably turns into desert (Durning 1989: 44–5; Eadie and Pettiford 2005).

Typically, the poor knowingly harm their environment to a serious degree only when under severe duress. Pushed to the brink of starva-tion, often evicted from familiar land by big commercial interests, such people will lack access to a sustainable livelihood with adequate land, water, and capital. Two common sequences, whereby poor people are involved in downward spirals of environmental degradation, are illus-trated by examples from Nepal, Costa Rica and Honduras. In Nepal, swift population growth threatens environmental viability; in Costa Rica large commercial interests have ousted numerous small holders from their land for cattle ranching in recent years; and in Honduras deforestation occurs in pursuit of valuable hardwoods for export (Stiefel and Wolfe 1994). In each case, however, the outcome is the same: large tracts of farming land are taken away from the rural poor who are, as a result, seriously disadvantaged, while environmental degradation and destruction is also a near certainty.

Environmental sustainability and religious traditions

We noted above in relation to climate change that when environmen-tal damage is clearly the result of discernible human influence then the issue moves beyond the realm of scientific and policy issues and enters the domain of moral and ethical concerns; and, as already noted, they are very often informed by religious convictions. Each of the four religious traditions focused upon in this book feature teach-ings that centrally reflect the idea that environmental sustainability is a crucial priority for each, highlighting the interaction of moral, ethical and ecological values. In each of the religious worldviews, eco-nomic gains are seen as a lesser priority than protection of the natural world, while excessive consumption of natural resources is often frowned upon because of the deleterious impact on environmental sustainability.

In the developing world, we have already noted, certain religious figures and the faith-based organisations with which they are often connected, views are important in several ways. These include the:

- Exercise of often considerable moral authority;
- Capacity to shape worldviews of large numbers of people through ability to 'talk to' large numbers – thousands or even millions – of followers;
- Control of often significant material resources;
- Considerable community building capacity (Gardner 2002; Ajit 2004).

Thus in the developing world religious leaders – either on their own or in partnership with the faith-based organisations with which they are connected – increasingly focus on issues of environmental and social responsibility that emphasise concerns not only for public welfare but also their followers' spiritual well-being. Overall, as Gardner observes, religious worldviews can 'shape attitudes towards the natural world' and such institutional power can help mould followers' 'behaviour and policies in ways that affect the environment, for better or worse' (Gardner 2002: 10).

Emphasising the role of religion from an ecological perspective, Anderson states that 'all traditional societies that have succeeded in managing resources well, over time, have done it in part through religious or ritual representation of resource management' (Anderson 1996: 166). Gardner notes that a growing urge to incorporate modern environmental concerns into religious worldviews can be seen in several recent examples of religious people's engagement in environmental issues (Gardner 2002; Tucker and Grim 2001). Before turning in the next section to practical examples of religious involvement in attempts at environmental sustainability in the developing world, it will be useful to highlight the religious traditions and worldviews which underpin and encourage this course of action.

In the monotheistic traditions of Christianity and Islam the natural environment is traditionally of only secondary importance; God/Allah is seen to transcend the natural world. As a result, the natural world can be seen primarily as a set of resources for human use, a perspective that has underpinned the wasteful and destructive economic development of the past two centuries, in both the developed and developing countries. On the other hand, these religious traditions can also find important grounds for encouraging the view that both traditions also have a foundation of strong environmental ethics. For example, the Christian focus on sacrament and incarnation can be understood as a focal point by which the natural world in its entirety is seen to be sacred. In addition, the Islamic concept of vice-regency emphasises that the natural world is not *possessed* by humans but merely passed to people in trust – and in this case trust involves a clear responsibility to try to preserve the balance of creation (Ammar 1995).

Individual religious leaders have specific things to say about protection of the natural environment. For example, speaking on behalf of the Catholic Church in 1990, Pope John Paul II said that, 'Christians realise their responsibility within creation and their duty towards nature and the Creator are an essential part of their faith'. In the same year, the Ecumenical Patriarchate speaking for the Orthodox Church, proclaimed that people 'ought to perceive the natural order as a sign and sacrament of God'. As a result, they should learn to respect the natural world because 'all creatures and objects have a unique place in God's creation'. In addition, the Orthodox Church also 'teaches that it is the destiny of humanity to restore the proper relationship between God and the world as it was in Eden'. Finally, Protestant Churches, speaking through the WCC in 1990, also 'committed themselves to conserve and work for the integrity of creation both for its inherent value to God and in order that justice may be achieved and sustained' (ARC 2004). Overall, it is clear that the major traditions in Christianity broadly share a view that underscores the importance of environmental sustainability and protection.

Turning to Islam, it is clear that for the world's more than one billion Muslims, Islam is more than a 'mere' religion. It is also a 'life code' for believers. The faith's sacred teachings – contained within the *Qur'an* and the *Sunnah* (sayings of the Prophet Mohammed and examples from his life) – collectively amount to a comprehensive and integrated code for life, which includes people's relationships with the natural world. Islam supplies a holistic approach to existence that neither distinguishes between sacred and secular nor the temporal from the natural world. Derived from the teachings of Islam's Prophet, Mohammed, attempts to formulate an ethical and moral system for Muslims developed over time into the Islamic legal system (*Shari'ah*). *Shari'ah* includes rules guiding environmental practices, covering such areas as: 'conservation and allocation of scarce freshwater resources, land conservation (with zones for various uses), and the establishment of pastures, wetlands, green corridors, and the conservation of wildlife' (The World Conservation Union 2006).

Key terms in Islam – *tawheed, khalifa,* and *akrah* – emphasise the importance of environmental concerns. *Tawheed* ('unity') is Islam's central concept. Allah is unity. His unity is reflected in the unity of humanity and nature. The import is that Muslims are enjoined to maintain earth's integrity, including flora, fauna, and overall the natural environment. For Muslims, a key responsibility is to keep balance and harmony in Allah's creation. *Khalifa* means 'trusteeship' and refers to the fact that Muslims believe that Allah created humans to be guardians of his creation. Put another way, people do not own nature; instead Allah entrusted nature to humans for them to look after it, not to exploit it. 'The world is green and beautiful, and Allah has appointed you his guardian over it', Mohammed said. Finally, *akrah* means 'accountability'. Muslims believe that on the day of reckoning Allah, who will assess how they undertook their responsibilities – including to the natural environment – following Islam's guidance of Islam, will judge them. The Qur'an points out that Allah wants people to enjoy the fruits of the earth. At the same time, he wants them to avoid excess leading to waste, 'for Allah does not love wasters' (Qur'an, Surah 7). These principles are collected in the *Shari'ah* where they are turned into practical directions covering how Muslims should live. In relation to the natural environment *Shari'ah* law 'protects animals from cruelty, conserves forests, and limits the growth of cities'.

Some Muslims regard natural disasters such as floods, hurricanes, and earthquakes as warnings from God indicating that people have embarked upon a fundamentally wrong course of action. Emerging environmental disasters, including the effects of global warming, are also seen by many Muslims in the same way (Folz *et al.* 2003). Seen as a 'wake-up' call from Allah, the greenhouse effect, a consequence of excessive consumption by humans of fossil fuels, creates serious problems for all people, including Muslims. This may be of especial concern in mainly Muslim countries, such as Saudi Arabia, Kuwait and UAE, whose economies rely heavily on the exploitation and sale of oil. For such countries, and for Muslims more generally, Islam's view of humanity as enjoying nature under Allah's trusteeship (*khalifa*) poses critical questions. A Muslim scholar, Nawal Ammar, points out that the Qur'an teaches that humans, as custodians of nature, are free to satisfy their needs only with an eye to the welfare of all creation. That is, 'the harmony and beauty God gave nature must be respected by humans in their stewardship of nature'. As a result, humans' use of natural resources must be in balance with nature. Ammar also explains that 'No one owns nature, therefore humans must share natural resources and population pressure will dictate limits to consumption so that there can be just access to resources by all'. In addition, although birth control 'is generally forbidden in the Qur'an, some Muslims now suggest that fertility control may be acceptable if seen as part of the self-discipline required from humans to avoid upsetting the divinely established balance of nature' (Ammar quoted in Coward 2002: 4).

Turning to Hinduism and Buddhism, both faiths contain teachings concerning the natural world that are however arguably in conflict. From these traditions, scholars sometimes emphasise both the illusory nature of the material world. For Hinduism, this implies the desirability of escaping suffering by turning to a timeless world of spirit. For some Buddhist schools, on the other hand, relief is sought through seeking release in nirvana. This other-worldly orientation is sometimes said to minimise the importance of environmental degradation, although both Hinduism and Buddhism place great emphasis on correct conduct and on fulfilment of duty, which includes obligations to environmental preservation (Narayanan 2000).

Hinduism has three central components: Life is sacred; simple living; and inner peace. On the first point, all living beings are regarded as sacred, because they are aspects of God. Consequently, they should be treated with both respect and compassion. The reasoning is that Hindus believe that the soul can be reborn into any form of life, and Hinduism features many stories where animals are seen as divine. These include the tale of the monkey Hanuman acting as the god Rama's faithful servant. Because of this belief in the sanctity of life, many Hindus are vegetarian, while trees, rivers and mountains are believed to have souls, and consequently humans should care for them. The second principle is 'simple living', a prized virtue among Hindus. *Brahmanas* ('teachers') are expected to live on the charity of others and not amass too much wealth. The *sadhu* ('sage') is the most highly respected people among Hindus, an individual who lives apart from normal society in forests or caves, travels on foot from one town to another, and takes pride in living simply and consuming very little. Finally, Hindus lay emphasis on inner peace, believing that true happiness comes from within; it is not achievable through a high level of ownership of possessions, and their pursuit should not be allowed to control life. Instead, it is important for people to discover their spiritual nature, as it brings both peace and fulfillment. Hindus regard rivers as sacred, and in the concept of *lila*, the creative play of the gods, Hindu theology engages the world as a creative manifestation of the divine (Gardner 2002: 14–15). In addition, '*vedas* and other religious scriptures have detailed discussions and descriptions on nature and how to protect it' (Ajit 2004: 12).

Buddhism has four central themes: all beings are connected; respect for life; simplicity and moderation; and right livelihood. For Buddhists, the idea of separateness is an illusion whereby well-being of the whole is inextricably linked to the health of individual parts, while the parts' health is indivisibly related to the health of the whole. As a result, caring for the environment begins with caring for oneself. As the Buddhist monk, the Venerable Maha Ghosananda of Cambodia, opines: If 'our hearts are good, the sky will be good to us' (http://Inweb18. worldbank.org/ ESSD/ envext.nsf/48ByDocName/BuddhistFaithStatementonEcologyt/$FILE/ FaithBuddhism2003Final.pdf). Respect for life is the Buddhist practice underpinning the belief that each individual's existence is only as important as everyone else's. It is important to treat nature as a friend and teacher, because one 'can then be in harmony with other creatures and appreciate the interconnectedness of all that lives'. Third, the notion of simplicity and moderation is contained in the idea that Buddha instructed people to live simply and appreciate the natural cycle of life. Only unhappiness can result from craving and greed. This is because demands for material possessions can never be satisfied, people will always demand more, and this seriously threatens environmental well-being. Therefore resolving environmental problems must begin with actions undertaken by the individual. Finally, right livelihood, according to Buddhism, is centrally concerned with how people earn their living. This should not be by killing, stealing, taking more than one needs, harming others or trading in dubious substances, including weapons, meat, alcohol or poisons. In addition, Buddhist environmentalists often stress the importance of trees in the life of the Buddha, and many examples of 'socially engaged' Buddhism have been noted in various Asian countries, including Thailand and Cambodia, where a key theme is forest protection (Gardner 2002: 14–15).

In summary, it is clear that Islam, Christianity, Hinduism and Buddhism collectively have a wealth of religiously-based precepts governing human behaviour in relation to the natural environment. In the next section, we shall see how such precepts are applied by faith-based organisations in various developing countries.

Case studies: Christianity in Honduras, Hinduism in India, Buddhism in Thailand and Islam in Malaysia

Earlier in the book we noted recent religious resurgence in many parts of the world, including some parts of the developing world. We saw that a context of this development was deepening globalisation, including the impact of structural adjustment programmes in many developing countries. There were also indications of diminishing belief in the ability of some governments to deal adequately with development shortfalls. As a result, some people looked to religion as a source of leadership in helping resolve such problems. We have already noted in this chapter that recent decades have seen increasing environmental problems of various kinds affecting the developing world. The case studies in this section – concerned with Christianity in Honduras, Hinduism in India, Buddhism in Thailand, and Islam in Malaysia – collectively emphasise a shared theme. It is that faith-based organisations and/or religious leaders, acting with regard to religious principles, have become increasingly involved in environmental sustainability campaigns. This often puts them into direct opposition to state-sponsored development projects, while highlighting the political and environmental dimensions to development projects in the developing world.

Liberation theology and environmentalism in Honduras

The Central American country of Honduras experienced growing concern about the natural environment in the 1980s, especially the swift rate of deforestation. 'Although Honduras is not overpopulated, its land resources have been overexploited, and there are numerous reasons for concern regarding deforestation and the prevalence of unsustainable agricultural practices. Enforcement of the few regulations already in effect is uneven'. Growing concern with environmental sustainability was reflected in the founding of the Honduran Association of Ecology (Asociación Hondureña de la Ecología, AHE) in the 1980s. A decade later, however, the organisation was under a cloud when it became clear that AHE had been run corruptly. However, this did not deter increasing environmental consciousness among many sectors of society, including peasant organisations, labour unions, and faith-based environmental groups ('Honduras' 1993).

In recent years, Honduras has experienced significant deforestation. The Department of Olancho, a 24,000 square kilometre land and forest reserve, has been seriously affected, with forests felled and timber removed and sold to make way for commercial agriculture. Unregulated logging has meant that about half of Olancho's five million hectares of forests had been destroyed by the early 2000s. The result was not only loss of the trees but also a significant reduction in Olancho's water supply. As a consequence, Olancho's fragile ecosystem, 'which includes over 500 unique birds, rare rainforest species, and many endangered plant and animals, is in danger of vanishing' (http://www.motherjones.com/news/qa/2005/06/tamayo.html). For many local people, the loss of forest and reduction in water supplies is bad enough, but there is also a third result. Many of the people who live in Olancho are poor and very few receive any of the wealth that derives from the sale of timber as a result of the logging. The financial rewards of cutting down the trees and selling the timber accrue to the already wealthy, including large landowners, businessmen, and members of Honduras' government (http://www.motherjones.com/news/qa/2005/06/tamayo.html). In addition, many local subsistence farmers have seen their crops ruined as a result of flooding that has occurred due to deforestation. In summary, despite the argument that Honduras' economic development requires exploitation of the country's natural resources – and these of course include timber – deforestation is very difficult to justify environmentally, economically, morally or ethically.

Honduras is 99% Christian, mainly Roman Catholic. In recent years, Christian environmental groups have emerged. Like many other regional countries Honduras has experienced the impact of liberation theology. A Catholic priest, Leonardo Boff, was instrumental in expounding its key tenets from the early 1970s (Boff 1987).

Liberation theology inspired local people in Orancho to try to do something about the unregulated logging that was causing such catastrophic consequences. A Roman Catholic priest, Father José Andrés Tamayo Cortez, has helped to organise a body of environmental activists, forming an organisation called the Environmental Movement of Olancho (EMO). The EMO protests both at the illegal logging in Olancho and the government forest policies that make it possible. Father Tamayo coordinated demands for a moratorium on logging until conservationists could inspect the forest and work out how best to protect the country's forest resources as well as find ways that local people would benefit financially from controlled harvesting of the forest resources. In 2003 Father Tamayo led a 3,000-person 'March for Life' that travelled the 200 kilometres to Honduras' capital, Tegucigalpa. The March brought environmental issues to national attention in a highly visible way. It was such a success that it was repeated the following year. This time around 5,000 people took part. Their main purpose was to protest at perceived corruption in the government's National Forest Agency. The 2004 March inspired other similar marches in the country, encouraging environmental activities in many parts of Honduras to demonstrate against environmental destruction (Plumer 2005).

Father Tamayo's activism in organising local people in Orancho to protest against unregulated logging has resulted in 'death threats, violent assault, and constant harassment' from Honduran business interests who have traditionally and consistently harassed environmental activists (http://www.motherjones.com/news/qa/2005/06/tamayo.html). For example, in 1975 two priests, a Colombian, Father Ivan Betancourt and a US citizen, Father Michael Cypher, as well as ten local activists were murdered after speaking out and organising local opposition in an attempt to expropriate land illegally. More recently, three members of Father Tamayo's EMO were shot and killed in 2003, including a 23-year-old priest (Plumer 2005). In recognition of his efforts to preserve Honduras' forests and seek just remuneration for local people for timber that is extracted, Father Tamayo was one of six recipients of the prestigious Goldman Prize for environmental activism in 2005 (Goldman Environmental Prize 2005).

In conclusion, Father Tamayo and his organisation, the EMO, has focused environmental activism of both secular and religious - individuals, collectively organised to defend their land against uncontrolled commercial logging. As a result, they have encountered opposition from the loggers and associated business interests. However, the EMO has been instrumental in getting the issue of environmental protection on to the political agenda in Honduras, as well as encouraging other groups in the country to fight environmental problems.

Hindu responses to environmental crisis in India

Alas! In the process of modernization and mimicking of western lifestyle and consumerism, modern Hindus have forgotten their ancestors' view on ecology, and have acquired the western exploitative attitude towards nature. Lush forests have been denuded, rivers, including the sacred river Ganga (the Ganges), have become polluted with industrial wastes. Delhi has become one of the most polluted cities in the world. Many beautiful birds and animals have become extinct. This devastation is taking place in the name of *progress* (Adhopia 2001).

How serious are India's environmental problems? A Delhi-based think tank for sustainable development Tata Energy Research Institute (TERI) has recently presented a shocking picture. A summary of a recent report indicates that India has undergone increasingly serious environmental degradation since independence in 1947 (www.teriin.org/

greenindia/sum.htm). TERI concludes that India's economic progress over the last six decades advancement has come at serious environmental cost. Problems include: 'falling water tables, soil loss, air pollution, water pollution, forest degradation, overgrazing, loss of species, and unmanageable municipal waste'. TERI estimates that India's industrialisation and accompanying urbanisation has resulted in a net loss in quality of life for Indians, when analysed in terms of financial costs and deleterious effects on human health. For example, according to TERI, air pollution led to '2.5 million premature deaths in 1997'. In addition, overall effects of soil degradation resulted in annual agriculture output falling by a quarter over the years. If environmental trends continue, TERI estimates, by 2050 not only will India have a population of 1.75 billion – an increase compared to now of over 0.5 billion people – but the country's rivers will be little more than 'open sewers'. In addition, erosion will have destroyed millions of hectares of once productive agricultural land, while forests would quickly disappear. In conclusion, TERI notes, a continued direction of economic development, without addressing environmental problems, conclude the scientists, is unsustainable (Mohanty 1999).

Vasudha Narayanan, a Hindu, summarises the situation in her essay, '"One tree is equal to ten sons". Hindu responses to the problems of ecology, population and consumption'. She writes that 'the Earth belongs to us only in our egos and avaricious hands' but 'in reality, it is we who belong to Earth, and by wrongly usurping what is not ours and what should be shared with the future generations of human beings, we are indulging in adharmic, unrighteous behavior' (Narayanan 2000: 115).

More than 80% of India's population of over one billion people are Hindus. What role have Hindu leaders and organisations sought to fulfil in relation to environmental protection? According to Vasudha Narayanan, professor of religion at the University of Florida, 'too few Hindu leaders and institutions are responding to the crisis of pollution, deforestation, soil degradation and unchecked development ...'. Narayanan contends that this is because many fall prey to the 'seductive power of consumer goods and the easy profits promised by large industries that have scant respect for the environment [and are] powerful enough to overcome any vestiges of respect for theology' (Narayanan 2001). On the other hand, several Hindu religious leaders have taken active roles in India's environmental movement in recent years. These include Swami Chidanand of Shivanand Ashram, Haridwar, who blessed the struggle against Tehri dam. He also blessed the Chipko movement.[1] In addition, 'Mahant from Brindaban temple is thinking about ecological issues and doing good works in Brajbhumi. Mahant in Banaras is taking up the issue of cleaning the Ganga' (Mohanty 1999: 12). There is also evidence of a significant level of environmental activism among some Hindu leaders and organisations. For example, several temples are now running programmes to restore entire forests in both Badrinath and Vrindaban. Activists, including Medha Patkar and Sunderlal Bahuguna, are working to try to cancel or at least moderate some of India's planned gigantic river development projects. In addition, India's richest temple, Tirumala Tirupati temple in Andhra Pradesh, has organised 'the planting of several million trees, both near the temple and across India. They've made the trees part of the pilgrims' devotional observances' (Mohanty 1999: 12–13). However, according to David Frawley, these are isolated examples of Hinduism-inspired environmental protection. More widely, he avers, the country's environmental movement 'is run by westernized elites, and based on western model. It has failed to become a mass movement, for it is devoid of spiritual foundation or content necessary to inspire Hindus'. In his book, *How I Became a Hindu* (2000), Frawley laments that

> Unfortunately, Hindus have forgotten this Vedic view of the earth and don't protect their natural environment. They have not added a (traditional) Hindu point of view to the ecology movement which is perhaps the main idealistic movement in the world today......part of the challenge of the modern Hinduism is to reclaim its connection to the earth (Frawley 2000: 13).

The overall conclusion is that India's environmental problems are much the same as those of the rest of the world. That is, there is growing awareness of multiple environmental problems but insufficient action on the part of many governments to resolve the concerns. Second, like many other developing countries that have seen fast economic growth in recent years, India faces impending catastrophic environmental crisis – unless changes are made promptly and fully across all levels of society. Third, India is four-fifths Hindu and theoretically Hindu philosophy provides a basis for the necessary changes; so far, however, Hindu leaders and organisations have a minor and ineffective role in helping resolve India's environmental crisis; they can do much more.

Buddhist monks and environmental activism in Thailand

Much of Asia is undergoing strong economic growth. Many regional governments as a result are struggling to achieve a balance between, on the one hand, economic development and, on the other, environmental protection and sustainability. Among the region's fast developers is Thailand, a country whose population is over 90% Buddhist. In the country there is a small but vocal group of monks who seek to use their religious prestige and societal influence to promote environmental sustainability among ordinary people. For example, environmentalist monks in Thailand have been at the forefront of opposition to shrimp farming, dam and pipeline construction and protection of mangroves, bird populations and trees, 'ordaining' the latter within 'sacred community forests' (Darlington 2000).

Often noted as one of the economically dynamic 'Asian tigers', Thailand has been experiencing an economic boom since the mid-1980s that was interrupted but not ended by the 1997 financial crisis that swept across Thailand, like much of Asia. The crisis served to focus attention on the negative environmental effects of Thailand's years of rapid industrialisation. These include:

- Severe degradation of water and coastal resources;
- Loss of natural habitats – primarily due to deforestation;
- Higher levels of air and water pollution;
- Increased levels of industrial waste water; and
- Dramatic rises in domestic sewage and hazardous wastes (Energy Information Administration 2003).

Seeking to recover from the 1997 financial crisis attention was focused on Thailand's serious environmental problems. For the first time, there began to be sustained awareness that to endure in the long term Thailand's economic development must also be environmentally sustainable. Prior to this, Thailand's government had indicated that it wanted to pay greater attention to environmental protection, so that the country could deal with environmental challenges linked to economic development. The Environmental Protection Act (EPA) was passed in 1992, a law that was heralded as the dawn of environmental awareness in the country. Following the EPA, Thailand's 1997 constitution required the government both to carry out public hearings and seek local communities' views before it commenced development projects with significant environmental impacts and conduct environmental impact assessments. This meant, first, that the government was now directly responsible for the deleterious environmental impacts of large infrastructure projects, intended or otherwise. Second, it highlighted that public participation in environmental issues was now an essential factor in economic development projects (Dearden 2002).

In the short term, however, the apparent awareness of environmental issues did not appear to make a great deal of difference to related outcomes. One reason was that Thailand's economic contraction that followed the 1997 financial crisis meant that attention was divided between two key issues: the problem of declining economic growth and the issue of environmental sustainability. The World Economic Forum 2000 produced an Environmental Sustainability Index in 2002, showing the state of the environment and how it was affected by human activities in various developing countries, ranked Thailand a poor 46th out of 56 countries. In 2006, a more comprehensive 'Environmental Performance Index', complied jointly by the Yale Center for Environmental Law & Policy at Yale University and the Center for International Earth Science Information Network (CIESIN), Columbia University Data, indicated that Thailand was rated 61st out of 146 countries (http://sedac.ciesin.columbia.edu/es/epi/downloads/2006EPI_AppendixC.pdf). The indications were that while Thailand was by no means the worst performer it was also clear that it was not making as much environmental progress as the government, much less local environmentalists, would have liked. According to the latter, Thailand's comparatively poor environmental performance was due to a lack of political will on the part of government to enforce existing laws and regulations (Dearden 2002). The relevant ministry, the Natural Resources and Environment Ministry, was said to lack influence within government. As a result, it was unlikely that the government would choose to take tough environmental decisions that would be necessary to regulate and monitor the environmental impact of economic development, from new building projects to increasing traffic (Energy Information Administration 2003).

Governmental failure to enforce its own environmental laws encouraged the rise of environmental protection NGOs, including both secular and faith entities. The latter have often developed under the aegis of Buddhist monks, a small but visible group known unofficially as environmentalist or ecology monks (*phra nak anuraksa*) (Darlington 1997, 2000). Such monks began to take a sustained and active role in seeking to help protect the environment, believing that it was a religious duty to help relieve ecological suffering. The monks understood that there was a direct connection between what in Buddhism is regarded as the root causes of suffering – greed, ignorance, and hatred – and the degradation and destruction of Thailand's natural environment. They believed that environmental activism was a religious duty, within the wider context of Buddhist activism. Environmentalist monks movement drew on Buddhist principles and practices and it was therefore natural for them to undertake traditional religious rituals and ceremonies to draw attention to environmental problems. These included tree ordination rituals (*buat ton mai*), during which trees were first blessed and then draped in saffron robes which signified sacred status.

Attempts were also made to raise environmental awareness among ordinary Thais. It was hoped that the monks would be able to inspire some at least to take part in practical conservation work. Both religious environmental ceremonies and practical conservation efforts were aspects of wider attempts by the environmentalist monks to generate and develop an ethic of conservation that would appeal to Thais. Several monks, including Phrakhru Pitak Nanthakhun, Phrakhru Manas Natheepitak, and Phrakhru Prajak Kuttajitto, personally initiated various grassroots conservation initiatives. These included not only the already mentioned tree ordinations and planting ceremonies but also the creation of wildlife preserves and sacred community gardens, long-life ceremonies for ecologically threatened sites or natural entities, initiatives in sustainable community development and natural farming, and campaigns against deforestation, shrimp farming, dam and pipeline construction, and the cultivation of cash-crops (Pipob Udomittipong 2000: 191–7).

In conclusion, our brief examination of the activities of environmentalist monks in Thailand highlights that exploitation of various types of natural resources in the country has caused various deleterious environmental effects. Forests have been continuously encroached and degraded due to the requirement of wood and more area for cultivation. In addition, often unregulated application of chemical fertiliser and pesticide for increasing agricultural yield, as well as booming tourist industry, has polluted the watershed environment. Environmentalist monks draw on Buddhist principles to seek to encourage ordinary Thais to join them in their efforts.

Islam and the natural environment in Malaysia

Folz (2005) has provided a useful overview of how environmental activists in various Muslim countries – including Malaysia, Egypt, Turkey, Iran, Pakistan and Nigeria – have sought to respond to environmental crises that are affecting their countries. The different accounts point to a shared conclusion. It is that poor people in these Muslim countries – like their counterparts in non-Muslim countries in the developing world – primarily feel detrimental effects of environmental degradation. So far in this chapter, our case studies – covering Christianity, Hinduism and Buddhism – indicate that religious individuals and faith-based organisations become involved in environmental campaigns for several reasons. First, environmental degradation and destruction is seen to be wrong according to religious tenets and, second, their effects can encourage liaisons between secular and faith activists who share a common goal: environmental protection and sustainability. Governments of Muslim societies may be slow to respond to environmental problems, while opposition parties and movements have usually focused on other issues, such as political reforms including democratisation. Folz (2005) also contends that throughout much of the Muslim world, albeit from small beginnings, environmental awareness and activism are growing. The overall point is that like other societies, the world's Muslim communities are facing significant challenges in seeking, on the one hand, to balance development and social justice and, on the other, to preserve the integrity of the globe's life support systems.

Like its neighbour Thailand, Muslim-majority Malaysia has been at the forefront of economic development in South-east Asia since the 1980s. Yet government efforts to legislate and deal with the consequences – environmental destruction and degradation – have, like Thailand, been stymied by lack of political will. In addition, there have been serious conflicts with indigenous peoples in Sarawak and elsewhere, focusing on demands for both land and social reforms and better protection of Malaysia's dwindling forests (Calvert and Calvert 1996: 246–7). More generally, conflicts between indigenous peoples and tree fellers are symbolic of contradictory interests involved in exploitation and conservation of forest resources. Use by subsistence-based people of forest resources for their survival is often in conflict with their use for industrial or cash crop purposes.

Malaysia has one of the strongest economies in South-east Asia. Malaysia is often said to be on a fast track to economic development, emerging as a major contributor to the global economy. Yet, like Thailand, Malaysia lacks appropriate infrastructures that also highlight problems of raw sewage and water shortages. Swift growth in personal ownership of cars has exacerbated a growing problem of air pollution (worsened by forest fires in neighbouring Indonesia in the early 2000s).

Deforestation, as a result of both logging and replanting of rubber plantations, has led to losses of both habitat as well as water retention problems on land stripped of trees. Since the early 1980s, as Malaysia's pace of growth has increased there have been few signs that the country's government takes environmental problems seriously. Government inaction or indifference has led to the emergence of local secular environmental NGOs as well as those with religious roots (Vincent and Ali 2005).

Unlike neighbouring Thailand, mainly a homogenous Buddhist culture, Malaysia is mainly but not exclusively Muslim: 60% of the population are followers of Islam. During the 1990s, as Malaysia became an increasingly significant economic force, the country's government, led at the time by Prime Minister Mahathir Mohamad, sought to reinforce the country's Muslim roots – an emphasis that still endures. The aim however was to emphasise that Malaysia was *developing but not westernising*. That is, the government sought to disseminate the message that its development path was a secular one, in line not only with Islam but also with the country's other main religions: Christianity, Buddhism, Taoism and Hinduism (Vincent and Ali 2005). As a result, the government sought to get the backing for this policy of various opinion formers, both secular – leaders in the environmental NGO community – and religious: Islamic scholars in the fields of law and the environment. The aim was to highlight the idea that environmental protection and sustainability in Malaysia was not only essential for long-term health and wealth but also this was a *secular* – rather than an *Islamic* – project. The consequence is that Malaysia does not currently have conservation projects that *explicitly* use Islamic principles as a key tool for education or awareness or any other aspect of environmental protection. In addition, no government environmental policies *explicitly* incorporate Islamic thought (Bankoff and Elston 1995).

There were reasons for this state of affairs that went beyond the desire of the Malaysian government not to be seen to be privileging Islam or any other religion. For example, although Malaysia has a majority Muslim population other minority populations might well have felt poorly used 'by conservation projects that focus on only one particular religious group'. In addition, for Muslim environmental NGOs there was generally another barrier to proclaiming Islamic credentials for conservation projects: it often made it difficult to acquire foreign funding for such initiatives – as few Western environmental groups seem explicitly prepared to support what they regard as Islamic conservation efforts (Arensberg 2004). As already implied, in addition, such initiatives would also struggle to get governmental support because, according to its constitution, Malaysia is technically secular – while claiming to use Islam as a guiding force in its policy making. Consequently, to use Islamic principles in environmental protection would be constitutionally inappropriate. Moreover, the government would also be hesitant to be seen espousing Islamic principles for a practical political reason. According to Arensberg, there is increasing tension in Malaysia, caused by attempts to install *Shari'ah* law by government parties in the north and east of the country. 'Politicians in parliament in Kuala Lumpur are facing immense pressure to not sound or act too extreme by proposing legislation based on Islam outlined in it for fear of being grouped with the separatist parties' (Arensberg 2004).

According to Abu Bakar Abdul Majeed, while Malaysia is a multi-ethnic country with a number of recognised religions, principles underlying Malaysia's development and environmental sustainability are compatible with Islamic definitions of a just society (Majeed 2003). In addition, Arensberg (2004) claims that the ideas and concepts of what he calls 'Islamic Environmentalism' are 'gaining popularity among intellectuals, Islamic leaders, and academics in Malaysia'. During his research in the country in the early 2000s, he discovered that many among such people 'were well versed in the connections between holy texts and basic environmental principles and that considerable thought had been given to ways these links could be exploited for conservation'. On the other hand, 'despite the good grasp people shared on the topic it was evident that little discourse had been shared across disciplines to take any further action'.

The wider point is that articulation of an Islamic environmental ethic in contemporary terms – that is, in recognising the urgency of the global crisis now facing humankind – is quite novel, not merely in Malaysia but also in the Muslim world more generally. Probably the first Muslim intellectual to do so was an American-trained Iranian Shi'ite philosopher, Seyyed Hossein Nasr, who argued that 'timeless truths' are seen as being expressed in a variety of historical, cultural and philosophical traditions. His environmentalist critique of Western modernity first appeared in 1967, in a book entitled *Man and Nature: The Spiritual Crisis in Modern Man*. Since then, Nasr has continued to explore the spiritual dimension of the environmental crisis through articles, lectures, and a later book, *Religion and the Order of Nature* (1996). The point in relation to Malaysia is that there is not at the moment a conducive intellectual climate in the country to link *Islamic* environmentalism with a critique of the government's economic development priorities. This is mainly because the government strives to present an essentially secular development vision which has no place for religiously-based concepts and critiques.

Overall conclusion

Recent years have seen rising concern for protection of the natural environment. Reflecting such concern, one of the MDGs is to 'ensure environmental sustainability'. We have seen that religious networks play an important and growing role with regard to the interaction of humans with nature and the environmental issues that inevitably arise (Coward and Maguire 2000, 2002). The religious traditions examined in this chapter have all developed environmental positions, including: 'ecotheology' in Christianity and 'Islamic environmentalism', while both Hinduism and Buddhism have also built up religiously-based critiques of environmental damage and how to achieve environmental sustainability. One result is growth in the numbers of religiously-based environmental NGOs in the developing world, several of which were examined in this chapter. In summary, these developments have made both nature and the environment new, cutting-edge topics in many religious worldviews.

6
Health

> Religion plays a central, integrating role in social and cultural
> life in most developing countries... there are many more reli-
> gious leaders than health workers. They are in closer and
> regular contact with all age groups in society and their voice is
> highly respected. In traditional communities, religious leaders
> are often more influential than local government officials or
> secular community leaders (UNICEF 1995).

Three of the eight MDGs are concerned with improving various aspects
of health in the developing world, underlining their crucial importance to more achievement of improved development outcomes. The
three relevant MDGs are to (1) 'reduce child mortality' by two-thirds,
especially among children under five years, the worst affected group,
(2) 'improve maternal health', and (3) 'combat HIV/AIDS ... and other
diseases'. The aim was that in relation to these health issues, both
faith-based organisations and secular development agencies, such as
the UNFPA, would work constructively together. As the quotation
above suggests, involvement of religious leaders and faith-based organisations was regarded as crucial in this regard both because of their
often high community standing and the sensitive nature of these
health issues.

In recent years, numerous religious leaders and faith-based organisations have begun to engage with partners in the secular development
community in relation to health issues in the developing world at
community, national, and international levels. When such partnerships work well, it reflects sustained dialogue, genuine willingness to
work together and a clear sense of shared objectives. On the other
hand, this is not to suggest that desirable health improvements will

necessarily come about only as a result of non-state secular and faith entities working together. To achieve essential long-term health improvements requirement, the leading role of government is crucial (Tessane 2005: 1).

The achievement of a variety of health goals in the developing countries can be undermined by various factors, internal and external. Turning to external factors first, we have already noted in earlier chapters that all developing countries must contend 'with the pressures of economic globalization on often fragile local economies ...'. In addition, various natural disasters, for example the tsunami of December 2004 that hit South and South-east Asia with particular force,[1] as well as floods, earthquakes and droughts, are vivid reminders of how such events can disrupt achievement of health objectives (UNICEF 2005a).

Among the relevant internal factors, we can note:

• Occasional rivalry between competing religious traditions over resources devoted to delivery of healthcare;
• 'Natural' disasters that affect many developing countries. On the other hand, as we noted in Chapter 5, many 'natural' disasters have human origins;
• Ethno-religious and political conflicts whose impact disproportionately falls on the weak and vulnerable in society, including children;
• Traditional social attitudes and cultural norms that can pose special challenges to health improvement;
• Budgetary constraints that impact on development programmes, including healthcare, in many developing countries.

Overall, to achieve greater success in relation to health would require both creative work and development of partnerships between both secular and religious entities. While such work is already taking place, it is generally not that well known and it deserves greater attention from development analysts. In particular, partnerships between religious and secular activists are of importance in relation to highly problematic health issues, such as HIV/AIDS. For example, UNICEF South Asia organised a conference in Kathmandu, Nepal, in April 2004 that brought together representatives of South Asia's many religious faiths. They included Buddhist monks from Thailand, Muslim imams from Pakistan's North West Frontier Province, one of the most religiously orthodox regions of South Asia, and Catholic priests from the Philippines. HIV/AIDS activists from the region also attended the conference.

Ven Phra Tuangsit from Nong Khai in Thailand was a keynote speaker at the conference. He is a Buddhist monk who leads a project called Sangha Metta that many want to see duplicated in other parts of South-east and South Asia. Under the Sangha Metta programme, Buddhist monks are involved in projects with young people, sex workers and others to spread awareness of HIV/AIDS, including demonstrating how to use condoms, if appropriate. 'At first people were worried that it was inappropriate', he noted, 'for a Buddhist cleric to work with condoms and things, but now people realise that I'm practising Buddhist compassion and helping people avoid painful, humiliating illness ... They listen and respect us because we are monks. So much has changed'. Numerous speakers at the conference also called for sympathy and forbearance for HIV/AIDS victims. Pointing to this collective concern, the conference organisers claimed that this was a sign that things had changed fundamentally: faiths and HIV/AIDS 'workers are converging, compromising and learning to live with each other's attitudes and priorities'. Because HIV/AIDS is soon set to become South Asia's biggest public health challenge, it is appropriate that the 'men and women who serve God have decided they have a role to play in helping the present and future victims of a dreaded epidemic' (UNICEF 2004). However, as Marshall and Keough note, to make such 'goals a reality ...depends largely on their ownership by local communities and on serious efforts to sustain a "development enabling environment", where local resources are tapped and mobilized to achieve these goals' (Marshall and Keough 2004: 17).

The next section provides an overview of health problems in the developing world that are focused upon in the MDGs: HIV/AIDS, maternal health and child mortality. It notes various international efforts to improve the situation that encourage interaction between secular and faith entities. The chapter then focuses on how Christianity, Buddhism, Islam and Hinduism perceive health issues in a development context, before examining case studies from Islam, Christianity, Hinduism and Buddhism in Asia, Africa and Latin America.

HIV/AIDS

Many would now agree that the human immunodeficiency virus/ acquired immunodeficiency syndrome (HIV/AIDS) pandemic is one of the greatest challenges now facing the international community. Around the world 40 million people now live with HIV/AIDS, with

females making up almost half of the victims. While sexual and reproductive healthcare and services contribute to the prevention of
HIV/AIDS and other sexually transmitted infections, suffering from
HIV/AIDS significantly increases for females the risk of complications
during pregnancy and childbirth. In addition, in many cultures victims
of the disease frequently have to contend not only with ill health and
eventually in most cases death, but also stigma and discrimination
(International Interfaith Network for Development and Reproductive
Health 2005: 1).

The first cases of AIDS were reported in the early 1980s. In the two-
and-half decades since, infections with HIV have grown to pandemic
proportions; there are now estimated to be 65 million infections and
25 million deaths. In 2005, nearly three million people died from
AIDS, over four million were newly infected with HIV, and around
40 million lived with the disease. HIV disproportionately affects certain
geographic regions, including sub-Saharan Africa and the Caribbean.
Effective prevention and treatment of HIV infection with antiretroviral
therapy (ART) is now available, even in countries with limited resources.
However, comprehensive programmes are 'needed to reach all persons
who require treatment and to prevent transmission of new infections'
(The Global HIV/AIDS Pandemic 2006).

A comprehensive report published in August 2006 on the eve of the
16th International AIDS Conference (August 13–18, 2006, in Toronto,
Canada), summarised selected regional trends in the HIV/AIDS pandemic. Primarily based on data from the *2006 Report on the Global AIDS
Epidemic* by the Joint United Nations Programme on HIV/AIDS, it
noted the following. *Sub-Saharan Africa* is home to about 10% of the
global population, yet the region is home to nearly two-thirds (64%) of
people living with HIV. 'Transmission is primarily through heterosexual contact, and more women are HIV infected than men'. Southern
Africa is the main focus of the AIDS epidemic; all countries in the
region except Angola have an estimated adult (15–49 years) HIV prevalence greater than 10%. Countries worst affected include Botswana,
Lesotho, Swaziland, Zimbabwe and South Africa. The latter country,
with an HIV prevalence of 18.8% and 5.5 million persons living with
HIV, has, along with India, the largest number of persons living
with HIV in the world.

Adult HIV prevalence is lower in *Asian* countries than in sub-Saharan
African nations. Of the estimated 8.3 million HIV-infected persons in
Asia, over two-thirds (5.7 million) live in India, while China, Thailand
and Cambodia also have relatively high infection rates.

Numbers of HIV infections are relatively low in *Latin America*. Brazil, the second most populous country in the Americas (after the United States), has an adult HIV prevalence of 0.5% and has approximately 30% of the population living with HIV in Latin America and the Caribbean. After sub-Saharan Africa, the Caribbean is the second most HIV-affected region of the world. While HIV prevalence has declined in urban areas of Haiti, it has remained constant in other areas of the Caribbean (UNAIDS 2006).

We have already noted that serious attempts to ameliorate the health of millions of people in the developing world might usefully recruit the energies of various religious leaders and faith-based organisations in the developing world. One such area is the HIV/AIDS pandemic. When the issue first surfaced in the early 1980s, most religions shunned or ignored the issue, despite the serious challenges it posed in and to their communities. This was often because, for many religious figures and faith-based organisations, 'HIV/AIDS was the disease of homosexuals and lesbians who needed to seek counselling to change their unnatural behaviour' (Bureau for Development Policy/Regional Bureau for Latin America and the Caribbean 2005: 5). This view seemed to reflect a belief that those who fell ill with the virus that causes AIDS were receiving divine punishment for their perceived 'immoral behaviour'. This conservative stance was reflected at the International Conference on Population and Development in Cairo in 1994. The issue of HIV/AIDS was high on the agenda and it appeared that conservative religious delegates – who collectively opposed measures like condom distribution to stop the spread of the disease – were at the time in the ascendancy.

Religion's role in combating HIV/AIDS is controversial. Yet improvements in HIV/AIDS hinge on the necessity of changing behaviours, and in this respect religious leaders and faith-based organisations can play a significant role. Over time, as we have already noted in respect to South Asia, it appears that because of the scale and consequences of the HIV/AIDS pandemic some religious leaders have changed their views. In recent years, often working together with secular development NGOs and/or government agencies, as we shall see below some religious leaders and faith-based entities have been notable for often energetic campaigns not only mobilising HIV/AIDS prevention efforts but also actively providing care and support services for sufferers of the disease.

Reflecting and seeking to coordinate grassroots religious initiatives, a United Nations (UN) AIDS Global Strategy Framework on HIV/AIDS has set out principles and elements that seek to deliver a coordinated and effective global HIV/AIDS response. The UN initiative highlights the necessity of involving key groups – government service providers, NGOs, and community groups – as well as religious leaders and faith-based organisations – in the fight against HIV/AIDS. The overall objective is to collect and focus relevant societal forces in a sustained drive against the HIV/AIDS pandemic (UNAIDS 2001).

The involvement of religious entities aims to build on many faiths' deep understanding of suffering and compassion and, wherever and whenever possible, provide relieve to them. Moreover, when seeking to assess the potential of religious entities to be active participants in the fight against HIV/AIDS, it is important to understand that many have long been engaged in seeking to improve the health of followers across the developing world. In Africa, Asia and Latin America, religious entities have delivered over time an array of welfare goods including health, social, and other communal services. For example, in many African countries, according to Ellis and ter Haar (2005: 2), 'faith groups provide an average of 40% of the healthcare'. Overall, the existing involvement of faith groups in healthcare in the developing world emphasises that the potential exists for similar initiatives in relation to HIV/AIDS. Such efforts could draw on preexisting infrastructures and large numbers of followers that might be used not only for implementing policies, but also in delivering and increasing in scope and coverage services delivery. In addition, many religious entities 'have the ability to mobilize at a grass-roots level because of their credibility and status' (Bureau for Development Policy/Regional Bureau for Latin America and the Caribbean 2005: 7).

This is not to suggest, however, that either working on their own or even in partnership with secular development agencies, do religious entities have all the resources and answers necessary to deal successfully with the HIV/AIDS pandemic. The involvement of both governments and the international community is also crucial. In addition, it is necessary to emphasise that partnerships – whether between religious entities or involving the latter and secular development organisations – are not always easy to institute or develop. In some cases, there is evidence of discord that 'have arisen among faith institutions and between faith and development actors as they struggle to come to terms with a new and devastating disease that defies traditional solutions and confronts them with a harsh picture of human behaviour' (Marshall and Keough 2004: 97). The very problematic characteristics of the pandemic – including, a lengthy time of silent, invisible incubation; its association with the most intimate of human behaviour; and its swift spread – have made the challenge exceptionally difficult. It is only now – when the disease has reached such significant levels as to threaten to devastate entire communities and even nations – that the response begins to come near equalling the challenge.

Maternal health and child mortality

The leading causes of death among women of reproductive age in many developing countries are complications linked to pregnancy and childbirth, including: severe bleeding (25%), infection (15%), unsafe abortion (13%), eclampsia (12%), obstructed labour (8%), other direct causes (8%), and indirect causes (20%). Around the world, over half a million women die every year from such causes. Over 99% of these deaths occur in developing countries, indicating that if the resources were available they could be avoided. In addition to maternal death, women experience more than 50 million maternal health problems annually. As many as 300 million women – more than one-quarter of all adult women living in the developing world – suffer from short- or long-term illnesses and injuries related to pregnancy and childbirth. While all women risk death and disability each time they become pregnant, women in developing countries face these risks much more often, since they bear many more children than women in the developed world. 'At least 40% of women experience complications during pregnancy, childbirth and the period after delivery. An estimated 15% of these women develop potentially life-threatening problems. Long-term complications can include chronic pain, impaired mobility, damage to the reproductive system and infertility' (Safe Motherhood Initiative 2002).

Women die for various reasons, but most maternal complications and deaths occur either during or shortly after delivery. Yet many women do not receive the essential healthcare they need either during pregnancy, during childbirth, or after delivery (World Health Organisation 1997). Various factors prevent women in developing countries from getting the life-saving healthcare they need, including: distance from health services, cost (direct fees as well as the cost of transportation, drugs and supplies), multiple demands on women's time and women's lack of decision-making power within the family. In addition, poor quality of services, including poor treatment by health providers, can also make some women reluctant to use the services (World Bank 1993).

Several steps could be taken to achieve improvements. The first is to ensure women's access to maternal health services, where the following essential services would be available: 'routine maternal care for all pregnancies, including a skilled attendant (midwife or doctor) at birth; emergency treatment of complications during pregnancy, delivery and after birth; and postpartum family planning and basic neonatal care'. Overall, 'such care would cost about $3 per person per year in low-income countries. Basic maternal care alone can cost as little as $2 per person'. However, access to appropriate services is not all that is required. In addition, there is an urgent need to 'improve women's status and raise awareness about the consequences of poor maternal health. Families and communities must encourage and enable women to receive proper care during pregnancy and delivery' (Safe Motherhood Initiative 2002). Religious leaders and faith-based organisations can play an important role, as they are very often significant sources of community norms and values.

The issue of women's health is closely connected to that of their children. Nearly eight million stillbirths and early neonatal deaths (deaths within one week of birth) occur annually. Most such deaths are found in the developing world. They are often caused by the same factors that result in maternal death and disability: poor health of women during pregnancy, inadequate care during delivery and lack of appropriate care for newly born infants. A study in Bangladesh undertaken in the 1990s found that 'a mother's death sharply increased the probability that her children, up to age 10, will die within two years. This was especially true for her daughters' (World Bank 1997: 27).

There are more than 2.2 billion children alive in the world, around one-third of the total global population of over 6.5 billion. Most live in developing countries – where around one billion children must survive on less than US$2 a day, and nearly half of all children are at least moderately underweight because they cannot get access to sufficient food. Malnutrition causes six out of ten of child deaths, two more die from pneumonia, while malaria, measles, diarrhoea, and HIV/AIDS also kill millions. Overall, nearly 11 million children – 70% of total child deaths – die each year from preventable diseases. Half of the child fatalities occur in just six countries: India (2.4 million), Nigeria, China, Pakistan, Ethiopia, and the Democratic Republic of Congo. 'Nine of the top ten problem countries are in Africa, with 43 percent of child mortality deaths; South Asia has 33%'. Moreover, in some developing countries, around 10% of children die before reaching the age of five years; the 'comparable rate in the USA is seven child deaths in *one thousand* live births'. Given such a position, it is unsurprising that one of the MDGs is to cut the mortality rate among children 'to approximately 28 deaths per 1000 births' (UNICEF 2005b). However, solutions to reduce significantly child mortality are achievable. Despite the fact that many developing countries have healthcare systems that are underdeveloped, inadequate, poorly funded and staffed, around two-thirds of such deaths could be prevented by known, low-cost, straightforward interventions, including: vaccinations, antibiotics, and providing education for mothers. They are not collectively expensive – even for countries with fragile health systems – and could be implemented relatively swiftly (Tessane 2005: 2).

Overall, it is important for secular development agencies and faith-based entities to work together to initiate and develop health improvements in the developing world. As we shall see below, even relatively small-scale initiatives involving faith-based organisations at community level can help catalyse national, regional, or even international social changes. Finally, as our case studies also indicate, working together with faith-based organisations and development agencies can make health services relevant and responsive in relation to cultural and religious norms and values.

Islam

Some Muslim countries, especially in Africa, are among the poorest and most underdeveloped in the world. To examine what can be done to improve matters in relation to health, the OIC, the Islamic Educational, Scientific and Cultural Organisation (ISESCO) and UNICEF jointly produced a comprehensive report in 2005, entitled *Investing in the Children of the Islamic World*. While focusing specifically on children, the report also usefully highlighted a range of health problems affecting Muslim countries. Overall, the report emphasised that action is urgently needed to tackle a range of problems facing over 600 million children in the Islamic world, from poverty and disease to education and protection. However, addressing these problems was not just the responsibility of governments but was also linked to initiatives initiated by various non-state actors, including religious entities. While governments are in the best position to provide financial and technical resources, as well as technical expertise and organisational skills of practical significance, required health improvements and lasting progress can also be facilitated by interaction involving both regional and international financial institutions and private sector, including religious entities. Finally, the report also called attention to the religious and moral duty of wealthier OIC member states significantly to increase development assistance and to seek to ensure that the most vulnerable sections of society, including children, women, and the poor, were assisted.

The overall focus upon child health in the report was timely because OIC member states – of which there were 57 in 2006 in Africa, Asia and the Middle East – collectively account for approximately 25% of the world's more than two billion children. OIC member states, including countries as developmentally and culturally different as Malaysia, Mali and Kuwait, account for nearly three-quarters of countries – 11 out of 16 – with the world's highest child mortality rates. Children living in Muslim countries in sub-Saharan Africa suffer the worst health deficiencies. For example, in sub-Saharan Africa child mortality rates are more than double the world average, while a child born there will on average live to only 46 years, compared to 78 in developed countries. Overall, more than four million children under the age of five years die each year in OIC countries from preventable disease and malnutrition, with around 2.5 million expiring before their first birthday. In 2005, only 25% of OIC member states – 14 out of 57 – were on track to achieve the MDG on child mortality (UNICEF 2005c).

In addition, many OIC countries have both high female fertility and a lack of access to skilled medical care. These factors contribute to some of the highest maternal mortality rates in the world. In Afghanistan, for example, one in six (17%) of all pregnancies leads directly to the death of the woman concerned, while in OIC member states in Sub-Saharan Africa, the average is slightly better – one death for every 15 pregnancies – although still much worse than the global average: one death in 74 (UNICEF 2005a). Overall, there is a troubling situation among OIC countries in relation to both children's and women's health. The dismal picture was highlighted by the OIC Secretary-General, Ekmeleddin Ihsanoglu, at the launch of the report. Dr Ihsanoglu pointed out that to improve the situation both the OIC

> and the broader Muslim community must demonstrate the true meaning of Islam's vision on childhood issues and the real spirit of Islamic solidarity by coming together for the sake of our children ... The future development of our countries depends on today's children, and the needs of these children are urgent (UNICEF 2005a).

Overall, there is much to be done in many Muslim countries to improve significantly both children's and women's health. To guarantee their rights in this regard, it would be necessary not only substantially to improve specific health indicators but also to make noteworthy progress on wider goals related to combating poverty and accelerating human development.

HIV/AIDS is also having a serious impact on many Muslims in the developing world. For example, among OIC member states in sub-Saharan Africa, adult prevalence rates were 5.4% (7.9 million cases) in 2005? Although HIV/AIDS rates are currently lower in other Muslim countries – for example, in Arab and Asian OIC member states they were respectively 0.3% and 0.1% – 'concentrated epidemics among intravenous drug users and commercial sex workers in some countries are major causes for concern' (UNICEF 2005a). The Director-General of ISESCO, Dr Abdulaziz Othman Altwaijri, stated that among OIC member states it was now necessary to make greater efforts not only to address high levels of maternal and child health, but also to 'break the silence on HIV/AIDS' (UNICEF 2005b). To achieve desired improvements OIC countries should seek to build upon the strength of Islamic traditions – such as, self-help, solidarity and protection of the vulnerable – in order to reaffirm commitment to health improvements for children, women and HIV/AIDS sufferers. While in some Muslim countries, as we shall see below, involvement of Muslim leaders and faith-based organisations in advocacy campaigns has proved to be an effective strategy to facilitate project ownership, achieving some encouraging successes, overall experience indicates that designing and implementing such interventions in religiously and socially complex contexts is often problematic. 'Designing rights-based advocacy messages that are neither in conflict with religious precepts nor carry negative value judgements are crucial to the achievement of related health improvement goals' ('Positive Muslims' 2004: 8).

To illustrate this contention, we focus next on Uganda's reproductive health project for the country's minority Muslim community, who comprise about 10% of the overall population (Haynes 1996b: 161). According to the coordinator of the country's Muslim Supreme Council Reproductive Health Programme, 'It was an extremely sensitive project'. At first, 'people thought that the project had come to promote family planning and further reduce the small numbers of Muslims, and they were determined to fight it till it failed' (UNFPA 2004: 41). Over time, however, the project achieved popular success because it worked with local Muslim communities rather than trying to impose a top down strategy that would have been more problematic and consequently less likely to succeed.

The main strategy was to encourage Muslim community leaders and scholars to consult and draw from Islamic texts at different phases of the project cycle. Muslim scholars were brought together to study various reproductive health messages and to relate them to texts in the Qur'an. Their participation turned out to be 'essential in gaining access to the Muslim community in Uganda and in promoting reproductive rights and service delivery among its members' (UNFPA 2004: 6). More generally, work to sensitise Muslim community leaders in Uganda was essential in opening up for public discussion a hitherto taboo subject: sexual and reproductive health. The all-important first step was to counter a prevalent fear among Uganda's Muslims: family planning was part of a conspiracy to reduce the size of the country's Muslim population. Credit here must go to the Mufti of Uganda, the country's most senior Muslim religious leader, whose support was instrumental in encouraging the view that reproductive health services among Muslim women needed both improving but spreading through the community. 'To ensure that these efforts were in line with Islamic thinking, reproductive health messages were studied and compared with teachings of the Koran and the Hadith. Specific strategies were also designed to reach women' (UNFPA 2004: 40).

The efforts to reach and involve Uganda's Muslim community were an essential aspect of the country's wider national population policy. Initially, when the policy was adopted in the mid-1990s, despite attempts to involve Uganda's Muslim Supreme Council (MSC), the country's Muslim community did not fully participate in related population and reproductive health activities. As a result, the Uganda MSC began to research into why the government's strategy had foundered, starting with the most senior religious figure, the Mufti. He, in turn, contacted the UNFPA, which has a Country Office in Uganda, to seek its advice. The result was a meeting between the Director of the National Population Secretariat and the Mufti concerning population policy in Uganda. They agreed (1) that the MSC would develop a project proposal to be presented to UNFPA for funding, and (2) to appoint a committee, whose personnel were chosen by the Mufti, to investigate why 'the Muslim community was not taking full advantage of the reproductive health services being offered'. To do this, a series of workshops – held at national, district and community levels – were undertaken to enable religious leaders to talk openly about previously taboo issues. These discussions were crucial in helping Muslim leaders to achieve improved cognisance of reproductive health among Muslim females. Five factors in particular were pointed to in this regard: (1) inability to reconcile specific population and reproductive health issues with the precepts of Islam, (2) confusion about the difference between reproductive health and 'birth control', (3) low priority for health issues in religious leaders' programmes, (4) lack of robust, evidence-based information and technical skills with which to promote health, and (5) poor management of the MSC's health infrastructure (UNFPA 2004: 40).

Once the deficiencies of the then current situation were highlighted, a programme of action was drawn up involving the MSC, the government and UNFPA. Its main components were, first, advocacy – needed to give a higher priority to reproductive health issues in the work of religious leaders. An improved communications regime was the second component, necessary to inform the Muslim community about reproductive health and rights and encourage men and women to utilise available services. Third, 'services improvements were implemented in order to provide better quality care and to make reproductive health services accessible, affordable and appealing to the community'. Initially improvements did not lead to increased use of facilities by females. The reason however was both obvious and easy to improve: their cost was too high for low-income Muslim women, the majority. Once this problem was identified and costs reduced, the take up improved significantly. The *Ndimugeni Mwete* ('Guest of the Centre') initiative was introduced. 'It enabled expectant mothers to receive antenatal, delivery and post-delivery services free of charge and greatly increased the number of women attending antenatal care clinics and delivering in health facilities' (UNFPA 2004: 41).

In conclusion, Uganda's reproductive health project for the country's minority Muslim community can be said to be successful as a result of the use of culturally sensitive approaches, which reflected the following concerns. First, it was important to consider as objectively as possible how religious sensitivities affected people's behaviour and then work out how to address them in such a way as to develop an environment of trust and mutual respect between secular and religious project partners. Prior to the project, public discussions on all aspects of sexuality, family planning and reproductive health did not take place within the Muslim community. Bringing in religious leaders at an early stage of the project was crucial to gain their trust and encourage them to spread the health message to the Muslim community.

Second, the project made especial effort to reach Muslim women. Initially, workshops were open only to men. Following the workshops, events that provided evidence-based information about the benefits of reproductive health services, men from the community were requested to support the participation of their wives in similar workshops. It appears that many did and, as a result, the turnout of women was 'overwhelming' (UNFPA 2004: 41).

Third, the use of Islamic references was crucial in ensuring the project's general acceptability among both religious leaders and the wider community, with specific reproductive health messages related to Qur'anic texts.

Fourth, from the project's beginning religious leaders – including the country's top religious leader, the Mufti – were identified as pivotal potential agents of change and, as a result, played a key role. This was crucial for gaining access to the wider Muslim community. In addition, in several press, local Imams transmitted reproductive health messages in their sermons in the mosques. This also emphasises how important it was to base the project strategy on a deep understanding of community values and needs.

Buddhism

The OIC focus on its 57 member countries emphasises that the 'Muslim world' – the *ummah* – is perceived as a joint entity that collectively binds together followers of Islam. Turning to Buddhism, it is immediately evident that no shared sense of community can be said to bind together its followers. In other words, there is no 'Buddhist world' comparable to the notion of a collective Muslim entity, which the OIC seeks to represent. On the other hand, like Muslim countries in the developing world, Buddhist countries – clustered in Asia – experience very similar health problems and, it might be thought, would be amenable to similar initiatives involving both secular development and faith entities that work to involve both religious leaders and communities more generally.

Despite the lack of a Buddhist collectivity that transcends national borders in the way that the notion of the *ummah* does, Buddhism does significantly focus on both spiritual and philosophical concerns that are together closely related to wider concern, including those to do with improving health. The preamble to the WHO charter reads: 'Health is a state of complete physical, mental and social well-being and not merely the absence of disease or infirmity' (http://www.who.dk/

main/WHO/Home/TopPage). In Buddhism, there is a similar understanding of what constitutes good health. Both Buddhists and the
WHO focus attention on the balanced interaction between the mind
and body as well as between life and its environment. Buddhists
believe that people have illnesses when this delicate equilibrium is dis-
turbed, and action according to Buddhist precepts is necessary both to
restore and strengthen the balance. This is not to imply that Buddhists
reject modern medicine and the related array of powerful diagnostic
and therapeutic tools to treat illnesses. Instead, stressing a holistic
approach, Buddhist belief stresses that most effective treatment is likely
to result from the use of conventional health improvement strategies
to combat illness, reinforced by a deeper understanding of the inner,
subjective processes of life. This emphasises the importance for
Buddhism of spiritual strength coupled with a powerful sense of
purpose or mission that is rooted in the desirability of compassionate
action for others.

To illustrate these points, the case study in this section focuses on
Cambodia, a country whose population is overwhelmingly Buddhist.
Like the example above from the Muslim minority in Uganda, our
concern is to examine a faith-based initiative to improve the health
of females. Cambodia has a relatively high maternal mortality rate of
590 deaths per 100,000 live births, while the infant mortality rate is
95 per 1,000 live births, that is, almost one in ten of babies born in the
country. This poor health position reflects the fact that Cambodia has
been wracked by serious conflict over the years that served to devastate
the healthcare infrastructure. Following the end of the conflict in
the early 1990s, the challenge was massive: to create an entirely
new healthcare system in a shattered, desperately poor country. In
1996, an external development agency, the United States Agency for
International Development (USAID) jointly founded, along with
Cambodia's government, the Reproductive and Child Health Alliance
(RACHA). The aim of RACHA was to improve healthcare by integrating
modern medical practices with the traditional structures that in many
places did manage to survive the years of war (http://rc.racha.org.kh/).

The RACHA initiative drew on the expertise and high community
standing of the country's Buddhist nuns. They became key advocates
and educators for breast-feeding among the country's women. This
strategy was chosen because, like Islamic leaders among Uganda's
Muslims, Buddhist nuns, like their male counterparts are widely perceived to occupy the moral high ground in Cambodia and, as a result,
their influence is pervasive (http://rc.racha.org.kh/rachaInfo.asp).

While many Cambodians came to distrust the government during the war years, the Buddhist religion remains one of the nation's unifying structures. Buddhist monks, nuns, and laypeople collectively have great social and religious influence on the beliefs and behaviour of most ordinary Cambodians. Reflecting this high regard many ordinary Cambodians regularly consult Buddhist figures, including monks and nuns in local monasteries, in relation to both physical and spiritual issues. Buddhist men and women also take active roles in various areas of health, including the construction of community medical centres, while also leading various community health initiatives in public health education and social development, including promotion of reproductive health and prevention of HIV/AIDS (USAID 2005).

Reflecting a strategy of tapping into existing social systems to promote good healthcare practices, the Nuns and Wat Grannies (N&WG) programme developed from within RACHA. It seeks to make use of Buddhist nuns' influence through engaging with local religious leaders as village healthcare educators. In one example, RACHA trained 30 nuns to spread knowledge on the promotion of proper breastfeeding techniques in the town of Pursat, capital of the Pursat province. Such information dissemination was necessary because, although most Cambodian women already breastfed their babies, there was a widespread – although erroneous – belief that the first milk, or colostrum, harms newly born babies. In addition, most Cambodian women are forced through the absence of clean supplies, to feed their babies contaminated water or foods in addition to breast milk. This practice often causes diarrhoea and in many cases, death. In Pursat, Nuns sought to encourage changes in both practices: First, as colostrum provides recognised health benefits, it is entirely appropriate that babies are breastfed straightaway after birth. Second, for the first six months, babies should only consume breast milk (Engender Health 2005).

While these principles seem clear and easy to put into effect, they were not widely followed in Pursat until the 30 nuns arrived as agents of change. They arrived in Pursat market on a Saturday in March 2000, 'in two trucks trimmed with banners illustrating correct breastfeeding practices'. The nuns immediately engaged with local women in discussions about breastfeeding, while passing out leaflets explaining in simple words and pictures health messages. This approach was successful – many women listened to the nuns and took their leaflets for two reasons: first, the nuns disseminated their health messages enthusiastically and, second, the nuns are trusted and respected.

The success of the initial Pursat initiative led to the approach being replicated elsewhere, involving partnerships between N&WG and local Buddhist community pagodas. Over the next five years, more than 900 pagoda workers were trained in Pursat and Siem Reap provinces. They visited nearly 300 villages and made over 30,000 house. RACHA undertook follow-up surveys and found an impressive increase not only in women's knowledge and acceptance of appropriate breastfeeding practices, but also significant changes in both behaviour and practices.

In conclusion, RACHA has managed successfully to disseminate a simple and effective health promotion campaign with the potential of changing for the better unsafe practices that could seriously affect the health of newly born and young babies. The key to the campaign's success was that it sought to work with local communities to engender and develop trust through the active involvement of Buddhist nuns, monks, and laypeople who worked as health educators and advocates in regard to breastfeeding and other reproductive and child health issues (Engender Health 2005; USAID 2005).

Hinduism

So far in this book, India has been the only focus of attention when examining the relationship between Hinduism and Hindu faith-based entities and development theory and practice outcomes. In this section, we focus on Mauritius, a country, like India, that has a Hindu majority population. We shall see that there are significant Hindu initiatives related to health in Mauritius, which primarily emanate from and link with wider transnational Hindu networks.

The island of Mauritius has a population of less than 1.5 million people. The 2000 census revealed that over 50% of Mauritians are Hindu, about a third Christian, while Muslims comprise just over 15%. Fewer than 1% of the population claims to be Buddhist, other faiths, atheist, or agnostic. There are no definitive figures for those who actually practice their faith, but there are estimates that the figure is around 60% for all religious groups. Religious affiliation is nearly always tied to ethnicity and to an extent geography. The north of the island is mainly Hindu, while the south is the home to many of the country's Christians. Large populations of Hindus and Catholics also live in the main population centres, including the capital, Port Louis, and the cities of Quatre Bornes and Curepipe (Seeworchun 1995).

Mauritius is a small island nation, and ethnic and religious groups, commonly known as 'communal groups' are tightly knit. As a result, intermarriage is relatively rare, although the 2000 census indicated that intermarriage was increasing. Normally, an individual's name easily identifies his or her ethnic and religious background, and there is a strong correlation between religious affiliation and ethnicity. Usually, citizens of Indian ethnicity are Hindus or Muslims. There is said to be concern among Hindu organisations that evangelical Christian churches are converting Hindus to Christianity, 'the 1990 and 2000 censuses show that the proportions of membership in the various faiths have remained the same during the last 10 years' (US Department of State 2003).

There are several important Hindu religious organisations in Mauritius, which have a concern with health issues. Both the Ramakrishna and Chinmayananda Missions are well-known organisations with centres on the island, which are extensions of well-established worldwide networks. In addition, the Arya Samaj, the Swami Lakshmanacharya Vishwa Santi Foundation and the Krishnanand Seva Ashram have ashrams in Mauritius that provide health services. The Krishnanand Seva Ashram has been described as being at the heart of Hindu spiritual life in Mauritius (Malik 2003: 5). Swami Krishnanand founded the Krishnanand Seva Ashram and the Human Service Trust in 1983. Swami Krishnanand, born in Rajasthan, India, in 1900 and died in Mauritius in 1992, spent a long, fruitful life as a spiritual teacher and mentor to literally thousands of Mauritian families. Both the ashram and the Human Service Trust are based in the town of Calebasses, in a building originally constructed as an Infirmary in 1888. The ashram currently supports 200 needy people in residence and also maintains a fully equipped ayurvedic healthcare centre that each week treats around 400 outside patients (Malik 2003).

The Arya Samaj is also active among Hindus in Mauritius. It is loosely affiliated to a supervisory organisation known as Arya Sabha, with 100,000 active priests around the globe. In Mauritius it provides health services to local Hindus (Bhuckory 1998). In addition, the Swami Lakshmanacharya Vishwa Santi Foundation (SLVF) is the third important Hindu institution in Mauritius. Directed by its founder, Swami Sri Lakshmanacharyulu, the SLVF provides free medicine, meals, yoga classes and lodging (Malik 2003).

Until recently, Mauritius was not regarded as having a serious HIV/AIDS problem. In 2001, only about 0.1% of the population was believed to be affected, with around 700 people living with the disease and with recorded deaths numbering less than 100 (CIA 2006). By 2005, however, over 900 people in Mauritius were estimated to have contracted HIV/AIDS. As a result of the worsening situation, the government, working with UNDP, established the Council of Religions' Action Plan on HIV and AIDS in 2006.

The HIV/AIDS epidemic in Mauritius is concentrated, characterized by prevalence below 1% among the general population (targeted group in sero-surveillance is pregnant women) and a higher prevalence of generally above 5% in specific vulnerable groups such as commercial sex workers (CSWs) and injecting drug users (IDUs). The country is experiencing a rapid increase in incidence due to the high vulnerability of IDUs. During recent years, the epidemic has risen exponentially with a concurrent marked shift in the predominant mode of transmission from unprotected heterosexual sex (64% in 2001 to 8% in 2004) to injecting drug use (7% in 2001 to above 88% in 2004). In 2005, 921 new HIV infection cases were documented (among which over 90% were in IDUs group), which corresponds to the highest annual incidence for the past 16 years (Government of Mauritius/Council of Religions 2006: 3).

The Council of Religions brings together representatives of the country's five major faiths: Baha'i Faith, Buddhism, Christianity, Hinduism and Islam. It seeks to 'support a collective vision to channel the power of religions, foster peace and bring about a better life in Mauritius' (Government of Mauritius/Council of Religions 2006: 2). The objective of cooperation among the religious and spiritual communities across Mauritius is to work together on an interfaith basis with effective guidance for shared understanding. Part of the vision of activities outlined since the inception of the Council has been to raise awareness through educational programmes. In addition, there is a desire to develop understanding among believers of all the faith communities in Mauritius of their shared core values and to combat prejudices of all sorts, particularly through targeting youth.

Previously the council existed as the 'Council of Religious and Spiritual Leaders', and over time demonstrated that it was a valuable vehicle for common social action. For example, in 1994 the Council worked with the Ministry of Women's Rights, Child Development and Family Welfare around the goals of the International Year of the Family, and subsequently acted as an advisory body to President Cassam Uteen. Furthermore for the General Election of 2005 the Council members boldly signed a joint Public Declaration to the electorate in promotion of responsible non-partisan voting. In view of their directive and in recognition of the invaluable contributions from faith-based initiatives to health promotion and to HIV/AIDS responses globally, an advocacy meeting with UN Secretary General, Kofi Annan, was organised in January 2005, in Mauritius. The Secretary General appealed to the members of the Council to work in partnership with other stakeholders in the fight against HIV/AIDS, and to particularly address the issue of stigma and discrimination in Mauritius (Republic of Mauritius, Ministry of Health and Quality of Life: www.gov.mu/portal/site/mohsite).

The Council was a key supporter of the country's HIV/AIDS action plan formulated in 2006–07 that would contribute to Mauritius' national strategic programme for 2006–10 devoted to reduction of HIV incidence and HIV/AIDS impact mitigation. In addition, the plan sought to create a facilitative environment that would encourage women to access relevant information and, as a result, to protect themselves from infection. The second objective was to contribute to a positive living environment for all People Living With HIV and AIDS (PLWHA). The main focal point of these efforts was to be through empowerment of the 'country's religious leaders to respond appropriately to HIV and AIDS issues, and thereby creating public awareness and respect of human rights and advocating for a coordinated multisectoral response' (Government of Mauritius/Council of Religions 2006; UNAIDS Mauritius Country Page: www.unaids.org/en/geographical+area/by+country/mauritius.asp).

From early 2006, when the initiative was established, the main outputs over the next 18 months were intended to be:

- A capacity development programme for Religious Leaders (on HIV&AIDS and outreach communication strategies) developed and implemented;
- Community mobilisation and awareness raising programmes on HIV&AIDS and respect of human rights implemented;
- Community level advocacy programme for empowering women against the HIV and AIDS pandemic implemented;
- Establishment of coordinating and project implementing capacity of Council of Religions (Government of Mauritius/Council of Religions 2006: 2).

In conclusion, individual faith-based organisations working on their own, including Hindu initiatives, were ineffective in dealing with the rise of HIV/AIDS in Mauritius. The chosen way forward – involving government, UNDP and faith leaders – established a cooperative initiative from 2006 that was seen as the best way forward to try to deal with the growing scourge of HIV/AIDS in Mauritius.

Christianity

Following the focus on HIV/AIDS initiatives in Mauritius, next we briefly examine HIV/AIDS activities of Christian churches in selected countries in Latin America and the Caribbean before turning to sub-Saharan Africa. The purpose is to provide a brief overview of what Christian religious leaders and faith-based organisations in both regions are doing in relation to rising numbers of HIV/AIDS sufferers in both regions. We saw earlier in the chapter, in a summary of numbers and geographical location of HIV/AIDS cases in the developing world, that sub-Saharan Africa is heavily affected by HIV/AIDS. The region has approximately 10% of the world's population but nearly two-thirds of known HIV/AIDs cases. Compared to Latin America and the Caribbean, African infection levels are high. Nonetheless Brazil, the second most populous country in the Americas (after the United States), has an adult HIV prevalence of 0.5%, that is, approximately 30% of the population living with HIV in Latin America. However, after sub-Saharan Africa, the Caribbean is the second most HIV-affected region of the world. The consequence of increased prevalence of HIV/AIDS in both regions is that Christian churches in recent years have made notable efforts to increase their involvement in both prevention and mitigation of its effects.

Religious leaders and representatives of faith-based organisations in Latin America and the Caribbean have sought to focus upon and address the issue of HIV/AIDS. Several have attended 'Leadership Development Programmes' sponsored by the UNDP. As a result, they began using leadership development tools and created new information resources on HIV/AIDS. In Cuba, a groundbreaking event took place during a regional leadership development programme. Religious leaders from Dominican Republic, Panama, El Salvador, Honduras, Jamaica and Ecuador requested UNDP's technical assistance and capacity enhancement to launch a Community of Practice on Religious Leaders in the Latin America and the Caribbean Region. The initiative aims to cement the basis for policy dialogue and decision-making that will ultimately lead to improved prevention efforts, expand the care, support and treatment of persons living with HIV/AIDS and others affected by the disease. The project has the potential to reach over

13,000 in each country. It is the UNDP's main contribution in supporting an integral leadership development programme focused on
religious leaders: pastors of Protestant churches, Catholic priests and
nuns and religious community activists working in the area of
HIV/AIDS and development issues at the country level. It is anticipated
that the initiative will also be of significance to faith-based organisations working in HIV/AIDS, as it will enable them to have greater
insight into how they can collaborate, contribute and provide leadership. The hope is that the lessons learned will spur and inform future
responses of FBOs in meeting the challenges of the epidemic (Bureau
for Development Policy/Regional Bureau for Latin America and the
Caribbean 2005).

Turning to sub-Saharan Africa, many of the region's Christian
churches are collectively in the vanguard of HIV/AIDS prevention and
mitigation efforts. For example, the Anglican Church is active in this
regard. The Church is said to be the region's fastest-growing Christian
denomination, with membership rising at more than 5% a year. As a
result, approximately 4% of Africans are members of the Church, that
is, some 25 million people (Minchakpu 2004). The serious HIV/AIDS
position in sub-Saharan Africa recently led the region's Anglican
churches to focus on HIV/AIDS prevention and consequences.
According to Bishop Charles Gaikia Gaita of the Anglican Church of
Kenya, the Church 'had been silent about the presence of HIV and
AIDS for a long time. There was discrimination, isolation and utter
rejection of people living with HIV and AIDS'. In addition, he stated,
the Church did not actively seek to help prevent the spreading of
both stigma and discrimination often associated with HIV/AIDS
(Tearfund 2006).

Reflecting this increased concern, by 2006 the Church was annually
spending nearly five billion dollars on fighting HIV/AIDS. However,
according to a 2006 report published by the Christian relief and development agency, Tearfund (n/d), this hugely significant effort fighting
HIV/AIDS 'barely rates a mention in global strategies for tackling the
pandemic'. Tearfund called for even greater resources for the African
Church to realise its potential to be one of the most effective agents in
the fight against HIV/AIDS in the region. George Carey, the former
Archbishop of Canterbury, writing in the foreword to a Tearfund
report, *Faith Untapped*, warned that 'with little recognition and scant
regard' for the work of churches in caring for HIV/AIDS sufferers and
their families, this hidden army is 'being stretched to breaking point'.
Lord Carey added that

Churches represent vast untapped potential to change behaviour and attitudes. If we put our own house in order and if we are properly resourced and trained, churches and other faith groups could become one of the single most effective strategies for tackling the pandemic. [Africa's churches and] their vast networks of volunteers are one of the few groups which are wrestling with the pandemic at close quarters every day (Tearfund n/d: 1).

However it is not only Africa's Anglican churches that focus on prevention and mitigation of the HIV/AIDS pandemic. *Faith Untapped* collected and collated growing evidence of Christian churches' collective involvement in health issues, including HIV/AIDS in sub-Saharan Africa:

*   Christian faith groups provide an average of 40% of the healthcare in many African countries;
*   97% of Christian congregations across six African countries are working with orphans and vulnerable children according to a Unicef survey;
*   A network of 600 churches in Zimbabwe is supporting more than 100,000 orphans;
*   1,500 church volunteers in one Kenyan project are supporting 29,000 people affected by HIV/AIDS;
*   Another survey showed that 79% of churches and Christian NGOs in Namibia were responding to HIV/AIDS (Tearfund n/d: 7).

One of the main contributions that Christian faith-based organisations make is by founding community support programmes for orphans and vulnerable children, and to integrate services for these children into existing prevention and care activities. For example, in Zambia, the Evangelical Fellowship of Zambia (EFZ), umbrella organisation for evangelical, pentecostal and charismatic churches, is active in HIV/AIDS concerns. For example, about 30% of adults are afflicted by HIV/AIDS in the town of Livingstone in southern Zambia. As a result, many children have been orphaned while school attendance statistics have dramatically declined. A group of 15 women volunteers from the EFZ were very keen to do something to help and formulated a plan for each individual to visit five families affected by AIDS each week.

'Typically these are households where grandparents are caring for orphans or a single-parent family; most don't have any regular income. Volunteers help with anything from housework to schoolwork.

The women often provide food from their own resources, though struggle to help with things like school fees. Where necessary they will try to put people in touch with trained counsellors and HIV testing facilities'. Having seen the effects of AIDS in their own families is what motivates many of the volunteers (Tearfund n/d: 18).

In Mozambique, the HIV/AIDS pandemic has advanced significantly, encouraged by three decades of war, 'labour migration, rapid urbanisation, high levels of poverty, insufficient health infrastructures and significant rates of sexually transmitted infections'. By 2002, 13.6% of the population were said to be living with HIV. While most sufferers lived in the country's central provinces, rising numbers of new cases were occurring along major transportation and commercial routes in the southern and central region. Of all new infections, more than 40% are found among the 15–24 age group, with the highest rate – 16% – found among 15–19-year-old girls compared to 9% of boys in the same age group (International HIV/AIDS Alliance 2006).

Like the government of Mauritius noted earlier, Mozambique's government has also taken steps, along with international partners, to combat the disease. So far, the emphasis 'has been on prevention, awareness-raising, voluntary counselling and testing and palliative care' rather than 'large-scale treatment programmes for people living with HIV/AIDS', although this has not prevented expanding provision of ART (International HIV/AIDS Alliance 2006).

Kubatsirana (which in the local language of Chitewe/Shona means 'to help one another') is a local Christian organisation comprising 58 member churches. Since the mid-1990s, it has developed into a key entity in Mozambique's HIV/AIDS response. Like the EFZ, a key aim is to mobilise and support volunteers within the local church to help families affected by HIV and AIDS. For example, 'in Chimoio city, there are 24 small groups of volunteers caring for 500 people who are too sick to work and more than 750 children orphaned by HIV/AIDS'.

Overall, Kubatsirana builds the capacity of local organisations to initiate community support programmes for orphans and vulnerable children, and to integrate services for these children into existing prevention and care activities. Secondly, the youth education programme provides information in its churches' youth groups on HIV/AIDS prevention. And in addition, 'Kubatsirana also trains and supervises church volunteers to provide quality home-based care and support to orphans, other vulnerable children, people living with HIV/AIDS and their families' (International HIV/AIDS Alliance 2006). As a result of the efforts of Kubatsirana, Mozambique's government invited the organisation to expand its work into every province in the country (Health Alliance International 2006).

In conclusion, in response to the HIV/AIDS pandemic Christian churches in both Latin America and the Caribbean as well as in sub-Saharan Africa, have sought to respond positively. Our examples from Africa suggest that Christian faith-based organisations and other NGOs help catalyse or develop government service provision, sometimes by showing that contentious and thorny issues – for example, provision of ART in Mozambique – are difficult yet, fundamentally, manageable with will and organisation. Further, we saw that faith-based organisations in, *inter alia*, Zambia and Mozambique initiate community-based initiatives that can make a real difference to the lives of HIV/AIDS sufferers and their families. Finally, to make HIV/AIDS initiatives effective seems to depend to a considerable degree on local communities believing not only that they have 'ownership' of them but also that they amount to serious efforts to sustain an environment where local resources are tapped and mobilised to achieve goals. Overall, Christian HIV/AIDS initiatives in Africa amount to a dedicated, creative, and caring partnership programmes that, in collecting both skills and assets of different partners together to confront HIV/AIDS, deserve wider encouragement and support from governments and secular development agencies.

Overall conclusion

In this chapter we have seen that in relation to health issues in the developing world, religion plays a highly significant role. This is because it is often central to the social and cultural life of most developing countries to the extent that religious leaders are often also health workers. Their relationship with the community encourages close and regular contact with all age groups, while their voice is highly respected. The result is that in many communities, both urban and rural, religious leaders can be more influential than government officials or secular community leaders.

Their importance was illustrated by our focus upon the three MDGs devoted to health: (1) to reduce child mortality by two-thirds, especially among children under five years, the worst affected group, (2) improve maternal health, and (3) combat HIV/AIDS and other diseases. We saw that in recent years, religious leaders and numerous faith-based organisations have begun to engage with partners in the secular development community in relation to health issues in the developing world at community, national, and international levels. When such partnerships worked well, and several of our examples support this conclusion, the outcome was sustained dialogue, genuine willingness to work together and clear sense of shared objectives. It is also important to recall, however, that necessary health improvements will not necessarily come about merely as a result of non-state secular and faith entities working together. In order to achieve the desired medium- and long-term health improvements, increased involvement from the government is crucial.

7
Education

Education is a human right and a key factor to reducing poverty and child labour and promoting democracy, peace, tolerance and development. Yet more than 100 million children of primary-school age, the majority of them girls, are not enrolled in school. Millions more are taught by untrained and underpaid teachers in overcrowded, unhealthy and poorly equipped classrooms. And one third of all children do not complete five years of schooling, the minimum required for basic literacy (UNICEF 2005c: 13).

The MDG on education can be seen as the central pillar on which all the others rest. But for people from faith communities it cannot be only a question of the number of children attending school. Of paramount importance to them is the content of the curriculum and above all the value system, implicit or explicit, underlying the education given. Very many of them abhor the idea of turning schools into individualistic, competitive, largely technical training grounds with jobs alone in mind (Tyndale 2004: 5).

There is no doubt that for any country literacy and primary education are the cornerstones of development and economic growth. In recent years there have been widespread calls to increase international spending on educational provision, in part as a perceived means to combat political extremism and terrorism (Krueger and Maleckova 2003). In addition, there are obviously sound educational reasons for wishing to improve the educational position of children in the developing world: approximately 125 million primary-school-aged children in the developing world are not in school; many of them are girls – often because when a family faces financial difficulties it is girls who are withdrawn first from school. Finally, access to both primary and secondary education is crucial in efforts to combat child labour, as well as reducing numbers of child soldiers in developing countries (UNESCO 2007).

The overall importance of improving education in the developing world is highlighted by the fact that two MDGs are concerned with the issue. By 2015, the aim is both to achieve universal primary education, as well as gender parity in education. Reflecting its developmental importance, that is, its critical importance as a yardstick of broader progress towards gender equality and women's empowerment, gender parity in education was placed on an accelerated timetable in 2000 (Global Campaign for Education 2002).

The United Nations Educational, Scientific and Cultural Organisation (UNESCO) is a leading driver are in improving education for better developmental outcomes, reflected in the following:

- Four years of primary education raises a farmer's output by 7% in Uganda;
- The child of a Zambian mother with a primary education has a 25% better chance of survival than a child of a mother with no education;
- Women with a secondary education are three times more likely to attend a political meeting in Bangladesh than those who lack education;
- Educated girls in the developing world generally have a significantly lower risk of HIV infection compared to females without education (UNESCO n/d).

The problem, however, is that while education's developmental benefits are very widely accepted, the goal of universal primary education will remain unachievable unless a major and sustained effort is immediately undertaken to accelerate current trends. At the moment, one in five of children aged 6–11 in developing countries – an estimated 113 million children – does not attend school, and three in five of them are girls. To achieve the MDG goal related to primary education by 2015, developing countries would need to accommodate over 150 million additional children compared to 1997, an increase of more than a quarter. During 2005, the United Nations Children's Fund (UNICEF; formerly United Nations International Children's Emergency

Fund) estimates that 86% of the world's primary-school-age children did attend school, rising from 82% in 2001. But to maintain this rate of progress would require at a minimum maintaining previous enrolment efforts, although in some regions, such as sub-Saharan Africa, especial efforts would be needed. It is estimated that an additional 88 million school places are needed in sub-Saharan Africa to accommodate population growth. Especially large increases in provision are needed in several African countries, including Angola, the Central African Republic, the Democratic Republic of Congo, Lesotho, Liberia, Niger and Somalia. South Asia is another region that will have to make particular efforts, as finding school places for an additional 40 million more children – an increase of one-third – will require at least the same pace of effort as in the 1990s (UNICEF 2005d).

Illiteracy is another profound educational problem in the developing world where the great majority of the nearly 900 million illiterates live. According to a recent report from Oxfam International, 'if all children of primary school age were to receive a good quality basic education lasting for a minimum of four years, the problem of illiteracy would be resolved in the space of a single generation'. Nine developing countries – Bangladesh, Brazil, China, Egypt, India, Indonesia, Mexico, Nigeria and Pakistan (known as the 'Education-9'; 'E-9') – are home to 70% of the world's illiterates. Girls and women are most at risk. In South Asia an estimated 60% of women are illiterate. Worldwide, one woman in four cannot read. To expand adult literacy by 50%, the number of adult literates would have to increase annually by some 92 million, implying sustained efforts at a greater level than before. In short, sub-Saharan Africa and South Asia face substantial challenges, where success will require significant extra efforts. On the other hand, some developing regions – such as, East Asia and Latin America and the Caribbean – will reach the goal by maintaining the same level of effort as during the past decade (UNESCO 2007).

According to UNESCO, the overall cost of providing the world's children with primary education by 2015 would require between $8 billion and $15 billion extra spending a year – less than 2% of the annual estimated military costs worldwide. UNESCO also estimates that the bulk of the necessary funds could be found in the developing countries themselves, 'through changing priorities and adopting cost-effective measures'. But to increase likelihood of success, 'a new global initiative' is needed that would 'ensure more effective donor co-ordination and increased aid to basic education, in particular through accelerated debt relief' (UNESCO n/d: 6).

The drive for education for all

Improving education in the developing world as a crucial aspect of achieving better overall development outcomes has been widely recognised for a long time. Twenty years ago, however, the dire consequences of uncontrolled demographic growth was *the* key concern expressed at many international development conferences (Simmons 1988). Many analysts regarded basic education as the main strategy to reduce untenable population growth rates. Because of the importance of the issue, a World Conference on Education for All (EFA) was held in Jomtien, Thailand, in 1990, with the aim of addressing such concerns by explicitly putting basic education high on the development agenda.

In 1993, the 'Education-9' (E-9) Initiative was launched in New Delhi, India, at the Education for All Summit of Nine High-Population Countries. The goal was to provide citizens of the E-9 countries – Bangladesh, Brazil, China, Egypt, India, Indonesia, Mexico, Nigeria and Pakistan – with basic education, both as a fundamental human right and as a way to curb very high population growth rates. As a result, governments of the E-9 countries 'pledged to universalize primary education and significantly reduce illiteracy in their respective countries'. They also adopted the Delhi Declaration, committing them to achieve the EFA goals in the spirit of the earlier Jomtien conference. Sponsored by UNESCO, UNICEF and UNFPA and hosted by India, the New Delhi summit 'provided a unique opportunity to mobilize high-level political support and financial and technical resources for primary education and literacy programmes'. A 'pre-summit' meeting also raised key issues of importance to achievement of educational goals, including: gender disparity, the link between population and education and the mobilization of funds (UNESCO 2000).

The EFA Fast-Track Initiative was a partnership between 15 developing countries and 30 bilateral and multilateral donors and agencies, led by the World Bank. It was created to help low-income countries achieve the goals of gender parity in primary education, as well as universal educational enrolment and completion. The Initiative addressed a broad range of educational concerns, including: teacher quality and curriculum content; pupil-teacher ratios; health, sanitation and nutrition in schools; understanding of HIV/AIDS and risk avoidance; and school governance. It also stressed the importance of the involvement of civil society and communities in the achievement of educational goals.

In 2000, a comprehensive assessment was undertaken of progress achieved to attain the educational goals related to primary school education and gender parity in education. The purpose was to assess the current status of basic education in more than 180 countries and to evaluate progress achieved over the decade since the Jomtien conference. The resulting data provided much relevant information that helped inform discussions conducted at the World Education Forum, held in Dakar, Senegal, from 26–28 April 2000 (UNESCO 2000). The Forum brought together more than 1,100 delegates from 164 countries to reaffirm their commitment to EFA. They adopted the Dakar Framework for Action, a document that set out agreed goals and strategies for achieving EFA. 'The Dakar framework for action – education for all: meeting our collective commitments', presented a UNESCO, G8, World Bank and IMF blueprint for the development of education globally by 2015, including achievement of MDG education goals. The six Dakar goals were as follows:

- Expand early childhood care and education, especially for the most vulnerable and disadvantaged children;
- Free and compulsory education of good quality for all children by 2015;
- Promote the acquisition of life-skills by adolescents and youth;
- Expand adult literacy by 50% by 2015, especially for women, and equitable access to basic and continuing education for all adults;
- Eliminate gender disparities by 2005 and achieve gender equality in education by 2015, with a focus on ensuring girls' full and equal access to and achievement in basic education of good quality;
- Enhance educational quality, especially in literacy, numeracy and essential life skills (UNESCO 2001).

In summary, the EFA initiative was to be a partnership involving: governments, civil society organisations, including faith-based organisations; and external bilateral and multilateral development agencies. Governments had the crucial responsibility of mobilising efforts and additional resources and securing involvement of stakeholders. 'Civil society' – understood as a collective term for various non-state actors, including: NGOs, both religious and secular, as well as teachers unions and parents – was also to play a key role. The intention was that civil society would work harmoniously together along with local communities to provide additional or alternative solutions where state provision was inadequate or absent. The aspiration was that such initiatives would be more flexible, innovative and closer to local communities and local cultures. Both bilateral and multilateral development agencies were expected to support the efforts of government and civil society by providing 'technical assistance, funding support, enhanced monitoring of EFA progress, greater co-ordination of efforts and strengthened partnerships between governments and civil society' (UNECSO n/d: 5).

Faith-based organisations and education

While EFA was designed to be a partnership between governments, civil society organisations and bilateral development agencies, concern was expressed that it would be primarily a top-down initiative, rather than a true joint venture linking interactively external development agencies, governments, civil societies and local communities (Tyndale 2004; World Faiths Development Dialogue 2003). We have consistently noted in this book that most successful development initiatives are not imposed top-down but have a significant bottom-up focus, including those significantly involving faith entities. The point is that people consistently requiring more and better development, especially the poor and women, should usefully play a full part in design, development and involvement in related development initiatives. This is not of course either a new idea or one restricted to involvement of faith-based organisations in development projects. As we saw in the Introduction, attempting to avoid charges of 'top down' development, in recent years both development theory and practice have increasingly employed the language of participation. Various techniques, including participatory rural appraisal, have been developed as a way to try to tap into local needs and priorities. On the other hand, many critics contend that there is still a strong tendency on the part of external aid donors to demand short time limits for the programme completion, thereby often practically excluding the possibility of community participation. Some observers allege that the World Bank's system of 'fast track' countries, that is, to reach the MDGs on education, is an example of this. In addition, problems often arise when external agencies send in '"experts" from outside who often fail to consult the poor and consequently make mistakes' (World Faiths Development Dialogue 2004: 5).

Turning to the general issue of the role of faith-based organisations in education in developing countries, several points emerge. First, many religious individuals may ask: What is education for? That is, is education simply for the purpose of achieving growing numbers of people to take part in economic development through skills accretion?

Or should it also be about increasing diversity and tolerance, enhancing the value placed on sharing and non-violence? Highlighting the belief that children and young people are the main hope for the future, many religious people would agree that primary school children should receive an education that includes a focus on peace-building, tolerance and overall living healthy lives. In addition, both school children and adults 'should learn non-violent approaches to conflict resolution, acceptance of the diversity of family structures and compositions and age-appropriate and comprehensive sexuality education' (International Interfaith Network for Development and Reproductive Health 2005: 3). The last point is especially important when thinking about girls in the context of early marriage and childbearing, events that can significantly impede girls' access to education.

Second, some governments in the developing world do not welcome faith initiatives in the field of development. For example, as we saw in relation to health in the preceding chapter, governments can be unwilling to work with faith-based organisations, despite the fact that in many cases they make a significant contribution towards the provision of health services, especially in contexts where the state is unwilling or unable to provide them. Some governments similarly find it difficult to work with faith-based organisations in educational provision, the focus of the current chapter. This is often because there is an unacceptable political dimension to such a partnership – for example, 'governments may choose to favour one tradition above others or to pursue a secular agenda that makes it impossible openly to liaise with faith groups' (World Faiths Development Dialogue 2004: 1).

On the other hand, education – like health – constitutes a field where faith-based organisations' involvement, development experts often note, can be of significance for educational achievement in the developing world. This includes a highly important role played by Christian churches in providing educational services in, for example, the Democratic Republic of Congo, where for years Christian schools have played a definitive role in educational provision (Ellis and ter Haar 2005; Haynes 1996b). This is a tradition that goes back to the colonial era. From the earliest days of European colonial expansion into Latin America, Asia and Africa, Christian missionaries were often significantly involved in provision of various welfare goods, including schools, hospitals, and raising funds to install clean drinking water and/or sanitation facilities. In short, during the colonial era churches were crucially important to development outcomes in many parts of the developing world.

Regarding education specifically, Christian mission churches – both Catholic and Protestant – were often given control of primary and (if it existed) secondary education during colonial rule in sub-Saharan Africa and Latin America. This enabled churches to acquire not only ideological and material power but also financial resources. The latter derived from collection of school fees, grants, ownership of land and buildings. In summary, during the colonial period, education was an important component of wider colonial policy, a focus of colonial administrations.

After colonialism ended, education was controversial in many developing countries. In particular, governmental attempts to nationalise education was a source of friction between churches especially in sub-Saharan Africa. Initially, African governments were often prepared to allow churches to continue their leading role in educational provision. Over time, however, many African governments sought to oust churches from their leading position because the former came to realise that education was a 'mere development good', over which governments could exercise control in order to ensure that educational benefits went to preferred constituencies and not others. Yet, as Hastings notes, 'there was (often) more [educational] continuity than could be expected in many African countries' (Hastings 1979: 189). This was because many Christian professionals, especially among the national Catholic churches, did manage – often quietly – to retain their educational positions despite often wholesale educational changes that many regional governments decreed in the decade following independence in the 1960s (Gifford 1998).

The political nature of post-independence education provision in Africa was exemplified by the situation in Zaire (now Democratic Republic of Congo). The state took over primary and secondary education in the early 1970s, only to hand back control to the country's biggest Christian churches – Catholic, Protestant and Kimbanguist – a few years later after it became clear that the government lacked the requisite ability to run education adequately (Hastings 1979; Haynes 1996b). In Togo, there was a similar situation: the state also took over education provision – only to hand it back to Christian churches a few years later for similar reasons (Gifford 1998). In Tanzania, the Catholic Church alone was handed control of the country's educational facilities in 1992, once again because of state inadequacies – but this led to serious Muslim protests over perceived 'favouritism' (Mbogoni 2004). The overall point is that educational provision in some African countries was often a politicised issue that could lead either to friction between state and religion or to inter-faith rivalry.

The politicised nature of educational provision in sub-Saharan Africa should not obscure the fact that faith-based organisations promoted education in many parts of the developing world – as a key source of social and human development – long before the emergence of international development as a global concern. Such religious initiatives were typically run on a voluntary and not-for-profit basis but they were not valued merely because to consumers they were often cheap or even free. Instead, as many accounts make clear, quality of education provided by many faith-based organisations was often good (World Faiths Development Dialogue 2004). But education in the developing world is also a highly political issue, raising the following question: 'Who controls education and for what purpose?' Throughout much of the developing world, control of education – whether by government, a faith-based organisation or a secular non-state entity – potentially offers the educational provider a good opportunity both to educate and to instil specific understandings of the world.

In the next section we focus upon non-state educational provision in the context of Islam, Christianity, Hinduism and Buddhism. The overall purpose is both to highlight the range of educational initiatives undertaken by non-state faith-based organisations, as well as to emphasise the often highly political nature of what they do.

Islam

Islamic schools in Africa and Asia

In Islam, education's importance is reflected in a one-word, divine message: 'Read'. It is also the case, however, that in some Muslim countries over half the adult population is illiterate, more than two-thirds of women cannot read, and primary school participation is relatively low, with fewer than six out of ten children regularly attending. As a result, such Muslim countries will need to make particular efforts to meet the MDG goal of universal primary completion by 2015. Around the world, 24 countries have primary school participation percentages below 60% and 17 of them have either Muslim majorities or large Muslim minorities (UNICEF 2005b).[1]

Islamic faith-based organisations have long played an extensive educational role in many parts of the developing world. Recent years have seen a rapid expansion in some regions, especially sub-Saharan Africa. There, the total number of Islamic NGOs, many of which have educational concerns, has grown from 138 (out of a total of 1,854 NGOs) in 1980, to 891 (out of 5,896) in the early 2000s (Salih 2002). Many of the most dynamic Muslim NGOs have adopted techniques introduced by Western NGOs, including those pioneered by Christian missionary organisations. In many cases, the latter combine provision of welfare services, including high standards of technical education, with religious proselytisation. Some modern Islamic schools in West Africa, for example, offer business studies and computer courses as part of their curriculum. Overall, however, there is a lack of reliable information on Islamic NGOs in sub-Saharan Africa, although Ellis and ter Haar note that many do valuable educational work (Ellis and ter Haar 2004, 2005). It is clear, however, both that there is a range of such institutions and that what they do educationally is linked to the particular national and religious contexts within which they work.

In Turkey, for example, imams – respected religious leaders who officiate at Friday prayers – have played a crucial role in a recent campaign to promote education for girls by urging parents to send their daughters to school (TDSH FH 2006). Turning to East Africa, the Aga Khan Foundation (AKF) works with local Ismaili Muslim communities in Kenya, Uganda and Tanzania. The AKF has developed the Madrasa Early Childhood Programme that aims to develop and extend early childhood schooling in local Islamic religious schools (*madrasas*). The initiative began on a small scale in Kenya in the mid-1980s and over time it developed more widely in Kenya, while also spreading to Uganda and Tanzania. In each country, there was a sustained attempt to involve local Muslims in the initiative. They made it clear that two issues were of particular importance: (1) their children should receive an education that drew on and celebrated their indigenous religious culture, while (2) also being appropriate to improve chances for access to and success in formal education, including ability to enrol in and succeed at university-level education.

Overall, the programme has three main objectives: (1) seeking to put local communities in charge, (2) insisting on quality, and (3) providing 'action-based learning'. It seeks to accomplish these goals by bringing together 'best practices, community preferences, and local values and customs to exert a significant influence on children's ability to perform well in school, career, and life'. It also aims to provide 'parents and community leaders with the knowledge, management skills, and mechanisms to facilitate long-term financing to enable them to sustain their efforts'. In addition, the Programme is widely regarded as both a dynamic and constructive effort to build on local religious schools – *madrasas* – while also benefiting from both international and national technical expertise. It is important to emphasise an important aspect of the Programme: the focus on girls' education and the general involvement of women as teachers, mothers, and administrators. Overall, the Madrasa Early Childhood Programme is a multifaceted Muslim initiative that now lobbies for national educational reforms in the three countries within which it is active, while also advocating creation of 'a broader regulatory space for other innovative educational projects' (Marshall and Keough 2004: 99, 183).

In neighbouring Ethiopia, Islamic education is a controversial issue. Ethiopia, a country of 73 million people (July 2005 est.) is divided between Muslims (45–50%) and Orthodox Christians (35–40%). In recent years, religion has become politicised, with growing friction between Muslims and Christians (Dickson 2005). The Ethiopian Muslim Relief and Development Association (EMRDA), an indigenous faith-based NGO established in 1994, legally registered with the Ministry of Justice, and working in Wollo, Arsi, and Amhara, Oromia and Afar regions. Its main concern is to ameliorate poverty and unemployment among the country's Muslims through community participation and sustainable integrated rural development. The EMRDA is also heavily involved in promoting basic formal and non-formal education, reproductive health and HIV/AIDS training, vocational and skill trainings, food security and civic education (Dan Church Aid 2006).

The EMRDA initiative is both educational and cultural. On the one hand, the Ethiopian government offers relatively little educational provision in many Muslim areas of the country (Dickson 2005). On the other hand, many Muslims in Ethiopia believe that, even when they do exist, government schools are too closely associated with Christian values and teachings. Sometimes, as a result, Muslim parents choose not to send their children to school at all. This applies particularly to girls, whom many local Muslim parents do not want to be educated in a mixed sex environment. Instead, there is scope for children's education in *madrasas*, established around mosques. But few *madrasas* engage in formal academic education and graduates from such schools are often disadvantaged in terms of future employment opportunities (World Faiths Development Dialogue 2004). The overall point is that the EMRDA is seeking to develop a network of Muslim schools in Ethiopia's Muslim areas that offer education that is seen by local Muslims as both culturally valid and educationally relevant.

Islamic NGOs in Africa, many of which engage in educational activities like the EMRDA, often cause nervousness and disquiet among many Western governments and development agencies, because of widespread suspicion that they can be a major source of anti-Western propaganda and even terrorism. For example, Salih argues that some Islamic NGOs in East Africa 'have been used as a vehicle for spreading political Islam at an accelerated rate combining faith and material rewards among the disfranchised Muslim poor'. As a result, they may become 'cronies to militant Muslim groups, including an emergent tide of indigenous African Islamic fundamentalist movements' (Salih 2002: 1–2; 2004). Ghandour (2002) contends that Islamic schools in sub-Saharan Africa often 'include not only an exclusive reference to Islam and an often powerful social legitimacy, but also sometimes ambiguous bonds with militant Islamists'. Agreeing with Salih, Ghandour avers that such links can place them in conflict with some African governments, as well as with Western development NGOs and governments. He claims further that some Islamic NGOs act as intermediaries between Islamic financiers and recipients operating in the environment of Islamist activists. However, Western intelligence services often find it extremely difficult to identify, localise and block financial flows that reach violent Islamic groups, because such NGOs can be very active mediators that also cover their tracks well. Rarely, however, are there '*direct* relationships between powerful Islamic financial backers and Islamic activist organisations' (Ghandour, 2002: 129; emphasis added). More generally, the September 11, 2001 terrorist attacks on the USA increased Western attention on *madrasas* in the developing world, including sub-Saharan Africa, the Middle East and Central and South East Asia. Some *madrasas* are adherents of Wahhabism, a purist version of Islam that serves as an inspiration to Islamic reform movements across the Muslim world – from India and Sumatra to North Africa and Sudan.

Critics of the Western approach contend that *madrasas* are often accused unwarrantedly of encouraging anti-USA and anti-Western opinions. Instead, they argue, *madrasas* frequently 'play an important role in countries where millions of Muslims live in poverty and the educational infrastructure is in decay' (Armanios 2003: 2). The educational and developmental ambivalence of *madrasas* can be illustrated by the case of Pakistan. Estimates of the numbers of *madrasas* in Pakistan range between 10,000–20,000. Many are said to focus their teaching along Wahhabist lines, including the *madrasas* where the leaders of the Taliban, former rulers of Afghanistan, studied (Armanios 2003: 5). The problem, however, is that Pakistan's educational infrastructure is crumbling. Living in a country whose economy is weak, with corresponding widespread and extreme poverty and underdevelopment, many Pakistanis understandably turn to what the state appears unable to provide: free education, accommodation, and board – which *madrasas* do provide. Thus while some *madrasas* may be focal points of extremism and militancy, observers believe that a wider and deeper process of fundamental educational reform and renewal in Pakistan would be necessary to reduce their influence. In recent years, following Western encouragement, Pakistan's government has encouraged *madrasas* to register with the state by offering financial inducements. The plan was to reward *madrasas* that agreed to comply with registration procedures with additional benefits, including better teacher training, salaries, text books, and computers. This would also involve *madrasas'* agreement that the government could monitor their curricula to ensure that they did not promote violence and extremism (Campbell 2006).

In addition, it is important to emphasise that *madrasas* are often significant educational resources for Muslims elsewhere in the developing world. For example, popularity of *madrasas* is said to be increasing in some parts of Southeast Asia, including Indonesia, the largest Muslim country in the world, home to nearly 200 million followers of Islam. In Indonesia, up to a quarter of primary and secondary school-age children attend local versions of *madrasas*, known as *pesantrens*. Overall, Indonesia's *pesantrens* are not widely noted for their extremism – but for adhesion to moderate forms of Islam that often encompass mystical Sufi teachings (Chew 2006).[2]

In conclusion, it is important, first, to differentiate between, on the one hand, the numerous Islamic religious institutions that play a constructive role in development and *madrasas* that teach a version of Islam that most Westerners and many Muslims would characterise as extremist. Second, our examples of Islamic educational provision in the developing world all underline the inherently political nature of education and its provision. Third, they emphasise the importance of involving local Muslim communities in planning and helping to undertake educational initiatives that are of direct relevance to them.

Christianity

We have already noted the emphasis in Islam on the importance of children's education, a concern also found in Christianity. The Christian scriptures highlight the special position of children in the faith, noting that: 'Whoever welcomes this child in my name welcomes me, and whoever welcomes me welcomes the one who sent me; for the least among all of you is the greatest' (Luke 9: 47–78). The Bible notes the importance of education, likening it to the sweetness of the drippings from honeycombs: 'Know that wisdom is such to your soul; if you find it, you will find a future, and your hope will not be cut off' (Proverbs 24: 14).

The above accounts of Islamic educational initiatives in various Muslim countries in the developing world all emphasise that children's education is an issue of crucial societal and often political concern. Turning to Christianity, we can see similar concerns for the same reasons: Whoever controls children's education is in an unrivalled position not only to proselytise but also to inculcate particular social and political worldviews. Consequently, as with Islam, Christian involvement in education in the developing world is often a controversial issue. Below we focus on Christian provision of education in Latin America in the context of jockeying for position between the region's traditionally dominant religious tradition, Catholicism, and a recent, yet sustained religious, challenge from Evangelical Protestantism. Both faiths are key providers of education in the region, where there is generally declining state ability to provide growing numbers of children with adequate schooling (*The Economist* 2002). Overall, the religious context of children's education in Latin America is contextualised by: (1) generally declining state ability to provide an adequate education, and (2) inter-religious rivalry between Catholics and Evangelical Protestants (Portillo 1999; Freston 2004).

As in sub-Saharan Africa, the issue of children's education in Latin America is intimately linked to the circumstances of earlier European colonisation. In Latin America, the *'conquistadores'* brought with them Dominican and Franciscan missionaries. This practice was said to justify the spread of Spanish and Portuguese rule because it brought Christianity in the form of Catholicism to the indigenous populations, resulting in Catholicism becoming Latin America's official religion (Pew Forum on Religion and Public Life 2006). As a result, the Catholic Church controlled children's education, established universities, and generally became central to educational life throughout the region. Over time, however, a struggle developed between liberals and conservatives over the societal and political position of the Catholic Church. Despite this, many regional governments continued to recognise Catholicism's special position as national religion well into the 20th century, with some regional countries, including Argentina and Venezuela, still providing at the present time to provide state financial support to the Church (Pew Forum on Religion and Public Life 2006; Freston 2004).

After World War II, provision of public education expanded throughout much of Latin America. The Catholic Church continued to dominate regional educational provision, although from the 1960s the ideological focus of its educational provision underwent a change. Following the Second Vatican Council ('Vatican II', 1962–65), the papacy began to give support to democratic ideas and religious freedom. The educational result was that 'religious instruction at Church schools in Latin America became supportive of freedom of religion and church hierarchies made special efforts to reach out to the representatives of other faiths in ecumenical cooperation' (Sigmund n/d). Another important ideological result of Vatican II was a growing significance for liberation theology in many parts of Latin America (Gutierrez 1973; Boff 1987). Liberation theology is a radical Christian view that believes that the Bible emphasises especial concern for the poor and underprivileged, and that it is a duty for Christians to work towards improving the developmental position of such unfortunates (Marshall and Keough 2004: 163).

A third development in the decades after Vatican II was that the Church found its dominant religious position in the region challenged by growing popular adherence Evangelical Protestantism. By the 1990s, surveys indicated that Protestants, mainly Evangelicals, comprised 15% or more of the populations in several regional countries, including: El Salvador, Guatemala, Peru, and Brazil. Many Evangelical Churches energetically proselytise their faith, and are often rewarded by an influx of new adherents – especially from among the recently-arrived poor who migrate in the hundreds of thousands from rural areas to rapidly increasing shantytowns in main population centres (Moreno 1997: 31; Carpenter 2003).

Part of the attraction of the Evangelical churches is that they often emphasise the importance of self-help and community initiatives in the context of poverty alleviation and as a result they are concerned with many of the same issues as liberation theology (Pew Forum on Religion and Public Life 2006). In addition, Evangelical Protestants in Latin America typically interpret the Gospel message with particular emphases, highlighting the importance of self-discipline, sobriety, family values, and active participation in a supportive community drawing its inspiration from the Bible. These are also the values that a burgeoning network of Evangelical schools in Latin America seeks to impart (Council of Evangelical Methodist Churches in Latin America and the Caribbean n/d). Some observers aver that Evangelical Protestants in Latin America are seeking to respond both to global economic and political conditions as well as local circumstances and factors. Critics argue however that such Evangelical initiatives in the region are the latest attempt by foreign – especially North American – churches to impose dependency and domination on locals, in effect seeking to establish and develop forms of 'neo-colonial Christianity' (Freston 2004; Pew Forum on Religion and Public Life 2006).

Overall, in Latin America both the overall culture and educational system has changed in recent years, shifting from Catholic dominance to a position of religious diversity, with growing importance for Evangelical Protestant churches. In the next section we focus upon an example of a Catholic educational network – Federación Internacional de Fe y Alegría – and an example of an Evangelical religious network, run by Latin America ChildCare, which is affiliated to a US-based Evangelical church, Assemblies of God.

Federación Internacional de Fe y Alegría

The Federación Internacional de Fe y Alegría ('International Federation of Faith and Joy') is a Catholic educational movement, rooted philosophically and religiously in liberation theology. Fe y Alegría's activities are focused on the most impoverished and excluded sectors of people, especially children, in Latin America. Its overall aim is to empower people, including children and young people, in order to improve their personal development and increase societal participation. Fe y Alegría's motto – 'Where the asphalt road ends, where there is no water or electricity, Fe y Alegría begins' – highlights its self-help purpose and philosophy (Marshall and Keough 2004: 166).

A Catholic priest, Fr Jose Maria Velaz, founded Fe y Alegría in Venezuela in 1955. Fr Velaz wanted to merge, strengthen and focus efforts to provide educational services in the slums of the capital city, Caracas. Over time the success of the movement's strategy was reflected in regional expansion to Ecuador (1964), Panama (1965), Peru (1966), Bolivia (1966), El Salvador (1969), Colombia (1971), Nicaragua (1974), Guatemala (1976), Brazil (1980), Dominican Republic (1990), Paraguay (1992), Argentina (1995), Honduras (2000) and Chile (2005). Recently, the movement has also established itself in Europe, with bases in both Spain and Italy (Fe y Alegría website: http://www.feyalegria.org/default.asp?caso=17&idrev=43&idedi=43).

Over the years, Fe y Alegría has become one of the most important faith-based providers of basic education in Latin America, reaching around one million children in poor communities in 15 regional countries. As the movement's guiding philosophy is rooted in the ideas of liberation theology then it is natural for it to focus attentions on the most impoverished and excluded sectors of society. To empower such people, by improving individual and collective societal participation, Fe y Alegría works to 'unite people in a process of growth, self-criticism and the search for answers to the challenges presented by human needs' (Marshall and Keough 2004: 166). The movement focuses much effort on poor children's education because it believes that it is important to promote 'formation of persons who are conscious of their own potential and of the reality about them; who are free, committed and open to transcendence; and who seek to be protagonists in their own development' (Marshall and Keough 2004: 167).

Fe y Alegría identifies itself as a Catholic educational movement for 'Integral Popular Education and Social Development'. It is *popular* as it sees education as a part of a pedagogical and political proposal for social transformation rooted in the local communities. It is *integral* because it presupposes that *education* involves the whole person in all his/her dimensions. It is concerned with *social development* as a consequence of regional socio-economic and political injustices, believing that individuals need assistance to confront and combat them, an essential step on the road to build societies that are overall more 'just, fraternal, democratic and participative' (Fe y Alegría website: http://www.feyalegria.org/default.asp?caso= 17&idrev=43&idedi=43).

Focusing its activities on education, Fe y Alegría offers not only formal – pre-school, primary and secondary – educational participation, but also opportunities for adults to advance their human development. The movement owns and runs nearly 70 radio stations, as well as adult education programmes, labour training and school equivalency programmes. Fe y Alegría also encourages workers' cooperatives and small businesses as well as community development projects focusing on: healthcare, indigenous culture, teacher training, and publication of educational materials. Overall, the Fe y Alegría network comprises over 2,000 centres in Latin America, involving around 1,000 schools for children, over 900 'extension education centres', and nearly 800 focal points for alternative education and other services. The movement employs nearly 35,000 people of whom 97.5% are lay people and 2.5% are religious professionals ('What is Fe y Alegría', at http://www.feyalegria.org/default.asp?caso=10&idrev=43&idsec=304&i dedi=43). In all its activities, Fe y Alegría acts in close coordination with local communities.

Latin America ChildCare

While Fe y Alegría has been growing for over 50 years since its inauguration in Venezuela, educational initiatives of Evangelical Protestants in Latin America are focused in what is known as the 'Christian school movement'. As a consequence of a growing shift to Evangelical Protestantism in many parts of Latin America there are growing numbers of such schools, now numbering over 2,000 in Latin America and the Caribbean. Many are recently established, since the early 1990s. Guatemala, El Salvador, Paraguay, and Puerto Rico are the regional countries with the highest number of Christian schools per capita. In addition, burgeoning Christian school movements can also be found in, *inter alia*, Bolivia, Mexico, Colombia, and Venezuela (Association of Christian Schools International n/d).

Latin America ChildCare (LACC), a ministry of the US-based Assemblies of God, is the leading provider of Christian schools in Latin America. LACC proclaims that its activities are centrally informed by the following religious principles:

1. 'To be an agency of God for evangelizing the world
2. To be a corporate body in which man may worship God
3. To be a channel of God's purpose to build a body of saints being perfected in the image of His son' (General Council of the Assemblies of God 2006).

Founded in 1963, LACC has grown over the years currently to involve over 300 educational projects affecting more than 100,000 children in 21 regional countries. Like Fe y Alegría, the educational philosophy of LACC is rooted in Christian principles, which are however somewhat different to those of Fe y Alegría's liberation theology perspective. LACC infuses its educational initiatives with what it calls 'the truth of the gospel', which seeks to equip the children the organisation teaches 'with the basic skills for competing in, and transforming, their society ... and to give them the things dreams are made of: a future' (Latin American ChildCare 2003).

LACC's self-proclaimed mission is to transform 'the lives of needy children with the Good News of Jesus Christ through education and ministries of compassion'. The organisation seeks to accomplish its goals via three main strategies:

- *Transformation*, by 'sharing the Good News of Jesus Christ through our words and deeds with children, their families and their community';

- *Education*, by 'applying knowledge and skills in the real-life context of students';
- *Compassion*, by 'caring for children through nutrition, healthcare and spiritual formation programmes' (Latin American ChildCare 2003).

In summary, LACC's mission is to provide poor children in Latin America with what it calls a 'Christian education'. The overall aim is to develop within the children it teaches the 'transforming belief in their God-given intrinsic value, a keen sense of their rich cultural identity, and the foundation for making free, responsible civic, moral and – most importantly – spiritual decisions' (Latin American ChildCare 2003).

John Bueno, a US-born, Chilean-reared pastor and his wife Lois founded LACC in El Salvador in 1963. The Buenos named their schools *Liceo Cristiano* ('Christian Schools'). Over the last four decades, LACC has developed into the largest integrated network of Christian schools in Latin America. The genesis for the schools' development came from the Buenos' desire to 'find a way to reach out to the children drowning in the poverty of a nearby barrio' (slum) by offering education that would highlight what they saw as the 'truth and hope and life-changing power of the gospel'. From small initial beginnings, the numbers of schools in El Salvador grew and a country-wide network developed. Today in El Salvador the LACC schools have a Salvadoran leadership, as well as 900 faculty and staff that operates 37 campuses. Of the 22,000 students enrolled at any one time, about a quarter receive financial assistance from the United States. In the course of the past four decades, more than 600,000 children have been through the Christian school programme in El Salvador alone – that is around 10% of the total population of a country of little more than six million people (Horn 2006). Overall, it seems fair to say that these schools have made a significant impact on children, families and the entire nation of El Salvador.

Yet while the LACC's educational network provides an education to tens of thousands of children at any one time, it works on what it calls 'indigenous missionary principles'. That is, LACC owns no schools itself – but instead works closely with local agencies, known as Programa Integral de Educacion de Las Asambleas de Dios (PIEDAD) that are autonomous in each country. Their main accountability is to the local Assemblies of God in their respective countries (Globalization of Pentecostalism 1996).

Overall, LACC provides a network of schools focusing on marginalised children in Latin America. Through its educational projects, LACC aims to provide philosophical and theological guidelines that centre on both evangelism and overt social concerns. In addition, LACC provides a channel of opportunity for North American and European donors to provide financial resources necessary to facilitate LACC projects in Latin America.

Hinduism

Hindu nationalism and the attempt to 'saffronise' education in India

India is an officially secular country – and has been since independence from British rule in 1947. In recent years, however, communalism has appeared as an important social and political issue. In particular, from the late 1980s, the strength of the *Hindutva* (Hindu Nationalist) movement grew. As a result, minority religions – including Islam, Buddhism, Christianity and Sikhism – came under pressure to define their own identities more fully than before, in order to combat *Hindutva*'s religious, political and social influence, manifested in various entities, including the Rastriya Swayansevak Sangh (RSS; 'National Volunteer Corps') and the leading Hindu nationalist political party, the Bharatiya Janata Party (BJP; 'Indian People's Party').

Regarding education, there was an associated controversy focusing on attempts to 'saffronise' it (Ram and Sharma 2005). This was a reference to saffron – the colour of the Hindu nationalist flag, and the neologism, to 'saffronise', referred to the increased influence of Hindu nationalist ideals both in education generally and in relation to primary, secondary and tertiary educational institutions. More than 32,000 educational establishments in India are now under the umbrella control of the RSS. During the late 1990s, following pressure from the BJP government, the National Council for Educational Research and Training (NCERT), India's main education policy-making body, sought to introduce 'religion to the classroom, where, since Independence in 1947, it was rarely seen'. The NCERT claimed that this course of action was justified in order to provide something hitherto lacking on school curricula: religious teachings, necessary, the Council averred in order to provide students with 'a universal value system' focusing on basic and inherent values of all religions. This in turn would provide to India's children, NCERT claimed, essential instruction in morals and values derived from India's rich religious traditions. Critics were concerned however that the strategy would not as claimed provide neutral and unbiased teachings about universal religious norms and values. Instead they feared that, to the detriment of India's other religious traditions, this would be a way of informing the school curriculum with divisive Hindu nationalist ideas, norms and values (Lall 2005; Sharma 2002: 215–18).

The initiative from NCERT followed election of the BJP to power in 1998, when it entered government as the largest party, heading a 19-party coalition government. The BJP proclaimed that its educational intentions included an attempt to recoup what it referred to as 'lost cultural values'. The main focus here was a (rewriting of) 'history project', which critics believed was a fundamental tenet of a wider strategy to saffronise India's education system (Lall 2005: 5). The BJP said it wanted to counter what it saw as the baleful influence of Christian missionaries in India, which both the BJP itself and the wider Hindu nationalist movement more generally believed was aggressively seeking converts, especially from among Hindus.[3] Rather than encouraging force to prevent what it regarded as a foreign Christian missionary 'invasion', Hindu nationalists instead supported the BJP and RSS campaign to teach 'Hindu values and culture' that, they believed, would undermine the appeal of Christian proselytisation. To this end, thousands of academics and teachers were recruited to help pursue Hindu nationalist educational goals (Sharma 2002: 215–18).

The BJP's Minister of Education, Murli Manohar Joshi, appointed scholars sympathetic to the Hindutva cause to national academic bodies, including the Indian Council of Historical Research, where he authorised replacing 14 of its 18 members with *Hindutva* supporters. This was particularly important because the Council is the sole government body responsible for distributing funds for historical research in India, where private research grants are virtually non-existent. Next, the minister focused his attentions on the Indian Council of Social Science Research and the Indian Institute of Advanced Studies, adding several pro-*Hindutva* scholars to each. Finally, the BJP government also began installing supporters in key positions at universities and colleges across India.

The BJP government's attempt to 'saffronise' India's education system was met with strong criticism from both conservative and liberal academics. The concern was that this was an attempt on the part of an extremist minority to destroy India's tradition of secularism, a step on the road to creation of a theocratic state. This was because of the comprehensive nature of the BJP plan. Among its most controversial features was the installation of compulsory courses in what it called 'Indian values' from preschool through to university level education provision; inclusion of Hindu religious texts in all educational syllabi; and instruction in 'Indian values and culture' during teacher training courses. Following an outcry, however, when over 12 (non-BJP) state education ministers protested at the plan, the minister shelved the proposal.

Yet this was not the end of the Hinduisation proposal. The tumult it generated developed into a country-wide debate on the generally poor state of the Indian education system, and what to do about it. And while this discussion served to some extent to legitimise the *Hindutva* campaign, many critics continued to maintain that, while accepting that many of India's schools needed refurbishing, it was fundamentally unhelpful to focus on the content of education only and ignore deep-rooted structural problems. In addition, critics averred, the *Hindutva* locus would likely exacerbate tensions between Hindus and religious minorities who, by being forced to accept a Hinduisation of India's education system, would lose rights guaranteed in the country's secular constitution. A particular concern was the proposal to include Hindu religious texts, dating back over 2,000 years, in the core curricula for all students irrespective of their own religious affiliation. As S.H. Chakravarty, Minister of Higher Education in West Bengal, a state not run by the BJP, puts it: 'The BJP is attempting to destroy the basic secular fabric of our country, because they don't believe in secularism' (Human Rights Watch 1999: 3). In summary, the BJP made an unsuccessful attempt, following its electoral victory in 1998, to try to redraw India's secular education curriculum at primary, secondary and tertiary levels.

The RSS also made efforts to try to saffronise further its own educational initiatives, focused in various organisations including the Vidya Bharati Sansthan (VBS; 'Indian Organisation for Education') (A Spreading Network 1998). Vidya Bharati runs around 14,000 primary and secondary schools, as well as dozens of colleges. Its educational network operates in 32 of India's 33 states, teaching nearly two million students. More generally, the RSS has sought to create a 'network of Sanskrit-language colleges that would further its campaign to make that ancient tongue the common language of all Indians' (Lloyd 1999).

However, perhaps the most controversial project involving the RSS and Vidya Bharati was the attempt to rewrite 'historical textbooks to highlight the achievements of Hindus or, as critics argue, to distort history to promote Hindu communalism' (Lloyd 1999). The main component of the strategy was to try to develop new historical principles that would stress the *Hindutva* ideological teachings. The policy also reflected the fact that unlike many other political parties in India, the BJP has a clear ideology recognising the potential of education to influence the mass of ordinary people (http://cac.ektaonline.org/resources/reports/sacw/appendixg.html).

The *Hindutva* educational campaign was undermined although not completely curtailed by the BJP's unexpected loss of power, to a coalition of parties led by the secular Congress Party, in the general election of May 2004 (Lall 2005; Mehta 2004). On coming to power, the Human Resource Development Minister, Arjun Singh, issued a statement 'cautioning people about [educational] institutions run by the RSS' following a cautionary report from the Central Advisory Board for Education. The minister also advised people to 'beware of the "venom" injected into the society by the educational institutions run by the saffron brigade', and hinted that the government would to try to control their further expansion (World Prout Assembly 2006).

In conclusion, the recent attempt to saffronise education in India by the Hindu nationalist movement, expressed largely through the BJP governments in power between 1998 and 2004, was an example of a faith-based political movement seeking to use education as a means to advance a more general religiously and ideologically motivated agenda. However, the attempt ran into controversy at once, and led to a strong counter-campaign that sought to focus upon the idea that to saffronise education in India went directly counter to the country's well-established secular traditions. At the same time, it should not be overlooked that the chain of schools established and run by the RSS satisfied a growing educational need in India where many believe the state-run educational system is failing to provide an adequate country-wide service (Lall 2005; Dreze and Sen 2003).

Buddhism

The focus in this section is on two Buddhist educational movements, the Sarvodaya Shramadana Movement (Sri Lanka) and Santi Sena (Cambodia). Each administers a network of schools and other education facilities inspired by Buddhist ideals. Their efforts are noteworthy, especially as both countries have endured years of conflict, insecurity and destabilisation, which have severely disrupted state ability to provide an adequate education service. In Sri Lanka, the Sarvodaya Shramadana Movement had to contend not only with the continuing civil war – between the Sinhalese-dominated state and the rebel mainly-Hindu Tamil Tigers[4] – but also the tragedy of the December 2004 tsunami and its after-effects. When the tidal wave struck the country, thousands of people were killed and huge numbers of homes and other buildings were destroyed. Education in Sri Lanka suffered a devastating impact; the tsunami 'destroyed hundreds of schools, drastically disrupted the lives of thousands of young children, and escalated the islands' educational shortcomings into a state of emergency' (Room to Read 2006). The context in Cambodia, on the other hand, was provided by the decades of conflict linked to the rule of the Khmer Rouge in the 1970s.

The Sarvodaya Shramadana Movement (Sri Lanka)

Ceylon became independent in 1948, changing its name to Sri Lanka (in Sinhalese: 'resplendent land') in 1972. In 1978, the country's legislative and judicial capital was moved from Colombo to nearby Sri Jayewardanapura Kotte, and the national flag was also changed: orange and green vertical bars were added, representing the mainly Hindu Tamil[5] and Muslim minority populations. Despite this attempt to indicate that Sri Lanka was not solely a Buddhist nation, 'Buddhist nationalism' has played a consistently preeminent political role in Sri Lanka, often serving as a unifying force among the Sinhalese majority. The mainly Buddhist Sinhalese comprise three-quarters of the population, Hindu Tamils make up around 18% and the rest – less than 10% – are mainly Muslims and Christians.

In Sri Lanka, education is free and compulsory in both primary and secondary schools. Nine out of ten students complete secondary school resulting in a corresponding adult literacy rate, among the highest in Asia. But while literacy rates in Sri Lanka are relatively high, overall the country's socio-economic environment is relatively poor: According to the UNDP's Human Development Index (1990–2003), 45% of Sri Lanka's population lives on less than US$2 per day. Moreover, the education system lacks sufficient schoolbooks, while students do not all have equal access to primary and secondary schools (Room to Read 2006). For example, many communities in the central highlands remain largely neglected and lag far behind the rest of the population. In one such community, Nuwara Eliya, female literacy rates (76%) are much lower than male literacy rates (87%). Overall, in many such communities, poverty is high and education levels very low; there are very few schools, those that exist are often poor, while it is common for girls to work long hours for low wages instead of going to school (Room to Read 2006).

Sri Lanka's patchy educational provision was the context within which the Sarvodaya Shramadana Movement was founded in 1958 by a young teacher, A.T. Ariyaratne (Premasiri 1997) (Use sarvodaya as eg http://ignca.nic.in/cd_05012.htm http://www.wfdd.org.uk/programmes/case_studies/sarvodaya.pdf). At this time, Ariyaratne was a teacher teaching science in a prestigious school in Colombo. Believing that many among the country's poor, rural communities were being neglected both in terms of development and educational opportunities, Ariyaratne organised work camps in villages, with the help of his students. His first project was in a poor, remote, outcast village. Ariyaratne asked his students to live on equal terms with the villagers, staying in their meagre huts, sharing their meals and work. The students assisted villagers to build roads, plant trees and dig wells and, as the result, the students intimately experienced the villagers' problems, including the constraints they faced. During the course of their work, many students came to learn the meaning of 'shramadana', a Buddhist term meaning giving one's time and labour as a gift.

Shramadana is part of the culture and tradition of Buddhism and, as already noted, in Sri Lanka Buddhism is the majority religion. The message of 'shramadana' is not new to most Buddhists, being a core concept that has developed since the time of the Buddha, 2,500 years ago. In addition, Buddhist values of loving kindness (*metta*), compassionate action (*karuna*), unselfish joy (*muditha*), and equanimity (*upekha*) are collectively the inner core values of the Sarvodaya Shramadana Movement, traditional Buddhist values that inspire, motivate and weld the community together (Chowdhry 2002).

Over time, the *shramadana* idea became widely accepted among many young Buddhist students in Sri Lanka, and within a few years the idea of working with the poor in their villages developed into an educational network involving hundreds of schools. Each weekend, thousands of school children participate in weekend village camps to share and donate their labour for development activities identified by local villagers (Premasiri 1997; Chowdhry 2002). More than 3,000 volunteers annually, participate in various development projects through the *shramadana* camps. They undertake a variety of tasks, including: building and repairing houses, digging wells, constructing latrines, cleaning irrigation canals, temples and sacred sites, planting trees and growing food crops and weeding and harvesting of paddy fields.

The educational objectives of the Sarvodaya Shramadana Movement are manifested in various ways at the village level. Typically, work commences with a preliminary survey to see what the local community lacks. Educational initiatives are focused on: children, mothers, young people, farmers and 'others' (including, teachers, government officials, artists, and crafts people). These constituencies form groups that meet regularly, while all groups usually get together collectively once a week. By the early 2000s, Sarvodaya Shramadana was working in more than 11,000 villages, while having a variety of national-level institutions, including: the Early Childhood Development Institute, Rural Technical Services, Legal Services, and *Sarvodaya* Enterprise Development Services. In addition, several thousand villages have established *Sarvodaya* Village Development Banks, largely staffed by local trained women. 'The main vehicle for this work is the network of *Shramadana* Societies in almost all the districts of Sri Lanka, including the conflict areas of the North and East' (Chowdhry 2002: 2).

Some 'development workers' of international agencies view religion and spiritual awakening as irrelevant or even a hindrance to the development process (Tyndale 2004). Yet the achievements of the Sarvodaya Shramadana Movement in Sri Lanka clearly show how the two communities in this context is significant spiritual awakening to achieving development goals. It is also of great relevance in dealing with and helping to overcome participants' fears and sense of powerlessness, thereby increasing in many cases participants' ability to resolve problems of poverty and more generally developmental shortfalls (Chowdhry 2002; Global Knowledge Partnership 2006).

Second, the overall purpose of Sarvodaya Shramadana programmes is social empowerment, a process that begins and ends with education. More and better education is the foundational basis of a concerted effort to change both conceptual and psychological aspects of society in rural Sri Lanka, through holistically addressing poverty, and achievability of sustainable lifestyles and the avoidance of war and violence. The movement seeks to achieve its goals through projects developed according to the needs of villagers, including: community capacity building, early childhood development programmes, disaster management, development education, biodiversity and environmental conservation.

Finally, a focus on the Sarvodaya Shramadana Movement also shows how religion and spirituality can serve as a basic resource for and in development. The Movement's overall aim is to make human life more meaningful – both for the giver and the receiver. Although the Movement involves the development of economic activities and capacities, it is also centrally concerned with facilitating the unfolding of participants' capacity to give and share. In other words, the Movement's main strength lies in its ability to awaken the self and achieve subsequent personal transformation. As Ariyaratne himself points out: 'The chief objective of *Sarvodaya* is personality awakening with the effort of the individual as well as with help from others' (Chowdhry 2002: 6).

Santi Sena in Cambodia

A frog in a well can see only a small part of sky. The one who can take the frog out of the well to see the whole sky, will make merit (Traditional Khmer saying).

Present-day Cambodia was part of the former French colonial empire in South East Asia, which included much of the eastern part of the Indochinese peninsula. French influence extended from roughly 1862 to the fall of Dien Bien Phu (1954). Prior to the organisation of a Western-style educational system established by the French, the Buddhist *wat* – that is, a temple and school with resident monks – had provided the only formal education in Cambodia. Buddhist monks have traditionally seen education as a key function of Buddhist doctrine and history, linked to the importance of acquiring merit. 'At the *wat* schools, young boys – girls were not allowed to study in these institutions – were taught to read and to write Khmer, and they were instructed in the rudiments of Buddhism'. Ten years after independence in 1954, Cambodia had nearly 600 Buddhist primary schools, teaching nearly 10,000 students. By the end of the 1960s, the number of students had nearly tripled to more than 27,000 being taught in Buddhist elementary schools (Federal Research Division of the Library of Congress 1997).

During the 1970s, Cambodia's development, including the country's educational system, was fundamentally destabilised and disrupted by several years of Khmer Rouge rule, which ended in 1979. During the Khmer Rouge era all *wat* schools were closed down. Despite the fact that more than 90% of Cambodians are Buddhists, throughout the Khmer Rouge era the faith had to contend with serious state attempts to eradicate it from society. During Khmer Rouge rule more than a million Cambodians people were killed and a further two million died as a consequence of state repression or hunger (Kamm 1998). Following the Khmer Rouge's overthrow in 1979 by a Vietnamese invasion, an initially hesitant state recognised the continuing popular appeal of Buddhism and allowed it a resurgent voice in national affairs.

After the Khmer Rouge era there followed a period of extended instability, during which the country's education system failed to recover. With an aim of helping improve the poor educational situation, a Buddhist education and development movement, Santi Sena (Sanskrit; in English: 'a group of people who work for peace and social welfare'), was founded in 1993 (Vikram Sarabhai Foundation & World Faiths Development Dialogue 2004). Santi Sena's 'mission' was

> To alleviate poverty through improving close co-operation with relevant governmental institutions; to encourage and support local initiatives; to focus the work on vulnerable and marginalized people; to reduce social violence; to promote human rights, democracy, social legislation and advocacy; to empower women; and to contribute to the conservation of natural resources (Venerable Nhem Kim Teng n/d: 3).

Within this context, Santi Sena has two specific educational goals:

- To promote good quality education for children and youth, including an awareness of ethics;
- To provide opportunities for informal education to women and people who lack access to accurate information (Venerable Nhem Kim Teng n/d: 3).

Santi Sena focuses on Buddhist teachings by offering *Dhamma Dana* (knowledge education). This does not imply a narrowly 'religious' education but an education concerned with wider, holistic goals, such as: 'building up skills, knowledge, self-confidence and mutual trust amongst community members and with outsiders, promoting self-help initiatives and engaging in natural resource management'. In addition, Santi Sena seeks to advise people 'on how to survive in the right way', conserve nature, build a peaceful society, and seek to provide 'security for human beings who are in need' (Venerable Nhem Kim Teng n/d: 1).

An example of Santi Sena's educational work comes from Prey Chlak pagoda in Svay Rieng provincial town. The organisation established a permanent library in Svay Rieng in 2000, with over 36,000 books. The aim of the library is 'to develop students' scientific knowledge in harmony with Buddhist values'. It specifically seeks to cater to the demands of both children and adults, and is a highly important educational resource – especially when seen in the context of state failure to provide sufficient books for children's education. By 2005, the library had been visited by over 700,000 students (Venerable Nhem Kim Teng n/d: 9).

Santi Sena also carries out a mobile library project in the region. A van equipped with reading and performance materials travels from primary school to primary school. The Santi Sena team performs different drama pieces, and the aim is to motivate children to attend school. By 2005, the mobile library project had visited over 60,000 school children in Prey Chlak province. Finally, in addition to the permanent and mobile libraries, Santi Sena has a training centre offering computer training courses, which take three months to accomplish. Between 2000–05, Santi Sena 'issued computer training certificates to 276 youths' (Venerable Nhem Kim Teng n/d: 9). The overall point about Santi Sena is that the movement has developed a series of practical educational initiatives in Cambodia that are centrally informed by its Buddhist values.

Overall conclusion

This chapter has argued that various forms of faith-based education in the developing world are of uniform educational validity if its potential audience is convinced that it can provide both formal educational opportunities within the context of a significant concern with religious and/or cultural values. Faith-based education is also important in a common context in the developing world: declining or patchy state ability to provide an adequate education service. Yet the issue is also widely controversial – not least because some critics see such educational initiatives as a serious challenge to what they regard as established societal values including, as in India, secular principles. On the other hand, many religious parents are of the opinion that faith-based education is entirely appropriate for their children; sometimes when state provision appears to favour a different religious group, as in Ethiopia. Moreover, the chapter points to the importance for societal cohesion of religious diversity being adequately incorporated into educational systems in the developing world. Finally, achievement of the MDGs in relation to education is only likely to be possible when educational initiatives – both state and faith-based – take into account societal diversity, not only in terms of a country's religious composition but also in other – culturally, geographically and economically – varied ways.

Conclusion

The most basic assumption underlying development studies – both in theory and practice – is that 'development' implies, if anything, poverty reduction and, by extension, accretions in well-being for the mass of ordinary people over time. Certainly, this was the underpinning assumption behind the emergence of development studies after World War II, when the concept of development first appeared on the international agenda. In the 1950s, there was growing realisation that, in fact, development was a rather complex concept that became even more problematic following the emergence of large numbers of post-colonial countries in Africa, Asia and elsewhere. By the 1960s and 1970s there was growing realisation of an increasingly developmentally polarised world. In the 1980s, leading Western governments and international financial institutions sought to deal with developmental imbalances by trying to 'roll back the state' in many developing countries, working on the presumption that many such states tried unsuccessfully to do too much: spending too much money and time but often developmentally achieving little.

By the 1990s, there was much acceptance of the view that to achieve broad-based 'development' in the developing world it was necessary to develop stronger partnerships between international donors, governments and local communities. This highlighted that it was incorrect to believe that all efforts towards improving development outcomes must emanate from the state alone. It also reflected the view that development goals are much more likely to be achieved when state and society work in tandem rather than in different directions. Not least in importance was the realisation – expressed in the notion of the 'third wave of democracy' (Huntington 1991) – that governments are more likely to propose, put into effect and implement pro-development policies and

205

programmes when they are encouraged to do by popular pressure – most obviously via the ballot box. Put another way, while across the board improvements in various development outcomes, including health and education, are fundamental to improvements in the development position of millions of people in the developing countries, such outcomes do not routinely occur. Often, indeed, such policies are strongly resisted by incumbent elites who see the issue of development as a zero-sum game: gains for anyone other than themselves, their families, friends, kin, and allies, are to be resisted. In short, analysis of development and its shortfalls necessarily starts from an understanding that developmental policies *always* have major resource implications and, as a result, (1) they are always highly *political* decisions, and (2) elites will normally try to prevent them if they can (Haynes 2005b).

Development is of course not only a domestic issue. It is also an international concern, and perceived development failures over the last six decades have led to periodic conceptual rethinks in this regard. Following perceived developmental 'failures' in the 1960s, the international focus shifted in the 1970s to concern with 'basic needs' strategies, whereby development would be catalysed through ensuring that all people had the necessary 'basics': clean water, basic healthcare, primary education, and so on. This strategy generally failed, however, for two main reasons: first, the developmental issue became subsumed into the wider Cold War ideological division, with development funds not necessarily going to the most 'deserving' cases but to allies of the key aid providing countries; and, second, because of the unwillingness of ruling elites and their supporters to allow the fundamental transfer of resources upon which the basic needs strategy depended. There was another directional shift in the 1980s: the perceived 'panacea' of SAPs, ubiquitously introduced and consolidated in dozens of developing countries. The key belief, articulated by the then World Bank President, Barber Conable in 1994, was that 'market forces and economic efficiency were the best way to achieve the kind of growth which is the best antidote to poverty' (quoted in Thomas and Reader 2001: 79).

Conable's statement reflected the intellectual dominance in the 1980s and early 1990s of neo-liberalism, an economic and political philosophy that ideologically underpinned the pro-market and monetarist ideas of influential governments, such as those of Britain's Margaret Thatcher (1979–90) and, in the USA, the administrations of Ronald Reagan (1980–88) and George Bush Sr (1988–92). The core belief of neo-liberalism was that to achieve development, government's role must be diminished, with private capitalists 'set free' from state control. Under pressure from Western governments and IFIs, many regimes in developing countries sought to put in place neo-liberal policies, albeit with variable – usually disappointing – effects.

The ideological power of neo-liberalism was at its zenith in 1989–91 when the Cold War came to an end and the Eastern European communist bloc collapsed. These developments not only appeared to offer spectacular evidence of the superior power of liberal democracy and capitalism over communism, but also provided pro-market forces with momentum. The dominant neo-liberal development strategy – the 'Washington consensus' – reflected the pre-eminence of such ideas among key, Washington, DC-based, opinion leaders: 'the IMF and the World Bank, independent think-tanks, the US government policy community, investment bankers, and so on' (Thomas and Reader 2001: 79). However, as – the growing numbers of – critics of the Washington consensus model subsequently pointed out, its studiously pro market view appeared to overlook the fact that only governments have the power to alter prevailing socio-economic realities through the application of appropriate policies and programmes. In other words, the market is not very good at allocating resources fairly; only governments can do that. And, whether they do or not, is strongly linked to the varying amounts of pressure put on governments by competing societal interests.

What is now clear is that, in the opening years of the third millennium, Washington consensus policies are not the answer to developmental shortfalls in the developing world. The point is that after 60 years of 'development' policies and programmes and three decades of neo-liberal economic policies, more than a billion people in the developing world still live on less than US$1 a day, over two billion – one-third of the global population – do not have access to potable clean water, while hundreds of millions of humans, especially women and the poor, do not have access to anything like adequate healthcare or basic educational opportunities. Overall, at the end of six decades of pro-development policies the global developmental picture is characterised by rising global poverty and polarising inequality. Reflecting such a concern, the international community has now set itself the challenge of a new 'onslaught' in the developing world on poverty and human deprivation. The deadline to achieve the United Nations' MDGs, declared in September 2000, was 2015 – less than ten years from now.

The MDGs reflect the fact that development thinking has undergone two important revisions since the 1990s. First, it is now widely accepted – by Western governments and development agencies alike – that to achieve beneficial developmental changes things cannot be left entirely to the market. Second, there is much agreement that early development successes, such as that of Britain, did not come about quickly or by chance. Instead, they were the outcome of specific governmental decisions to:

- Reduce the power of business interests;
- Adopt relatively high levels of taxation to fund growth of welfare states;
- Pursue policies for full employment; and
- Redistribute wealth from rich to poor via progressive taxation policies.

In the early 2000s, the World Bank also admitted the need for a changed emphasis to achieve development goals. The Bank noted in its *World Development Report 2000/2001* that adjustments would be necessary at both global and national levels to record widespread developmental gains. Nationally, goals of promoting opportunity were inherently linked to increases in overall economic growth, as were patterns and quality of growth. While market reforms could be central in expanding opportunities for poor people, reforms needed to reflect local institutional and structural conditions. And this, the Bank admitted, was difficult to achieve – not least because it would necessitate a significant shift in power between groups, an outcome that would likely be fought against by those currently enjoying disproportionate shares of wealth and power.

Second, shifting focus on how to facilitate popular capacities, the Bank stated that the 'choice and implementation of public actions that are responsive to the needs of poor people *depend on the interaction of political, social, and other institutional processes*' (World Bank 2001: 7; emphasis added). But to facilitate the abilities of ordinary citizens not only depends on 'active collaboration among poor people, the middle class (sic), and other groups in society', but is also linked to wider changes in governance style and outcomes. These would be necessary in order to make public administration, legal institutions, and public service delivery both more efficient and accountable to all citizens – rather than only serving the interests of a privileged few (World Bank 2001: 7). In short, the Bank accepted that to deliver enhanced participation in development required the inclusion of both poor and middle class people in decision-making structures and processes.

Third, in order to enhance security in various ways, the Bank noted that effective national actions were necessary to manage the risk of economy-wide shocks – as well as to build effective mechanisms to reduce the risks faced by poor people, including health- and weather-related risks. In respect of the national aspects necessary to lead to more and better development, the Bank explicitly referred to and discussed not only the necessity of *collective, political* actions to try to achieve development gains – but also the fact that national governments must necessarily interact with processes of globalisation in order to get what they can from it. In summary, the Bank noted the significance of both domestic and global factors in relation to development outcome in the developing world.

In summary, the 2001 Report was cautiously optimistic, with a basic presumption that, for millions of impoverished people in the developing countries, major reductions in dimensions of poverty were now theoretically possible. It was also notable for the adoption of some of the critical alternative approach's concerns. Whereas the World Bank's chief concern in the 1980s and early 1990s was to roll back the role of the state in development and leave it to the market, the 2001 Report emphasised the possibility that stated development goals might be achieved by a three-way collective effort, involving domestic markets, state institutions, and civil society. However, the Report also accepted that to attain these 'international development goals will require actions to spur economic growth and reduce income inequality, but even equitable growth will not be enough to achieve the goals for health and education' (p. 6). However, it remained to be seen whether relevant actors could actually work together to 'harness' globalisation, via economic integration and technological changes, so as to better serve the developmental interests and goals of poor people and facilitate an increase in their share of society's prosperity.

A more recent World Bank Development Report (2004) – subtitled, *'Making Services Work For Poor People'* – basically restates the same kind of themes and concerns as those referred to in the 2001 Report. It notes that to improve service delivery, institutional changes are necessary to strengthen relationships of accountability – between policymakers, providers, and citizens. The then-president of the World Bank, James Wolfensohn, proclaims in his foreword that

We enter the new millennium with great hopes. For the first time in human history, we have the possibility of eradicating global poverty in our lifetime. One hundred and eighty heads of state signed the

Millennium Declaration in October 2000, pledging the world to meeting the Millennium Development Goals by 2015. In Monterrey, Mexico, in the spring of 2002, the world's nations established a partnership for increasing external assistance, expanding world trade, and deepening policy and institutional reforms to reach these goals. Foreign aid, which declined during the 1990s, has begun to increase again. ...

These changes will not come overnight. Solutions must be tailored not to some imaginary 'best practice' but to the realities of the country or the town or the village. One size will not fit all. But I am convinced that this new way of thinking about service delivery, and indeed about development effectiveness, will bear fruit, particularly when matched with adequate resources and a desire to assess what works and what does not, and to decide what must be scaled up and, indeed, what must be scaled down (Wolfensohn 2004).

Although relatively optimistic in tone, the 2004 Report also acknowledged that the early years of the 21st century were characterised by highly significant developmental challenges, including HIV/AIDS and other diseases, as well as illiteracy, unclean water, conflict within and between states, and widespread examples of misused foreign developmental assistance in many developing countries.

The stated aim of the 2004 *World Development Report*, the 26th in the World Bank's 'flagship' series, was to 're-ignite and reinforce' development hopes by setting out ways to confront and deal with extant development challenges. In a focus reminiscent of the 'basic needs' approach to development first adopted in the 1970s, the Report stressed how important for development outcomes are the provision of basic services – particularly health, education, water, and sanitation – for all citizens, while stressing that governments in the developing world should not bear full responsibility for provision of such development goods. In addition, the 2004 Report acknowledged that to achieve the MDGs by 2015 much more would be necessary beyond providing necessary sums of financial assistance – difficult though that in itself would be. The 2004 Report also noted that to achieve the MDGs by 2015 it would be necessary to encourage both religious and secular community organisations, organised in a variety of ways and according to various criteria, in pursuit of a variety of objectives.

But the Report also noted that services all too often fail poor people in the developing world, and that while these failures may be less spectacular and immediate than financial crises, such as the 1997–98 Asian Financial Crisis, over time their effects are just as – if not more – profound. The Report also provided various examples of what happens when services *do* work for poor people; and that they can be provided by variety of sources, state and non-state, secular and religious. The main point is that development outcomes in the developing world often improve when local people believe that they have a stake in their success, for example, 'when girls are encouraged to go to school, when pupils and parents participate in the schooling process, when communities take charge of their own sanitation'. Services are also likely to function better when corruption is curtailed, particularly when it affects provision of basic health services, which of course poor people need greatly. Instead, development needs to be viewed comprehensively by recognising, for example, 'that a mother's education will help her baby's health, which building a road or a bridge will enable children to go to school' (World Bank 2004. 121).

In summary, the 2004 Report emphasised that to bring about broad improvements in human development, poor people in the developing world needed urgently to get better access to affordable, better quality services in health, education, water, sanitation, and electricity. If such improvements were not forthcoming, the Report reiterated, then 'freedom from illness' and 'freedom from illiteracy' – two of the most important ways poor people can escape poverty, and central among the MDGs announced in 2000 – would remain for many elusive.

Religion and development in the developing world

The strategies and objectives stated in the 2004 World Development Report were central to the World Bank's two-pronged strategy for development: (1) investing in and empowering people, and (2) improving the climate for financial investments from both domestic and external sources. The focus on communities in the 2004 World Development Report was welcome, not least because it served to emphasise more generally that development outcomes, ultimately can only be measured in the extent to which they affect poor people's quality of life.

Our starting point in this book was a realisation that development outcomes need improving dramatically across much of the developing world. To achieve such objectives, the book focused on the various relationships between 'religion' and 'development' in sub-Saharan Africa, Asia and Latin America. The aspiration was to provide a commentary on what has taken place, and is currently happening, in the spheres of religion and development in these regions. In summary, the book sought to provide a comparative treatment of these issues – in order to appreciate and comprehend the rich variety of extant national and regional situations in sub-Saharan Africa, Asia and Latin America. The overall purpose of the book was to serve as an introduction and overview of the topic, with the intention to stimulate further examination and discussion of the relevant issues.

We saw an important developmental role of religion in relation to the following:

- Engendering and influencing values, which in turn can affect the formulation of underlying policy considerations and governmental policies;
- Worsening or help resolving political conflicts depending on the circumstances.

There is now much more awareness – on the part of governments, academics and NGOs – of the variable role of religious individuals and faith-based organisations in relation to development outcomes in sub-Saharan Africa, Asia and Latin America. There was not, however, one single event to explain this changed emphasis; there was no '9/11 moment' in relation to religion's role in development, analogous to the impact of the murderous attack by a transnational religious extremist organisation – al-Qaeda – against the world's most conventionally powerful country, the USA. Indeed, the 9/11 attack was indicative of a wider conflict between the USA – and by extension, the West – and Islamic extremism. As we have seen in this book, however, 9/11 and its aftermath certainly did not exhaust the ways that religion can affect political and developmental outcomes in the contemporary world.

A further assumption of the book was that the current role of religion in development in the developing world can usefully be seen in relation to three interlinked developments: widespread religious resurgence, deepening globalisation and extensive concern with the quality of governance in many developing countries. The collective impact of these developments is that we cannot any longer ignore religion influence on development in the developing world.

To examine the issue in detail we focused upon two generic kinds of religious actors: (1) faith-based organisations that operate transnationally, and (2) faith-based organisations that work within a country.

We saw that both can impact significantly on development outcomes, in relation both to policy formation and execution. In relation to the first category, we saw that various transnational religious actors, including, Islamic, Roman Catholic and Protestant Evangelical groups, collectively bring religious concerns into development discourses. In the second category, we examined various faith-based organisations from four religious traditions – Islam, Christianity, Hinduism and Buddhism – in various countries in sub-Saharan Africa, Asia and Latin America. They too collectively represent an important development, overtly aligning religious traditions and principles with attempts to deliver better development outcomes.

Because of its potentially vast subject matter, the book did not set out to examine each and every area where religion has an impact on development in the developing world. For example we did not look at one of the potentially most fruitful regions of the world to examine the relationship between religion and development: the Middle East. Instead, we were concerned with examining how religion affects two general sets of issues: (1) various aspects of human development, and (2) conflict, conflict resolution and peacemaking, in three major regions of the world: sub-Saharan Africa, Asia – especially East, Southeast and South Asia – and Latin America. In short, the book had a comprehensive – although not global – focus that encompassed major parts of the developing world.

The book arrived at three main conclusions:

- Developments associated with modernisation – that is, socioeconomic and political change involving urbanisation, industrialisation, and centralisation of government – and globalisation – that is, increasing multifaceted interaction between states and societies around the global – are crucial to an understanding of the current involvement of religion in development in the developing world regions focused upon in this book;
- Rather than fading from relevance as modernisation theory prophesised, religion is now of major – and almost certainly growing – developmental importance in the developing world regions focused upon in this book;
- The nature and characteristics of faith-based organisations we have examined are not only linked to their structural and systemic attributes but also reflect particular features of the religion and culture that produces them.

After the Cold War: religion, development and modernisation

In recent years, and especially after the Cold War ended in the late 1980s, there was much speculation about how developmental outcomes in the countries of the developing world would now be different now compared to the past. In what respects have things changed? What do the changes, if they are in fact occurring, mean for peace, prosperity, and justice – in short, for prospects of enhanced development – in the developing world?

The first point is that it was once widely assumed that nations would invariably secularise as they modernised. It was believed that associated loss of religious faith and secularisation would dovetail with the idea that technological development and the application of science to overcome perennial social problems of poverty, environmental degradation, hunger, and disease would result in long-term human progress. However, it is plausible to surmise that lack of success in this regard was one of the factors behind the recent increased focus on the developmental role of religion in the developing world (Berger 1999).

Over the last two or more decades religion has had significant impact upon development outcomes in many parts of the developing world. And, as a result, confidence that the growth and spread of urbanisation, education, economic development, scientific rationality and social mobility would combine to diminish significantly the sociopolitical position of religion was misplaced. Two broad trends can be noted. First, religion was often used politically – often as a vehicle of opposition or as an ideology of community self-interest. Threats emanating either from powerful, outsider groups or from unwelcome symptoms of modernisation (breakdown of moral behaviour, overliberalisation in education and social habits) served to galvanise such groups. Second, failure of governments to push through programmes of developmental improvements have also encouraged faith-based organisations which typically develop a faith-based ideology of solidarity and development – for example, the Basic Christian Communities found in Latin America and elsewhere in the developing world, and various Islamic development entities.

A key factor in the rise of faith-based organisations in many parts of the developing world was the impact of globalisation on many local communities. This included the economic range and clout of transnational corporations and a perception that they are taking economic power from governments – and thus from citizens and their efforts to

control their own fates (Haynes 2005a). We also noted widely perceived downsides to economic globalisation more generally, especially
worsening impoverishment of already poor people especially in the
developing world. These circumstances helped lead to a new or renewed
focus from numerous faith-based organisations seeking to ameliorate
social and human rights imbalances often perceived as exacerbated by
the effects of economic globalisation. As a result, there was widespread
religious concern with development and human rights concerns
during the period of post-Cold War globalisation. This was manifested
in various ways, including: new religious fundamentalisms and support
for various anti-globalisation activities, including anti-WTO protests
and North/South economic justice efforts (Spickard 2001). Overall, this
underlines that religious responses to globalisation now often include a
stress on social interests that go way beyond the confines of what
Christians might call 'church life'.

Alkire (2006) emphasises that in relation to social development and
human rights, ideas of desirable outcomes expressed by religious
organisations and more generally by faith perspectives may well differ
significantly from those advanced by non-religious economic development models, for example, those advanced by the IMF or the World
Bank. This is because from a general religious perspective development
programmes and policies appear to be 'one-eyed giants' which 'analyse,
prescribe and act *as if* man could live by bread alone, *as if* human
destiny could be stripped to its material dimensions alone' (Goulet
1980, quoted in Alkire 2006).

We also noted rather similar objections to non-religious developmental programmes and policies emanating from individual religious
perspectives. For example, writing from an Islamic viewpoint, Seyyed
Hussein Nasr focuses on the link between modernisation and development, and emphasises how important it is for them to be concerned
about religion. For him, development without such a concern will
fatally distract Muslims from what is their true – that is, religious –
nature and, as a result, seriously undermine their chances of living
appropriately (Nasr 1967, 1975, 1996).

Second, in recent years Roman Catholic social teachings have often
articulated what might be called a faith-based view of development.
This emphasises the contributions of 'spiritual disciplines and of
ethical action to a person's "vocation to human fulfillment", addressed
alongside contributions made by markets, public policy, and poverty
reduction' (Alkire 2004: 10). Another articulation of concern about the
goals and purpose of human development from a Catholic perspective

is to be found in a radical approach, liberation theology. Liberation theology emphasises what it regards as structural developmental and political injustices and demands increased engagement of Catholics with political and economic institutions in order to try to gain better outcomes. A Peruvian priest, Gustavo Gutierrez, famously articulated liberation theology in his *A Theology of Liberation. History, Politics and Salvation* (1973). Representatives of other religious faiths, including Judaism and Buddhism, have also advanced similar kinds of development interpretations to that of Gutierrez, underlining that religious faiths tend to work from similar positions in relation to some social development issues. In addition, distinct liberation theologies have also been articulated by other major faiths. For example, various popular books have also explicated a similar people-centred development perspective, for example, Bernardo Klicksberg's *Social Justice: A Jewish perspective* (2003) and Sulak Sivaraksa and Ginsburg's *Seeds of Peace* (1992), from a Buddhist perspective.

In addition to that emanating from specific faiths, there are also recent examples of interfaith religious involvement in relation to a variety of human development issues. A key example in this regard is the WFDD, an initiative that sought to map areas of convergence among religious faiths' visions of development agendas, with a focus on: relationships of service and solidarity, harmony with the earth, and the vital but limited contribution of material progress (World Faiths Development Dialogue 2003).

In a speech delivered in June 2005, a senior World Bank figure, Katherine Marshall, emphasised that the Bank did not believe 'that religion and socio-economic development belong to different spheres and are best cast in separate roles – even separate dramas'. Her observation was based on recognition that around the world many religious organisations and development agencies share similar concerns: how to improve (1) the lot of materially poor people, (2) the societal position of those suffering from social exclusion, and (3) unfulfilled human potential in the context of glaring developmental polarisation within and between countries, partly as a result of the impact of globalisation (Marshall 2005a). Marshall's speech emphasised that while religion has often in the past been understood by the Bank as 'otherworldly' and 'world-denying', it is now accepted that religion can significantly contribute to developmental goals in the developing world, not least because issues of right and wrong and social and economic justice are central to the teachings of the world religions, including: Buddhism, Christianity, Hinduism, Islam and Judaism.

Reflecting such concerns, a series of 'Leaders Meetings' were convened to pursue avenues to address these issues. In their book, *Millennium Challenges for Development and Faith Institutions* (2003), Marshall and Marsh report on a meeting, in Canterbury, England in October 2002, hosted by Jim Wolfensohn and George Carey. The purpose of the meeting was to bring together an important group of leaders from the world's faith communities, key development organisations, and from the worlds of entertainment, philanthropy and the private sector. Linked to the MDGs, themes of the meetings included: poverty and hunger, children's education, gender equality, health, HIV/AIDS and other diseases, and environmental sustainability. Many participants accepted that poverty, HIV/AIDS, conflict, gender concerns, international trade and global politics explicitly link all the world's countries and peoples – rich and poor – into a global community. This sense of one-ness highlighted the urgency of developing shared responsibility and partnership to deal with collective problems facing humanity. The overall conclusion was that more is needed to be done to move from expressions of solidarity in the face of shared problems to the realisation of practical plans involving collaboration between the worlds of faith and development in confronting major development issues (Marshall and Marsh 2003).

In summary, shared concerns – with poverty and human development more generally – encouraged closer links between faith-based organisations and development agencies, notably the World Bank. Second, collectively cognisant of economic globalisation's apparent polarising impact, there was common ground linking them, encouraging what might be an emerging global consensus underpinning the pursuit of the MDGs.

Religion, conflict, conflict resolution and peacemaking

Another issue of central concern for this book was the role of religion in conflict, conflict resolution and peacemaking – because resolving inter- and intra-societal conflict is a fundamental prerequisite for human development. A starting point to analysis in this regard is to note that globalisation both highlights and encourages religious pluralism. Some religions, especially Islam, Christianity and Judaism (the so-called 'religions of the book', as their authority emanates principally from sacred texts, actually, similar texts) claim what Kurtz calls 'exclusive accounts of the nature of reality', that is only *their* beliefs are regarded as *true* beliefs (Kurtz 1995: 238).

Religious exclusivist truth claims can be a serious challenge to religious toleration and diversity, essential to our co-existence in a globalised world. On the other hand, most religious traditions have within them beliefs that can make a contribution to a multicultural world. For example, from within Christianity comes the idea of non-violence, a key attribute of Jesus, the religion's founder, who insisted that all people are children of God, and that the test of one's relationship with God is whether one loves one's enemies and brings good news to the poor. As St Paul said, 'There is no Jew or Greek, servant or free, male or female: because you are all one in Jesus Christ' (Galatians 3: 28).

Because globalisation results in increased interaction between people and communities, it implies that encounters between different religious traditions are both increasingly common yet not invariably harmonious. Sometimes, the result is what Kurtz labels 'culture wars' (Kurtz 1995: 168). Kurtz contends that this is because, as already noted, various religious worldviews encourage different allegiances and standards in relation to various areas, including the family, law, education and politics. Increasingly, it appears, conflicts between people, ethnic groups, classes, and nations are framed in religious terms. Such religious conflicts seem often to 'take on "larger-than-life" proportions as the struggle of good against evil' (Kurtz 1995: 170).

This contention seems to be borne out when we focus upon the issue of religious involvement in current conflicts. For example, stability and prosperity in the Middle East is a pivotal goal, central to achievement of peace and the elimination of poverty. The Middle East is particularly emblematic in this regard as it is the birthplace of the three monotheistic religions (Christianity, Islam, and Judaism), with a legacy not only of shared wisdom but also of conflict – a complex relationship that impacts on countries as far away as Indonesia and the United States. A key to peace in the region may well be achievement of significant collaborative efforts among different religious bodies, which along with external religious and secular organisations, for example from Europe and the United States, may through collaborative efforts work towards developing a new model of peace and cooperation to enable the Middle East to escape from what many see as an endless cycle of religious-based conflict.

This emphasises the fact that religion may be intimately connected, not only in the Middle East, *both* to international conflicts and their prolongation *and* to attempts at reconciliation of such conflicts. In other words, in relation to many international conflicts, religion can play a significant, even a fundamental role, contributing to conflicts in various ways, including how they are intensified, channelled or reconciled. Many international conflicts have religious roots and religion is driving both hatred and violence. Hans Kung, an eminent Roman Catholic theologian, claims that

the most fanatical, the cruelest political struggles are those that have been colored, inspired, and legitimized by religion. To say this is not to reduce all political conflicts to religious ones, but to take seriously the fact that religions share in the responsibility for bringing peace to our torn and warring world (Hans Kung, quoted in Smock 2004).

On the other hand, it is important not to overestimate religion's potential for and involvement in large-scale violence and conflict if that implies ignoring or underestimating its involvement and potential as a significant source of conflict resolution and peace-building. It is important to recognise that, especially in recent years, numerous religious individuals, movements and organisations have been actively involved in attempts to end conflicts and to foster post-conflict reconciliation between formerly warring parties (Bouta *et al.* 2005). This emphasises that various religions collectively play a key role in international relations and diplomacy by helping to resolve conflicts and build peace. For David Smock (2004), Huntington's 'clash of civilisations' thesis oversimplifies causal interconnections between religion and conflict, in particular by disregarding important alternate variables, including the numerous attempts from a variety of religious traditions to help resolve conflicts and build peace. When successful, religion's role in helping resolve conflicts is a crucial component in wider issues of human development because, as Ellis and ter Haar note: 'Peace is a precondition for human development. Religious ideas of various provenance – indigenous religions as well as world religions – play an important role in *legitimising or discouraging violence*' (Ellis and ter Haar 2005: 4 emphasis added).

More generally, we have noted much involvement of religion in developmental issues in the developing world over time. The recent developmental impact of religion falls into two – not necessarily mutually exclusive – categories. First, if most people in a community are not especially religious, then religious actors may well be developmentally marginal. However, in most developing countries, for the most part people are – sometimes fervent – religious believers. In some cases, unsuccessful attempts by many political leaders to modernise and develop their countries have led to sustained responses from various religious actors. Religion can serve to focus and coordinate opposition, especially – but not exclusively – that of the poor and ethnic minorities. Religion is often well placed to benefit from a societal backlash against the perceived malign effects of modernisation. In particular, various religious fundamentalist leaders have sought support from ordinary people by addressing certain crucial issues. These include: the perceived decline in public and private morality and the insecurities of life, the result of an undependable market where, it is argued, greed and luck appear as effective as work and rational choice. On the other hand, we have also noted many examples of faith-based organisations that appear to be wholly focused on development issues and do not appear to have an oppositional relationship with government.

Religion and development: the future

And what of the future? If the issues and concerns that have helped stimulate widespread religious resurgence – including, socio-political and economic upheavals, patchy modernisation, increasing encroachment of the state upon religion's terrain – continue (and there is no reason to suppose they will not), then it seems highly likely that religion's developmental role will continue to be significant in many parts of the developing world. This will partly reflect the continuing impact of secularisation – set to continue in many countries and regions, linked to the spread of globalisation – which will be fought against by many religious leaders and faith-based organisations (Norris and Inglehart 2004).

In the early years of the third millennium it is increasingly clear that approaches to development, as well as development outcomes in the regions of the developing world, are polarised. On the one hand, in relation to *theorising* about development, there are both 'radical' and 'reformist' interpretations of what needs to be done to ameliorate development outcomes in developmentally under-achieving countries in the developing world. Radical approaches argue that they are necessary in order to resolve fundamental development impasses (Rai 2005; Taylor 2005). Critics contend, on the other hand, that many radical approaches are excessively concerned with often purely theoretical criticisms of the status quo. The perceived problem is that this does not allow sufficient attention to the actual experiences and developments on which such theories and theoretical perspectives are focused: the conditions in which, for example, women or the poor live and work, and the actual effects of greater (and lesser) degrees of involvement with global markets and forces on national economies and sectors. It might be that future insights on development are likely to be provided by an amalgamation of both theory and practice, so that the various subject matters that collectively comprise the issue area of 'development studies' benefit from clear and robust theorising underpinned by various forms of empirical evidence from a number of sources.

The field of development studies more generally currently features an unresolved – perhaps unresolvable tension – between radicalism and reformism, for example, between those who view 'liberal' democracy as hopelessly formal and manipulative and who dismiss calls (by the World Bank, the United Nations Economic Commission for Latin America, and others) for the reform of neo-liberal schemes as merely cosmetic and window-dressing. It may be however that evident divergences between radical and reformist solutions to developmental quandaries are but the tip of the iceberg. What I am referring to is the general manner in which many of the problems and issues identified in the book – poverty, health, education, conflict, the natural environment – are examined. Such issues are not of course unfamiliar more generally in social science. This might in turn suggest that what we examined as 'development studies' is not actually a distinct discipline, or set of disciplines. Instead, its subject matter is not especially distinctive – as it is actually at the heart of social science issues anyway, and has been since the time of Adam Smith.

On the other hand, in the developing world, developmental successes and failures in relation to attempts to democratise and then consolidate democracy, develop and sustain successful economies, protect natural environments, and pay more attention to human and women's rights, are best explained by allusion to – different mixes depending on context and a host of other factors – both domestic and external factors, probably in most cases with the main emphasis on the former. Overall, the book's chapters have emphasised that various unhelpful structural factors can be overcome by the determination of individual religious leaders and faith-based organisations, encouraged by civil society organisations and more generally bottom-up pressure on rulers.

Notes

Introduction: Religion and Development

1 A faith-based organisation is an entity whose inspiration or main funding draws from their faith. It can be an institution, association or group formed by people of the same religious affiliation. Within the Christian tradition, for example, faith-based organisations include – but are not limited to – churches and church-affiliated organisations for both men and women, youth groups and Sunday schools, as well as church-based NGOs, social welfare bodies, schools and health institutions, and both national and international church organisations and networks (Byamugisha *et al.* 2002: 1).

2 According to the WFDD website, 'The World Faiths Development Dialogue was set up in 1998 as an initiative of James D. Wolfensohn, President of the World Bank and Lord Carey, then Archbishop of Canterbury. Its aim is to facilitate a dialogue on poverty and development among people from different religions and between them and the international development institutions'. The focus is on the relationship between faith and development and how this is expressed, both in considering decisions about development policy and in action with impoverished communities all over the world.' (http://www.wfdd.org.uk/).

3 The World Council of Churches (WCC), founded in Amsterdam in 1948, is an international, interdenominational organisation bringing together most major Protestant, Anglican, and Eastern Orthodox Christian churches. WCC headquarters are in Geneva.

4 Graduate of Wellesley College and the Woodrow Wilson School, Princeton University, Marshall was a Visiting Scholar at Harvard University. At the time of the establishment of the DDVE, Marshall had over 30 years' experience in the field of international development, having worked since 1971 for the World Bank. Formerly, she directed the World Bank's programmes in East Asia, Africa and Latin America. She is currently (late 2006), a Senior Officer responsible for a broad range of issues focusing on ethics, values, rights and faith in development work, while serving as Counsellor to the President of the World Bank. She also serves on the boards of several non-governmental organisations, and has written numerous articles and several books on international development issues for (http://www.weforum.org/site/knowledgenavigator.nsf/Content/Marshall%20Katherine).

5 An Abrahamic religion (also known as a Judeo-Abrahamic Faith) is any religion that derives from a common ancient Semitic tradition, traced by followers to Abraham. The latter was a figure whose life is noted in the Hebrew Bible/Old Testament, the Qur'an and in the Christian Bible, in Genesis 20: 7. Thus Abraham has significance for Judaism, Islam and Christianity, a group of monotheistic religions. More than half of the world's population – over three billion people – are followers of Abrahamic religions.

6 Immanentism refers to something existing in the realm of the material universe and/or human consciousness.

Chapter 1 Religious Resurgence, Globalisation, and Good Governance

1 Defined as organisations (1) generally possessing specific values based on religious conviction that pervade the organisation's work, and (2) an often extensive network of co-religionists who support the organisation as an expression of religious community.

2 The main area of the globe that did not conform to the trend was Western Europe (Norris and Inglehart 2004).

3 Note, however, that not all observers accept the claim of widespread religious resurgence. See for example Bruce (2002).

4 G7 is an international organisation that was officially established in 1985. Its purpose is to facilitate economic cooperation among the world's largest industrial nations, among which 'summit meetings' of member states began over 30 years ago, in 1975. G7 members are: Canada, France, Germany, Italy, Japan, the United Kingdom and the United States. G7's remit is to discuss and coordinate members' actions on economic and commercial matters and to work to aid other states' economies. The leaders of the G7 states meet annually in member countries. Anti-globalisation protesters regard the G7 as little more than 'a rich man's club', meeting periodically in order to plot how to dominate the world through self interested capitalist policies (Held and McGrew 2002: 75–6).

5 This section draws on Haynes (2006).

6 At the time of writing (late 2006), the WFDD appeared to be in a state of 'suspended animation', with no clear decision taken about its future following James Wolfensohn's retirement from the Bank in June 2005, when he was replaced by Paul Wolfowitz.

Chapter 2 Religion and Development: The Ambivalence of the Sacred

1 This is a reference to R. Scott Appleby's, *The Ambivalence of the Sacred: Religion, Violence and Reconciliation* (2000). Appleby describes how both terrorists and peacemakers can emerge from the same community, and be followers of the same religion. One kills while the other strives for reconciliation. Appleby explains what religious terrorists and religious peacemakers share in common, what causes them to take different paths in fighting injustice, and how a deeper understanding of religious extremism can and must be integrated more effectively into our thinking about tribal, regional, and international conflict. More generally, the book highlights how religious actors can be motivated by a variety of concerns.

2 Ebaugh (2002) usefully highlights four factors that have brought religion back into general social science discourse, from whence it was (re)moved by modernisation and secularisation theories. They are:

- *rational choice theory;*
- *civic culture;*
- *globalisation;*
- *social movements.*

3　Spirituality, in a narrow sense, concerns itself with matters of the spirit. The spiritual is usually perceived to be concerned with eternal verities regarding the ultimate nature of people, contrasting with the temporal or with the worldly. The central defining characteristic of spirituality is a sense of connection to a much greater whole which includes an emotional experience of religious awe and reverence.

4　WFDD was particularly active in this regard. Go to http://www.wfdd.org.uk/ programmes.html#prs for a list of relevant projects.

5　The Anglican Church has 70 million members around the world.

6　Paul Wolfowitz replaced Wolfensohn as head of the World Bank in June 2005. From that time the WFDD was in abeyance and at the time of writing (late 2006) its future is uncertain.

7　The United Nations estimates that if funds for debt repayment were diverted back into health and education, the lives of seven million children a year in the developing world could be saved.

8　The Faith Action for People-Centered Development Policy network brings together the following churches and faith-based organisations: Africa Faith and Justice Network, American Friends Service Committee, Washington Office, Bread for the World, Churches for Middle East Peace, Church of the Brethren, Washington Office, Church World Service, Columban Fathers' Justice and Peace Office, Episcopal Church, USA, Episcopal Migration Ministries, Evangelical Lutheran Church in America, Lutheran Office for Governmental Affairs, Lutheran Immigration and Refugee Service, Lutheran World Relief, Maryknoll Office for Global Concerns, Mennonite Central Committee, Washington Office, National Council of the Churches of Christ in the USA, NETWORK: A National Catholic Social Justice Lobby, Presbyterian Church (USA), Washington Office, Reformed Church in America, and United Methodist Church, and General Board of Church and Society, Washington Office on Africa, and Washington Office on Latin America(http://www.trincoll.edu/depts/csrpl/RINVol4No1/ jubilee_ 2000.htm).

Chapter 3　Conflict, Conflict Resolution and Peace-building

1　Interview with Tom Lantos (2001) BBC Radio 4, *Today* programme, 20 November 2001, quoted in Hurrell 2002: 195.

2　Such remarks did not seem to affect Congressman Lantos' electoral popularity. In the March 2004 democratic primary in California's 12th Congressional District he gained 71.6% of the votes case. His nearest challenger acquired less than 20% (19.8%) (http://www.lantos.org/).

3　A clan is smaller than an ethnic group, a collection of families of variable overall size often bearing the same family name, under the control of a single chieftain.

Chapter 4   Economic Growth, Poverty and Hunger

1   There is a notable exception to this general rule. The UNDP has sought to emphasise *human economic development* in a broadly defined sense.
2   The Christian community in Kerala consists of Latin and Syrian Catholics, Orthodox and Protestants.
3   In Sanskrit, Santi Sena means a group of people who work for peace and social welfare improvements.
4   Afghanistan, Bangladesh, Bosnia, Burkina Faso, Democratic Republic of Congo, Côte d'Ivoire, Egypt, India, Iran, Kazakhstan, Kenya, Kyrgyz Republic, Madagascar, Mali, Mozambique, Pakistan, Syria, Tajikistan, Tanzania, Uganda and Zanzibar.
5   Find information about the Ismaili Imamat and its head, the Aga Khan, at: http://www.akdn.org/hh/highness.html.

Chapter 5   Environmental Sustainability

1   A Hindu activist called Sundarlal Bahuguna started the *Chipko* movement in the 1970s for the preservation of forestlands according to Hindu ecological ideas.

Chapter 6   Health

1   A 9.1 magnitude off the coast of Indonesia on 26 December, 2004, caused a tsunami – or tidal wave – that reached as high as nine metres and killed at least 213,000 people in 11 regional countries.

Chapter 7   Education

1   Eight developing countries with Muslim-majorities or significant Islamic minorities are participants in the EFA Fast-Track Initiative designed to deal with this shortfall: Burkina Faso, The Gambia, Guinea, Guyana, Mauritania, Mozambique, Niger and Yemen (www1.worldbank.org/education/efafti/).
2   Sufism is a mystical movement within Islam that seeks to find divine love and knowledge through direct personal experience of God.
3   Christians account for 2.5% of India's more than one billion people; Hindus are in the majority, with more than 80% of the total population, while Muslims make up the largest minority, around 12%.
4   In Sri Lanka, religious instruction is compulsory. All children study Buddhism even if they are of a different faith tradition.
5   Tamils are an ethnic group, predominantly Hindu, whose language is also Tamil, a Dravidian language. In Sri Lanka, Tamils are mostly located in the country's Northern and Eastern provinces. They are also in the majority in the neighbouring Indian state of Tamil Nadu State, in the south-east of the country; the two communities have strong links. In Sri Lanka, some Tamils are indigenous, others are descendants of estate labourers brought into the island during British colonial rule.

Bibliography

'A spreading network' (1998) *Frontline*, 'India's national magazine', 15, 23, November 7–20, pp. 15–18.

Abraham, C.M. (1996) *Fish Workers' Movement in Kerala*, Mumbai: Institute for Community Organisation Research.

Adhopia, A. (2001) 'Hinduism promotes environment protection', Boloji.com. Available at: http://www.boloji.com/analysis/018.htm Last accessed 16 December 2006.

Ahmad, S.I. (2003) 'Principles of self development in Islam'. *IslamOnline.net*, 2 October. Available at: http://www.islamonline.net/english/Contemporary/2003/11/Article01.shtml Last accessed 4 October 2006.

Ajit, S.K. (2004) 'Quest for good governance: Contribution and potential of religious institutions as stakeholders'. Paper presented at 'The Quest for Good Governance' conference, organised by the Monash Governance Research Unit & Monash Institute for the Study of Global Movements, 27 August.

Al-Akwa'a, A. (2005) 'Human dignity: Governance implications', Almansour Cultural Foundation. Available at http://www.mansourdialogue.org/English/lecs%20(5).html Last accessed 6 October 2006.

Alkire, S. (2004) 'Religion and development', draft chapter for D. Clark (ed.) *The Elgar Companion to Development Studies*, October 2004.

Alkire, S. (2006) 'Religion and development', in D. Clark (ed.) *The Elgar Companion to Development Studies*, Cheltenham, UK: Edward Elgar.

Ammar, N.H. (1995) 'Islam, population and the environment', in H. Coward (ed.) *Population, Consumption and the Environment*, Albany: State University of New York Press, pp. 123–36.

Anderson, E.N. (1996) *Ecologies of the Heart: Emotion, Belief, and the Environment*, New York and Oxford: Oxford University Press.

Appleby, R. Scott (2000) *The Ambivalence of the Sacred: Religion, Violence and Reconciliation*, Lanham, MD: Rowman and Littlefield.

Appleby, R. Scott (2006) 'Building sustainable peace: The roles of local and transnational religious actors'. Conference paper prepared for the Conference on New Religious Pluralism in World Politics, Georgetown University, 17 March.

Aquaviva, S. (1979) *The Decline of the Sacred in Industrial Society*, Oxford: Blackwell.

ARC (Alliance of Religions and Conservation) (2004) 'What does Christianity teach about ecology?' Available at http://www.arcworld.org/faiths.asp?pageID=39 Last accessed 14 November 2006.

Arensberg, A. (2004) 'Islamic environmentalism in Malaysia'. Available at: http://www.austinarensberg.com/?page_id=389 Last accessed 16 December 2006.

Armanios, F. (2003) 'CRS Report for Congress. Islamic Religious Schools, *Madrasas*: Background', RS21654, Washington, DC: The Library of Congress.

Armstrong, K. (2001) *The Battle for God: Fundamentalism in Judaism, Christianity and Islam*, London: HarperCollins.

The Ashden Awards for Sustainable Energy (2006) 'Micro-hydro power for remote communities in the Hindu Kush, North West Frontier Province, Pakistan'. Available at: http://www.ashdenawards.org/winners/akrsp Last accessed 21 December 2006.

Association of Christian Schools International (n/d) 'Welcome to ACSI's Latin America Office'. Available at: http://www.acsi.org/web2003/default.aspx?ID=1692&#43 Last accessed 20 December 2006.

Bankoff, G. and Elston, K. (1995) 'Environmental regulation in Malaysia and Singapore', Asia Paper no. 2, University of Western Australia Press in association with Asia Research Centre.

Barringer, T. (2006) 'Taking faith seriously in International Relations and Development Studies'. Paper presented at the conference, 'Governance in the Commonwealth: Civic Engagement and Democratic Accountability', the Institute of Commonwealth Studies, London, 11–13 March. Available at: http://commonwealth.sas.ac.uk/events/csc_march11/barringer.pdf Last accessed 3 August 2006.

Barrow, G. (1995) 'Ethnic riots leave five Kenyans dead', *The Guardian* (London), 18 October.

Barrow, S. (2006) 'Good governance needs bridges not barriers to relating to Muslims', *Ekklesia*, 6 October Available at http://www.ekklesia.co.uk/content/news_syndication/article_0610101bridges.shtml Last accessed 11 December 2006.

Bartoli, A. (2005) 'Conflict prevention: The role of religion is the role of its actors', *New Routes*, 10, 3, pp. 3–7.

Baylis, J. and Smith, S. (eds) (2005) *The Globalization of World Politics*, Oxford: Oxford University Press.

Berger, P. (1969) *Sacred Canopy: Elements of a Sociological Theory of Religion*, New York: Anchor Books.

Berger, P. (1975) *Pyramids of Sacrifice*, New York: Basic Books.

Berger, P. (1999) (ed.) *The Desecularization of the World: Resurgent Religion in World Politics*, Grand Rapids/Washington, DC: William B. Eerdmans/Ethics & Public Policy Center.

Berger, P. (2003) 'The cultural dynamics of globalization', in P. Berger and S. Huntington, *Many Globalizations: Cultural Diversity in the Contemporary World*, New York: Oxford University Press, pp. 1–17.

Berger, P. and Hefner, R. (2003) 'Spiritual capital in comparative perspective'. Paper written for the Planning Meeting, Spiritual Capital Research Program, Metanexus Institute, Philadelphia, USA. Available at: http://www.metanexus.net/spiritual_capital/pdf/Berger.pdf Last accessed 10 August 2006.

Beyer, P. (1994) *Religion and Globalization*, London: Sage.

Beyer, P. (2006) *Religions in Global Society*, London: Routledge.

Bhuckory, S. (1998) 'Manilal Maganlal Doctor', in U. Bissoondoyal and M. Banymandhub (eds) *Major Figures of the Mauritius Arya Samaj*, Moka, Mauritius: Mahatma Gandhi Institute Press, pp. 32–45.

Bock, J. (2001) 'Communal conflict, NGOs, and the power of religious symbols', in D. Eade (ed.) *Development and Culture*, Oxford: Oxfam, pp. 78–91.

Boff, L. (1987) *Introducing Liberation Theology*, Maryknoll: Orbis Books.

Bouta, T., Kadayifci-Orellana, S. and Abu-Nimer, M. (2005) *Faith-Based Peace-Building: Mapping and Analysis of Christian, Muslim and Multi-Faith Actors*, The Hague, Netherlands: Institute of International Relations.

Bratton, M. and van de Walle, N. (1997) *Democratic Experiments in Africa*, Cambridge: Cambridge University Press.

Brecher, J. and Costello, T. (1994) *Global Village or Global Pillage: Economic Reconstruction from the Bottom Up*, Cambridge, MA: South End Press.

Brown, P. (2001) 'World deal on climate isolates US', *The Guardian*, 24 July.

Bruce, S. (2002) *God Is Dead: Secularization in the West. Religion and Spirituality in the Modern World*, Oxford: Blackwell.

Bureau for Development Policy/Regional Bureau for Latin America and the Caribbean (2005) *Shifting Perspectives and Taking Action. UNDP's Response to HIV/AIDS in Latin America and the Caribbean*, New York: UNDP.

Burke, J. (2004) *Al-Qaeda: The True Story of Radical Islam*, Harmondsworth: Penguin.

Burke, J. (2006) *On the Road to Kandahar*, Harmondsworth: Allen Lane.

Burnell, P. and Morrissey, O. (eds) (2004) *Foreign Aid in the New Global Economy*, Cheltenham: Edward Elgar.

Byamugisha, G., Steinitz, L., Williams, G. and Zondi, P. (2002) 'Journeys of faith: church-based responses to HIV and AIDS in three southern African countries. Strategies for hope', Hatfield, South Africa: Southern African Regional Poverty Network. Available at: http://www.sarpn.org.za/documents/d0001614/index.php Last accessed 10 March 2006.

Calvert, S. and Calvert, P. (1996) *Politics and Society in the Third World*, Harlow: Pearson Education.

Calvert, S. and Calvert, P. (2001) *Politics and Society in the Third World*, 2nd edn, Harlow: Pearson Education.

Campbell, D. (2006) 'Under suspicion', *The Guardian*, 22 August.

Canadian International Development Agency (2006) 'Coastal Rural Support Program'. Available at: cida.gc.ca/cidaweb/cpo.nsf/f7a3cbaf96ca2a4985256-d1d0052ee15/9ac75832fcc3f376852570190031856e Last accessed 21 December 2006.

Cardenal, R. (1990) 'The martyrdom of the Salvadorean church', in D. Keogh (ed.) *Church and Politic sin Latin America*, London: Macmillan, pp. 235–54.

Carlson, J. and Owens, E. (2003) *The Sacred and the Sovereign. Religion and International Politics*, Washington, DC: Georgetown University Press.

Carpenter, J. (2003) 'The new Evangelical universities. A dynamic new element in mission lands', *Mission Frontiers*, March–April, pp. 6–7.

Casanova, J. (1994) *Public Religions in the Modern World*, Chicago and London: University of Chicago Press.

Center for the Study of Global Christianity (2006) 'Status of global mission, 2006, in the context of 20th and 21st centuries', South Hamilton, MA: Center for the Study of Global Christianity.

Chew, A. (2006) 'Starting young: JI targets schools', CNN.com, International Edition. Available at: http://www.cnn.com/2003/WORLD/asiapcf/southeast/08/11/indonesia.schools/ Last accessed 20 December 2006.

CGAP (Consultative Group to Assist the Poor) (2004) 'How donors can help build pro-poor financial systems', Donor Briefs, no. 17, Washington: CGAP.

Chowdhry, K. (2002) 'The Sarvodaya Shramadana Movement in Sri Lanka'. Available at: http://www.wfdd.org.uk/programmes/case_studies/sarvodaya.pdf Last accessed 20 December 2006.

CIA (Central Intelligence Agency) (2006) 'World Factbook – Mauritius'. Available at: https//www.cia.gov/cia/publications/factbook/print/mp.html Last accessed 18 December 2006.

Cleary, L. and McConville, T. (eds) (2006) *The Governance and Management of Defence*, London: Taylor & Francis.

Conflict and Resolution Forum (2001) 'Faith-based peacemaking: The role of religious actors in preventing and resolving conflict worldwide', 10 April, Washington DC.

Council of Evangelical Methodist Churches in Latin America and the Caribbean (n/d) 'ELADE (Latin American School of Evangelization)' Available at: http://www.ciemal.com.ar/english/ELADE.asp Las accessed 20 December 2006.

Coward, H. (2002) 'Population and consumption: Contemporary religious responses'. Unpublished manuscript, University of Victoria, Australia.

Coward, H. and Maguire, D.C. (eds) (2000) *Visions of a New Earth: Religious Perspectives on Population, Consumption and Ecology*, Albany: State University of New York Press.

Cox, H. (1968) *The Secular City*, Harmondsworth: Penguin.

Cox, H. (1984) *Religion in the Secular City Towards a Postmodern Theology*, New York: Simon & Schuster.

Crawford, S. Cromwell (1989) 'Hindu ethics for modern life', in S. Cromwell Crawford (eds) *World Religions and Global Ethics*, New York: Paragon House, pp. 5–35.

Crawley, M. (2003). 'Two men create bridge over Nigeria's troubled waters', *Christian Science Monitor*, 28 February. Available at: http://www.csmonitor.com/2003/0228/p07s01-woaf.html Last accessed 3 October 2006.

Dahl, A. (1998) 'Spiritual dimensions of sustainable development'. 'Baha'i Library Online'. Available at: http://bahai-library.com/index.php5?file=dahl_spiritual_dimensions_development Last accessed 14 December 2006.

Dan Church Aid (2006) 'The Ethiopian Muslims' Relief and Development Association'. Available at: http://www.dca.dk/sider_paa_hjemmesiden/where_we_work/africa/ethiopia/read_more/the_ethiopian_muslims_relief_and_development_association Last accessed 18 December 2006.

Dark, K. (ed.) (2000) *Religion in International Relations*, Basingstoke: Palgrave.

Darlington, S. (1997) 'Not only preaching – The work of the ecology monk: Phrakhru Nantakhun of Thailand', *Forest, Trees and People Newsletter*, No. 34, pp. 17–20.

Darlington, S. (2000) 'Tree ordination in Thailand', in S. Kaza and K. Kraft (eds) *Dharma Rain: Sources of Buddhist Environmentalism*, Boston: Shambhala Publications, 2000, pp. 198–205.

Dearden, P. (2002) *Environmental Protection and Rural Development in Thailand*, London: White Lotus.

Dickson, D. (2005) *Political Islam in Sub-Saharan Africa: The Need for a New Research and Diplomatic Agenda*, Washington, DC: United States Institute of Peace.

Dreze, J. and Sen, A. (2003) 'Basic education as a political issue', in B.G. Tilak (ed.) *Education, Society and Development: National and International Perspectives*, New Delhi: APH, pp. 1–18.

Durning, A. (1989) *Action at the Grassroots*, Worldwatch Papers no. 88, Washington, DC: Worldwatch Institute.

Eadie, P. and Pettiford, L. (2005) 'The natural environment', in J. Haynes (ed.) *Palgrave Advances in Development Studies*, Basingstoke: Palgrave, pp. 181–200.

Ebaugh, H.R. (2002). 'Presidential address 2001, Return of the sacred: Reintegrating. Religion in the social sciences', *Journal for the Social Scientific Study of Religion*, 41, 3 p. 385.

Eccleston, B. (1996) 'NGOs and competing representations of deforestation as an environmental issue in Malaysia', *The Journal of Commonwealth and Comparative Politics*, 34, 2, pp. 116–42.

Economist, The (2002) 'Education in Latin America. Cramming them in', 9 May. Available at: http://www.economist.com/world/la/displayStory.cfm?story_id=1121601 Last accessed 20 December 2006.

Ekins, P. (1992) *A New World Order. Grassroots Movements for Global Change*, London: Routledge.

Ellis, S. and ter Haar, G. (2004) *The Worlds of Power: Religious Thought and Political Practice in Africa*, London: Hurst.

Ellis, S. and ter Haar, G. (2005) 'Religion and Development in Africa'. Background paper prepared for the Commission for Africa.

Embassy of India (n/d) 'Kerala: Asia's Cradle of Christianity' Available at: http://www.indianembassy.org/new/NewDelhiPressFile/kerala_christianity.html Last accessed 21 December 2006.

Energy Information Administration (2003) 'Thailand: Environmental issues', 'County Analysis Briefs'. Available at: http://www.eia.doe.gov/emeu/cabs/thaienv.html Last accessed 16 December 2006.

Engender Health (2005) 'In Cambodia, Buddhist nuns take charge as breastfeeding advocates and educators' Available at: http://www.engenderhealth.org/itf/cambodia-3.html Last accessed 18 December 2006.

Esposito, J. and Burgat, F. (2002) *Modernising Islam: Religion in the Public Sphere in Europe and the Middle East*, London: Hurst and co.

Ezzat, H. Raouf (2005) 'Beyond methodological modernism: Towards a multicultural paradigm shift in the social sciences', in H. Anheier, M. Galsius, and M. Kaldor (eds) *Global Civil Society 2004/5*, London/Thousand Oaks, New Delhi: Sage Publications, pp. 40–59.

Federal Research Division of the Library of Congress (1997) 'Cambodia. Buddhist education'. Available at: http://www.country-data.com/cgi-bin/query/r-2142.html Last accessed 20 December 2006.

Ferret, G. (2005) 'Africans trust religious leaders', BBC News. Available at: http://news.bbc.co.uk/1/hi/world/africa/4246754.stm. Last accessed 8 December 2006.

'Final Declaration of the World Forum on Food Sovereignty' (2001) Havana, Cuba, 7 September.

Fisher, J. (1993) *The Road from Rio. Sustainable Development and Nongovernmental Movement in the Third World*, Westport, Connecticut, Praeger.

Fisk, R. (2005) *The Great War for Civilisation: The Conquest of the Middle East*, New York: Fourth Estate.

Folz, R. (ed.) (2005) *Environmentalism in the Muslim World*, Waltham, MA: Nova Biomedical.

Folz, R., Denny, F. and Baharuddin, A. (2003) *Islam and Ecology: A Bestowed Trust*, Cambridge, Massachusetts: Harvard University Press.

Frawley, D. (2000) *How I Became a Hindu*, New Delhi: Voices of India.

Freston, P. (2004) *Evangelicals and Politics in Asia, Africa and Latin America*, Cambridge: Cambridge University Press.

Fukuyama, F. (1992) *The End of History and the Last Man*, Harmondsworth: Penguin.

Gardner, G. (2002) *Invoking the Spirit: Religion and Spirituality in the Quest for a Sustainable World*, Washington, DC: Worldwatch Institute.

General Council of the Assemblies of God (2006) 'Our mission and vision'. Available at: http://ag.org/top/About/mission_vision.cfm Last accessed 20 December 2006.

Gervais, S. (2004) 'Local capacity building in Title II food security projects: a framework', Occasional Paper, no. 3, Washington DC: USAID Office of Food for Peace.

Ghandour, A.-R. (2002) *Jihad humanitaire, Enquête sur les ONG islamiques*, Paris: Flammarion.

Gifford, P. (1998) *African Christianity. Its Public Role*, London: Hurst and Co.

Global Campaign for Education (2002) 'An action plan to achieve the MDGs in education'. Briefing for EFA Ambroul uu conterence, April.

Global Knowledge Partnership (2006) 'Sarvodaya Shramadana Movement of Sri Lanka'. Available at: http://www.globalknowledge.org/gkps_portal/form-master.cfm?&menuid=9&parentid=8&action=view&orgid=336 Last accessed 20 December 2006.

Globalization of Pentecostalism (1996) 'Report of globalization of Pente-costalism conference, 10–13 June in San Jose, Costa Rica'. Available at· http://www.pctii.org/ag.html Last accessed 20 December 2006.

Goldman Environmental Prize (2005) 'Internationally acclaimed Goldman Environmental Prize names 2005 Winners' Available at: http://www.gold-manprize.org/node/563 Last accessed 15 December 2006.

Gopin, M. (2000) *Between Eden and Armageddon: The Future of World Religions, Violence and Peacemaking*, New York and London: Oxford University Press.

Gopin, M. (2005) 'World religions, violence, and myths of peace in inter-national relations', in G. ter Haar and J. Busutill (eds) *Bridge or Barrier. Religion, Violence and Visions for Peace*, Leiden: Brill, pp. 35–56.

Goulet, D. (1980) 'Development experts: The one-eyed giants', *World Development*, 8, pp. 481–9.

Government of Mauritius/Council of Religions (2006) '2006–2007. Council of Religion's (sic) Action Plan on HIV and AIDS in Mauritius'. Available at: http://un.intnet.mu/UNDP/html/mauritius/Council%20of%20Religions%20Pro%20Doc.pdf Last accessed 18 December 2006.

Grey, M. (2003) *Sacred Longings: Ecofeminist Theology and Globalisation*, London: SCM Press.

Gunaratna, R. (2004) 'Defeating Al Qaeda – The pioneering vanguard of the Islamic movements', in R. Howard and R. Sawyer (eds) *Defeating Terrorism. Shaping the New Security Environment*, Guilford, Connecticut: McGraw-Hill/Dushkin, pp. 1–28.

Gupta, R.K. (2004) 'Vedantic wisdom as a source of developmental ima-gination'. Paper presented at the International Institute of Social Studies Conference: 'Religion and Development', 3 November, The Hague, The Netherlands.

Gutierrez, G. (1973) *A Theology of Liberation. History, Politics and Salvation*, New York: Orbis Books.

Harrison, P. (1993) *The Greening of Africa: Breaking Through in the Battle for Food and Land*, Harmondsworth: Penguin Books.

Harsch, E. (2003) 'Africa builds its own peace forces', *Africa Recovery*, 17, 3, pp. 1, 14–16, 18–20.

Hastings, A. (1979) *A History of African Christianity, 1950–75*, Cambridge University Press, Cambridge.

Haynes, J. (1993) *Religion in Third World Politics*, Buckingham, UK: Open University Press.

Haynes, J. (1996a) *Religion, Fundamentalism and Identity A Global Perspective*, Discussion Paper no. 65, Geneva: UNRISD.

Haynes, J. (1996b) *Religion and Politics in Africa*, London: Zed.

Haynes, J. (1998) *Religion in Global Politics*, Harlow, UK: Longman.

Haynes, J. (ed.) (1999) *Religion, Globalization and Political Culture in the Third World*, Basingstoke, UK: Macmillan.

Haynes, J. (2002) *Politics in the Developing World*, Oxford: Blackwell.

Haynes, J. (2005a) *Comparative Politics in a Globalizing World*, Cambridge: Polity.

Haynes, J. (ed.) (2005b) *Palgrave Advances in Development Studies*, Basingstoke, UK: Palgrave.

Haynes, J. (2005c) 'Islamic militancy in East Africa,' *Third World Quarterly*, 26, 8, pp. 1321–39.

Haynes, J. (2006) 'Principles of Good Governance', in L. Cleary and T. McConville (eds) *The Governance and Management of Defence*, London, Taylor & Francis, pp. 17–31.

Haynes, J. (2007) *An Introduction to International Relations and Religion*, Harlow/London: Pearson Longman.

Health Alliance International (2006) 'Programs: Mozambique. Community partner: *Kubatsirana*'. Available at: http://depts.washington.edu/haiuw/html/programs/mozambique/partners/Kubatsirana/index.htm Last accessed 18 December 2006.

Held, D. and McGrew, A. (2002) *Gloablization/Anti-Globalization*, Cambridge: Polity.

Hewitt, W. (1990) 'Religion and the consolidation of democracy in Brazil: the role of the Commundades Eclesias de Base', *Sociological Analysis*, 50, 2, pp. 139–52.

Hill, J. (2001) 'Global ethics: What we can learn From Christians overseas', *Christian Ethics Today*, 7, 4. Available at: http://www.christianethicstoday.com/Issue/035/Global%20Ethics%20What%20We%20Can%20Learn%20From%20Christians%20Overseas%20By%20Jack%20A%20Hill_035_23_.htm Last accessed 2 September 2006.

Hirohita, M. (2002) 'Muslims and Buddhists dialogue', Unitarian Universalist Fellowship of Frankfurt, 10 November. Available at: http://www.uufrankfurt.de/MuslimsBuddhists021110.htm Last accessed 28 March 2006.

Holenstein, A.-M. (2005) 'Role and significance of religion and spirituality in development co-operation. A reflection and working paper'. (Translated from German by Wendy Tyndale.) Bern: Swiss Agency for Development and Co-operation, March.

'Honduras' (1993) Library of Congress Country Studies. Available at: http://lcweb2.loc.gov/cgi-bin/query/r?frd/cstdy:@field(DOCID+hn0068) Last accessed 16 December 2006.

Hopkins, D. (ed.) (2001) *Religions/Globalizations: Theories and Cases*, Durham: NC: Duke University Press.

Horn, K. (2006) 'The inspiration of one, Today's pentecostal evangel'. Available at: http://www.ag.org/Pentecostal-Evangel/Articles2006/4795_InspireOne.cfm Last accessed 20 December 2006.

Houghton, J.T. (1992) *Climate Change: The IPCC Scientific Assessment*, Cambridge: Cambridge University Press.

Howard, R. and Sawyer, R. (eds) (2004) *Defeating Terrorism. Shaping the New Security Environment*, Guilford, Connecticut: McGraw-Hill/Dushkin.

Human Development Report (1996) New York: UNDP.

Human Rights Watch (1999) 'India', New York: Human Rights Watch.

Huntington, S. (1991) *The Third Wave. Democratization in the Late Twentieth Century*, Norman, OK: University of Oklahoma Press.

Huntington, S. (1996) *The Clash of Civilizations*, New York: Simon and Schuster.

Hurrell, A. (2002) '"There are no rules" (George W. Bush): International order after September 11', *International Relations*, 16, 2, pp. 185–204.

Hutanuwatr, P. and Rasbach, J. (2004) 'Engaged Buddhism in Siam and South East Asia', Case study for WFDD, University of Birmingham.

Ibrahim, J. (1991) 'Religion and Political Turbulence in Nigeria', *Journal of Modern African Studies*, 29, 1, pp. 115–36.

International Consultancy on Religion Education and Culture (1998) 'World Faiths and development'. Paper presented at the World Faiths Development Conference, Lambeth Palace, London.

International HIV/AIDS Alliance (2006) 'Mozambique'. Available at: http://www.aidsalliance.org/sw7217.asp Last accessed 18 December 2006.

International Interfaith Network for Development and Reproductive Health (2005) 'A faith-filled commitment to development includes a commitment to women's rights and reproductive health. Religious reflections on the Millennium Development Goals'. Paper prepared for the 2005 World Summit, 14–16 September.

Johnston, D. and Sampson, C. (1994) *Religion, the Missing Dimension of Statecraft*, Oxford: Oxford University Press.

Jubilee USA Network (2001) 'Justice found in Islamic texts & taught by our imams'. Available at: http://www.jubileeusa.org/jubilee.cgi?path=/jubilee_congregations/worship_resources/&page=islamjustice_texts.html Last accessed 7 September 2006.

Juergensmeyer, M. (2000) *Terror in the Mind of God: The Global Rise of Religious Violence*, Berkeley, CA: University of California Press.

Juergensmeyer, M. (2005) 'Religion in the new global order'. Available at: http://www.maxwell.syr.edu/moynihan/programs/sac/paper%20pdfs/marks%20paper.pdf Last accessed 18 April 2006.

Kamm, H. (1998) *Cambodia: Report from a Stricken Land*, London: Arcade.

Kamrava, M. (1993) *Politics and Society in the Third World*, London: Routledge.

Keohane, R. (2002) 'The globalization of informal violence, theories of world politics, and the "liberalism of fear"', *Dialog-IO*, Spring 2002, pp. 29–43.

Khan, M.A. Muqteda (ed.) (2006) *Islamic Democratic Discourse*, Lanham, MD: Rowman and Littlefield.

Klicksberg, B. (2003) *Social Justice: A Jewish Perspective*, Jerusalem: Gefen Publishing House.

Klicksberg, B. (2003) 'Facing the inequalities of development: some lessons from Judaism and Christianity, *Development*, 46, 4, pp. 57–63.

Knott, K. (2000) *Hinduism: A Very Short Introduction*, Oxford: Oxford Paperbacks.

Köhler, H. (2002) 'Working for a better globalization'. 'Remarks by Horst Köhler Managing Director, International Monetary Fund Conference on Humanizing the Global Economy, Sponsored by the Canadian Conference of Catholic Bishops, El Consejo Episcopal Latinoamericano, and The United States Conference of Catholic Bishops Washington, DC, January 28, 2002'. Available at: http://canberra.usembassy.gov/hyper/2002/0129/epf214.htm Last accessed 20 December 2006.

Kollapen, J. (2005) 'Identity and democracy: Building multicultural democracies'. Presentation at the Forum on Global Development convened by the UNDP and the French Ministry of Foreign Affairs, Paris, France, 17–19 January.

Korieh, C. (2005) *Religion, History, and Politics in Nigeria: Essays in Honor of Ogbu U. Kalu*, Lanham, MD: University Press of America.

Krueger, A. and Maleckova, J. (2003) 'Seeking the roots of terrorism', *The Chronicle of Higher Education*, 49, 39, Page B10.

Kubálková, V. (2003) Kubálková, V. (2002) 'Toward an international political theology', *Fathom: The Source for Online Learning*. Available at: http://www. fathom.com/feature/35550/ Last accessed 14 October 2005.

Kubálková, V. (2006) 'Religion in the international relations classroom'. Paper presented at the panel, 'Religions Facing Globalization', 20th International Political Science Association Congress, Fukuoka, Japan, 11 July.

Kukha, M. and Falola, T. (1995) *Religious Militancy and Self-assertion: Islam and Politics in Nigeria*, Aldershot: Ashgate.

Kurien, J. (1996) *Towards a New Agenda for Sustainable Small-Scale Fisheries Development*, Calicut, India: South India Federation of Fishermen's Societies.

Kurtz, L. (1995) *Gods in the Global Village*, Pine Forge: Sage.

Lall, M. (2005) 'The challenges for India's education system', Briefing paper ASP BP 05/03, Chatham House, London.

Lane, J.-E. and Ersson, S. (1994) *Comparative Politics. An Introduction and New Approach*, Cambridge: Polity.

Latin American ChildCare (2003) 'About Latin American ChildCare'. Available at: http://latinamericachildcare.org/cgi-bin/webc.cgi/about.html Last accessed 20 December 2006.

Lean, M. (1996) 'Changing the in-vironment', *Our Planet*, 8, 2, August. Available at: http://www.ourplanet.com/imgversn/82/lean.html Last accessed 21 December 2006.

Levine, D. (1984) 'Religion and politics in comparative perspective', *Comparative Politics*, October, pp. 95–122.

Levinsohn, J. (2003) 'The World Bank's Poverty Reduction Strategy Paper approach: Good marketing or good policy', G-24 Discussion Paper Series, New York: United Nations Conference on Trade and Development.

Lillard, D. and Ogaki, M. (2005) 'The effects of spiritual capital on altruistic economic behavior', Cornell University and the Ohio State University, unpublished manuscript, September. Available at: http://paa2006.princeton. edu/download.aspx?submissionId=61119 Last accessed 11 August 2006.

Lloyd, M. (1999) 'Hindu nationalists campaign to remake education in India. Ruling party and its allies enlist academics to revise the canon', *The Chronicle of Higher Education*, p. A56.

Loy, D. (2000) 'The religion of the market', in H. Coward and D. Maguire (eds) *Visions of a New Earth*, Albany: State University of New York Press, pp. 15–28.

MacDowell, M. and Utukuru, P. (2005) 'Duality and non-duality in science and religion', *Science and Theology News*, Online edition, 26 May. Available at: http://www.stnews.org/commentary-548.htm. Last accessed 2 October 2006.

Maier, K. (1991) 'Blood Flows in Kano streets in Christian-Muslim battles, *The Independent* (London), 16 October.

Maier, K. (2001) *This House Has Fallen: Nigeria In Crisis*, Harmondsworth: Penguin.

Mainwaring, S. and Viola, E. (1984) 'New social movements, political culture, and democracy: Brazil and Argentina', *Telos*, 61, pp. 17–52.

Majeed, Abu, Bakar Abdul (2003) 'Islamic Environmentalism: A matter of interpretation', in R. Folz, F. Denny and A. Baharuddin (eds) *Islam and Ecology. A Bestowed Trust*, Cambridge, Mass, Harvard University Press.

Malek, C, (2000) 'Identity (inter-group) conflicts'. The Conflict Resolution Information Service, University of Colorado. Available at: http://v4.crinfo.org/ CK_Essays/ck_identity_issues.jsp Last accessed 25 October 2005.

Malik, R. (2003) 'The Hindus of Mauritius', *Hinduism Today*, April–June, pp. 3–5.

Malloch, T. (2006) 'Social, human and spiritual capital in economic development'. Available at. http://www.metanexus.net/metanexus_online/show_ article2.asp?id=9483) Last accessed 10 August 2006.

Mansfield, P. and Pelham, N. (2003) *A History of the Middle East*, Harmondsworth: Penguin.

'Married adolescents ignored in global agenda, says UNFPA' (2004). Press Release, 4 June.

Marshall, K. (2005a) 'Religious Faith and Development: Rethinking Development Debates', Religious NGOs and International Development Conference, Oslo, Norway, 7 April, 2005.

Marshall, K. (2005b) 'Faith and development: Rethinking development debates', World Bank paper, June, Washington, DC: World Bank.

Marshall, K. (2006) 'Religion and international development. Interview with *Katherine Marshall*, Director, Development Dialogue on Values and Ethics, The World Bank, The Pew Forum on Religion and Public Life, March 6. Available at: http://pewforum.org/events/index.php?EventID=100 Last accessed 21 December.

Marshall, K. and Keough, L. (2004) *Mind, Heart and Soul in the Fight against Poverty*, Washington, DC: World Bank.

Marshall, K. and Marsh, R. (eds) (2003) *Millennium Challenges for Development and Faith Institutions*, Washington, DC: World Bank.

Marty, M. and Appleby, R. Scott (eds) (1993) *Fundamentalisms and Society: Reclaiming the Sciences, the Family, and Education*, Chicago: University of Chicago Press.

Marty, M. and Appleby, R. Scott (1993) 'Introduction' in M. Marty and R. Scott Appleby (eds) *Fundamentalism and the State. Remaking Polities, Economies and Militance*, Chicago: University of Chicago Press, pp. 1–9.

Marty, M. and R. Scott Appleby (eds) (1995) *Fundamentalisms Comprehended*, Chicago: University of Chicago Press.

Marty, M. and J. Moore (2000) *Politics, Religion and the Common Good: Advancing a Distinctly American Conversation About Religion's Role in Our Shared Life*, San Francisco: Josey-Bass Publishers.

Mayotte, J. (1998) 'Religion and global affairs: The role of religion in development', *SAIS Review* 18, 2, pp. 65–9.

Mbogoni, L. (2004) *The Cross Versus the Crescent: Religion and Politics in Tanzania from the 1880s to the 1990s*, Dar es Salaam: Mkuki na Nyota Publishers.

McFague, S. (1993) *The Body of God: An Ecological Theology*, Minneapolis: Fortress Press.

Medhurst, K. (1989) 'Brazil', in S. Mews (ed.) *Religion in Politics*, Harlow, UK: Longman.

Mehta, P.B. (2004) 'BJP looking out for more allies to isolate Congress', *The Hindu*, 8 January 2004, p. 10.

Miles, J. and Hashmi, S. (2002) *Islamic Political Ethics: Civil Society, Pluralism and Conflict*, Princeton: Princeton University Press.

Minchakpu (2004) '"African Church has come of age", say African Anglican Bishops', 1 October. Available at: http://ctlibrary.com/11992 Last accessed 18 December 2006.

Mitchell, R. and Tanner, C. (2002) *Religion and the Environment*, Basingstoke, UK: Palgrave.

Mittelman, J. (1994) 'The globalisation challenge surviving at the margins', *Third World Quarterly*, 15, 3, pp. 427–41.

Moghadam, A. (2003) 'A Global Resurgence of Religion'. Working paper, no. 03–03, Weatherhead Center for International Affairs, Harvard University, Cambridge, MA, USA.

Mohanty, M. (1999) Environment: India's ecological mess', *Hinduism Today*, May, pp. 12–14.

Moix, B. (n/d) 'Peace is divine, preach it'. 'Mission Statement, The Muslim-Christian Dialogue Forum Kaduna, Nigeria'. Available at: http://www.sipa.columbia.edu/cicr/research/journal/features/kaduna.html Last accessed 13 December 2006.

Moreno, P. (1997) 'Rapture and renewal in Latin America', *First Things*, 74, June–July, pp. 31–4.

Mulvany, P. and Madeley, J. (2006) 'Hungry for change', *The Guardian*, 25 October.

Narayan, D. with Patel, R., Schafft, K., Rademacher, A. and Koch-Schulte, S. (2000) *Voices of the Poor: Can Anyone Hear Us?* New York: Oxford University Press.

Narayanan, V. (2000) 'One tree is equal to ten sons', in H. Coward and D. Maguire (eds) *Visions of a New Earth*, Albany: State University of New York Press, pp. 111–30.

Narayanan, V. (2001) 'Water, Wood, and Wisdom: Ecological Perspectives from the Hindu Traditions', *Daedalus*, Fall. Available at: http://www.amacad.org/publications/fall2001/narayanan.aspx Last accessed 21 December 2006.

Nasr, S.H. (1967; revised ed. 1997) *Man and Nature: The Spiritual Crisis of Modern Man*, Chicago: Kazi Publications.

Nasr, S.H. (1975) *Islam and the Plight of Modern Man*, London: Longman.

Nasr, S.H. (1996) *Religion and the Order of Nature*, New York: Oxford University Press.

Nasser, N. (n/d) 'The Aga Khan Development Network. An Ismaili perspective on culture, transnationalism and development in Pakistan'. PowerPoint presentation, Birmingham School of Architecture and Landscape, University of Central England. Available at: http://bcgit.berkeley.edu/nasser_ppt.ppt Last accessed 21 December 2006.

National Commission on Terrorist Attacks (2004) *The 9/11 Commission Report: Final Report of the National Commission on Terrorist Attacks Upon the United States*, New York: W.W. Norton and Company.

National Religious Partnership for the Environment (n/d) 'Press Release: Earth's climate embraces us all. A plea from religion and science for action on global climate change'. Available at: http://www.nrpe.org/ Last accessed 21 December 2006.

Needham, A. and Rajan, R. (eds) (2007) *The Crisis of Secularism in India*, Durham, NC: Duke University Press.

Norris, P. and Inglehart, R. (2004) *Sacred and Secular: Religion and Politics Worldwide*, Cambridge: Cambridge University Press.

Nye, J. (2002) 'Globalism versus globalization', *The Globalist* ('The daily online magazine on the global economy, politics and culture'. 15 April. Available at: http://www.theglobalist.com/StoryId.aspx?StoryId=2392 Last accessed 13 April 2006.

Olsson, J. and Wohlgemuth, L. (eds) (2003) *Dialogue in Pursuit of Development*, Stockholm: Almqvist and Wiksell International.

Oommen, T.K. (1992) 'Religion and development in Hindu society', *Social Compass* 39, 1, pp. 67–75.

Parliament of the Worlds Religions (2004) 'An ecumenical view of globalisation for the common good'. Available at: http://www.barcelona2004.org/eng/banco_del_conocimiento/documentos/ficha.cfm?IdDoc=1331 Last accessed 11 December 2006.

PARPA (2001) 'Strategy document for the reduction of poverty and promotion of economic growth', Government of Mozambique. Available at: http://www.govmoz.gov.mz/parpa/eindex.htm Last accessed 4 October 2006.

Pawlikowski, J. (2004) 'Ethics & globalization: The interreligious challenge', *Interreligious Insight*, April, pp. 17–20.

Peluso, N. (1993) 'Coercing conservation: the politics of state resource control', in R. Lipschutz and K. Conca (eds) *The State and Social Power in Global Environmental Politics*, New York: Columbia University Press, pp. 46–70.

Pettifor, A. (ed.) (2003) *Real World Economic Outlook. The Legacy of Globalization: Debt and Deflation*, New York and Basingstoke: Palgrave.

Petito, F. and Hatzopoulos, P. (eds) (2003) *Religion in International Relations. The Return from Exile*, New York and Basingstoke: Palgrave Macmillan.

Pew Forum on Religion and Public Life (2006) 'Event transcript. Christianity and Conflict in Latin America'. Symposium on 'Religion, Conflict and the Global War on Terrorism in Latin America'. Available at: http://www.speroforum.com/site/article.asp?idCategory=33&idsub=135&id=3540 Last accessed 21 December 2006.

Pimbert, M., Tran-Than, Khan, Deleage, E., Reinert, M., Trehet, C. and Bennett, E. (eds) (2005) 'Farmers' Views on the Future of Food and Small-Scale Producers. Summary of an Electronic Conference, 14 April to 1 July, 2005', London: International Institute for Environment and Development.

Pinkney, R. (2005) *The Frontiers of Democracy: Challenges in the West, the East and the Third World*, Aldershot: Ashgate.

Pipob Udomittipong (2000) 'Thailand's ecology monks', in S. Kaza and K. Kraft (eds) *Dharma Rain: Sources of Buddhist Environmentalism*, Boston: Shambhala Publications, pp. 191–7.

Poethig, K. (2002) 'Movable peace: Engaging the transnational in Cambodia's Dhammayietra', *Journal for the Scientific Study of Religion*, 41, 1, pp. 19–28.

Portillo, Z. (1999) 'Latin America Gets Poor Marks', Latin America Report, Wellington, New Zealand: InterPress Third World News Agency.

Positive Muslims (2004) *HIV, AIDS and Islam. Reflections Based on Compassion, Responsibility & Justice*, Observatory, South Africa: Positive Muslims.

Plumer, B. (2005) 'Marching for life; an interview with Jose Tamayo', *Mother Jones Magazine*, 1 June 29. Available at: http://www.motherjones.com/news/qa/2005/06/tamayo.html Last accessed 16 December 2006.

Premasiri, P. (1997) 'Sri Lanka and the Sarvodaya model', in B. Saraswati (ed.) *Integration of Endogenous Cultural Dimension of Development*, New Delhi: IGNCA, pp. 78–87.

Przeworski, A. (1986) 'Som eprobelms in the study of the transition to democracy', in G. O'Donnell, P. Schmitter and L. Whitehead (eds) *Transitions from Authoritarian Rule: Southern Europe*, Baltimore, MD: Johns Hopkins University Press, pp. 47–63.

Przeworski, A., Alvarez, M., Cheibib, J.A. and Limongi, F. (1996) 'What makes democracies endure?', *Journal of Democracy*, 7, 1, pp. 39–55.

Rai, S. (2005) 'Gender and development', in J. Haynes (ed.) *Palgrave Advances in Development Studies*, Basingstoke, UK and New York: Palgrave Macmillan, pp. 226–45.

Ram, A. and Sharma, K.D. (2005) *National Policy on Education: An Overview*, Delhi: Vikas Publishing House.

Ramadan, T. (2006) 'Before the trap springs shut on the Palestinian people, resign!'. Available at: http://www.tariqramadan.com/rubrique.php3?id_rubrique=43&lang=en Accessed 6 June 2006.

Ramet, S. (1998) *Nihil Obstat: Religion, Politics and Social Change in East-Central Europe and Russia*, Durham, NC: Duke University Press.

Ratzinger, J. and Pera, M. (2006) *Without Roots: The West, Relativism, Christianity and Islam*, New York, Basic Books.

Religious Working Group on World Bank and IMF (1997) 'Moral imperatives for addressing structural adjustment and economic reform measures'. Available at: http://www.sedos.org/english/maryknol.htm Last accessed 21 December 2006.

Reychler, L. (1997) 'Religion and conflict', *The International Journal of Peace Studies*, 2, 1, pp.?? Available at: http://www.gmu.edu/academic/ijps/vol2_1/Reyschler.htm Last accessed 14 April 2006.

Robertson, R. (1995) *Globalization: Social Theory and Global Culture*, London: SAGE.

Room to Read (2006) 'Sri Lanka'. Available at: http://www.roomtoread.org/countries/sri_lanka.html Last accessed 20 December 2006.

Rosen, D. (2005) 'Religion, identity and Mideast Peace'. The 10th Annual Templeton Lecture on Religion and World Affairs. Available at: http://www.fpri.org/enotes/20050923.religion.rosen.religionidentitymideastpeace.html Last accessed 25 May 2006.

Sabia, D. (1997) *Contradiction and Conflict: Popular Church in Nicaragua*, Tuscaloosa, Alabama: University of Alabama Press.

Sacks, J. (2003) *The Dignity of Difference: How to Avoid the Clash of Civilizations*, London: Continuum.

Safe Motherhood Initiative (2002) 'Maternal mortality'. New York: Family Care International.

Salih, M.A. (2002) 'Islamic NGOs in Africa: The promise and peril of Islamic voluntarism', Occasional Paper, Centre of African Studies, University of Copenhagen.

Salih, M.A. (2004) 'Islamic NGOS in Africa. The promise and peril of Islamic voluntarism', in A. de Waal (ed.) *Islamism and its Enemies in the Horn of Africa*, London: Hurst and Company, pp. 146–81.

Scholte, J.A. (2005) *Globalization*, 2nd edn, Basingstoke: Palgrave Macmillan.

Scruton, R. (2005) *The West and the Rest: Globalization and the Terrorist Threat*, London: Continuum.

Seeworchun, C. (1995) *Hindu Festivals in Mauritius*, Birmingham: African Books Collective.

Selinger, L. (2004) 'The forgotten factor: The uneasy relationship between religion and development', *Social Compass*, 51, 4, pp. 771 11.

Sen, A.K. (1999) *Development As Freedom*, New York: Knopf Press.

Serageldin, I. and Barrett, R. (eds) (1996) *Ethics and Spiritual Values: Promoting Environmentally Sustainable Development*. Washington, DC: World Bank.

Serra, L. (1985) 'Ideology, religion and class struggle in the Nicaraguan revolution', in R. Harris and C. Vilas (eds) *Nicaragua: A Revolution under Siege*, pp. 151–74.

Sharma, R.N. (2002) *Indian Education at the Cross Road*, Delhi: Shubhi.

Shaw, T. (2005) 'The global political economy', in J. Haynes (ed.) *Palgrave Advances in Development Studies*, Basingstoke, UK: Palgrave, pp. 249–67.

Sigmund, P. (n/d) 'Education and religious freedom in Latin America', International Association for Religious Freedom, Oxford, UK. Available at: http://www.iarf.net/REBooklet/LatinAmerica.htm Last accessed 20 December 2006.

Simmons, O. (1988) *Perspectives on Development and Population Growth in the Third World*, London: Springer.

Simonse, S. (1998) 'Steps towards peace and reconciliation in Northern Uganda. An analysis of initiatives to end the armed conflict between the Government of Uganda and the Lord's Resistance Army, 1987–1998'. Commissioned by Pax Christi Netherlands.

Sinding, S. (2005) 'Does "CNN" (Condoms, Needles, Negotiation) work better than "ABC" (Abstinence, Being Faithful and Condom Use) in attacking the AIDS epidemic?', *International Family Planning Perspectives*, 31, 1, pp. 38–40.

SIPA (School of International and Public Affairs) (2006) 'His Highness the Aga Khan, the Ismaili Imamat and the Aga Khan Development Network', SIPA, Columbia University. Available at: http://www.sipa.columbia.edu/news_events/announcements/aga_khan.html Last accessed 21 December 2006.

Sivaraksa, Sulak and Ginsburg, T. (eds) (1992) *Seeds of Peace: A Buddhist Vision for Renewing Society*, Berkeley, CA: Parallax Press.

Smith, B. (1982) *The Church and Politics in Chile*, Princeton, NJ: Princeton University Press.

Smock, D. (2001) 'Faith-Based NGOs and international peacebuilding'. Special report no. 76, United States Institute of Peace, October. Available at: http://www.usip.org/pubs/specialreports/sr76.html Accessed 4 February 2006.

Smock, D. (2004) 'Divine intervention: Regional reconciliation through faith', *Religion*, 25, 4. Available at: http://hir.harvard.edu/articles/1190/3/ Last accessed 1 September 2005.

Smock, D. (ed.) (2006) *Religious Contributions to Peacemaking. When Religion Brings Peace, Not War*, Washington, DC: United States Institute of Peace.

Society for the Scientific Study of Religion (2001) 'Symposium on globalization at the conference of the Society for the Scientific Study of Religion held in Ohio in October, 2001. Available at: http://www.cra.org.au/pages/00000061.cgi Last accessed 19 April 2006.

Soka Gakkai International (2000) 'Debt Cancellation: A Moral and Economic Imperative'. Available at: http://www.sgi.org/english/Features/quarterly/0007/interview.htm Last accessed 6 September 2006.

Spickard, J. (2001) 'Tribes and cities: Towards an Islamic sociology of religion', *Social Compass*, 48, pp. 103–16.

Spickard, J. (2003) 'What is happening to religion? Six sociological narratives'. Unpublished manuscript, available at: http://www.ku.dk/Satsning/Religion/indhold/publikationer/working_papers/what_is_happened.PDF Accessed 14 April 2006.

Stiefel, M and Wolfe, M. (1994) *A Voice for the Excluded. Popular Participation in Development: Utopia or Necessity?*, London/Geneva: Zed/UNRISD.

Stiglitz, J. (2006) *Making Globalization Work: The Next Steps to Global Justice*, London, Allen Lane.

Tarrow, S. (1998) *Power in Movement. Social Movements and Contentious Politics*, 2nd edn, Cambridge: Cambridge University Press.

Taylor, I. (2005) 'Globalization and development', in J. Haynes (ed.) *Palgrave Advances in Development Studies*, Basingstoke, UK: Palgrave, pp. 268–87.

Tearfund (n/d) 'Faith untapped. Why churches can play a crucial role in tackling HIV and AIDS in Africa'. Available at: http://www.tearfund.org/webdocs/Website/Campaigning/Policy%20and%20research/Faith%20untapped.pdf Last accessed 18 December 2006.

Tearfund (2006) 'African church in urgent call for resources as it spends equivalent of £2.5 billion on AIDS fight', 11 August. Available at: http://www.tearfund.org/News/Press+release+archive/August+2006/African+church+in+urgent+call+for+resources+in+AIDS+fight.htm Last accessed 18 December 2006.

ter Haar G. and Busutill J. (eds) (2005) *Bridge or Barrier: Religion, Violence and Visions for Peace, Brill.*

Tessane, J. (2005) 'Reduce child mortality. A public lecture by Sabina Alkire', *Boston Theological Institute Newsletter*, 35, 7, October 25, pp. 1–2.

'The Global HIV/AIDS Pandemic, 2006' (2006) *Morbidity and Mortality Weekly Report*, August 11, 55, 31, pp. 841–4.

Thomas, A. (1994) *Third World Atlas*, 2nd edn, Buckingham: Open University Press.

Thomas, C. and Reader, M. (2001) 'Development and inequality', in B. White, R. Little and M. Smith (eds) *Issues in World Politics*, Basingstoke: Palgrave, pp. 74–92.

Thomas, S. (2000) 'Religious resurgence, postmodernism and world politics', in J. Esposito and M. Watson (eds) *Religion and Global Order*, Cardiff: University of Wales Press, pp. 38–60.

Thomas, S. (2005) *The Global Resurgence of Religion and the Transformation of International Relations: The Struggle for the Soul of the Twenty-First Century*, New York and Basingstoke, UK: Palgrave Macmillan.

Thürer, D. (1999) 'The "failed State" and international law', *International Review of the Red Cross*, 836, pp. 731–61.

Tickner, A. (2005) 'On taking religious worldviews seriously'. Paper presented at the Robert Keohane *festschrift* conference, Princeton University, February.

Tokatlian, J. (2006) 'The partition temptation: Iraq to Latin America', 'Open Democracy. Free Thinking for the World'. Available at: http://www.open-democracy.net/democracy-protest/partition_temptation_4140.jsp Last accessed 13 December 2006.

'Towards an Islamic jurisprudence of the environment' (2002) IslamOnline.net. Available at: http://www.islamonline.net/english/Contemporary/2002/08/Article02b.shtml Last accessed 15 December 2006.

Tucker, M. and Grim, J. (2001) 'Introduction· The emerging alliance of world religions and ecology', *Daedalus*, 130, 4, pp. 1–13.

Tyndale, W. (n/d) 'National Forum of Fish Workers: a spiritually inspired movement for alternative development'. 'Case study' produced for the World Faiths Development Dialogue. Available at: http://www.wfdd.org.uk/programmes/case_studies/fishworkers.pdf Last accessed 21 December 2006.

Tyndale, W. (2001) 'Faith and economics in 'development': a bridge across the chasm?', in Deborah Eade (ed.) *Development and Culture*, Oxford: Oxfam, pp. 45–59.

Tyndale, W. (2004) 'Religions and the Millennium Development Goals: Whose agenda?'. Paper prepared for the 'Religion and Development Conference', The Hague, The Netherlands, 3 November.

UN Millennium Project (2005) 'Investing in Development: A Practical Plan to Achieve the Millennium Development Goals'. Available at: www.unmillenniumproject.org/reports/index.htm Last accessed 4 October 2006.

UNAIDS (2001) *The Global Strategy Framework on HIV/AIDS*, New York: UNAIDS.

UNAIDS (2006) *Report on the Global AIDS Epidemic 2006*, Geneva: UNAIDS.

UNESCO (n/d) *Education for All. An Achievable Vision*, Paris: UNESCO.

UNESCO (2000) *Education for All: Evaluation of the Year 2000*, New York: UNESCO.

UNESCO (2001) 'Monitoring Report on Education For All', New York: UNESCO.

UNESCO (2007) *EFA Global Monitoring Report. Strong Foundations*, New York: UNESCO.

UNFPA (2004) *Culture Matters. Working with Communities and Faith-based Organizations: Case Studies from Country Programmes*, New York: UNFPA.

UNICEF (1995) 'Religious Leaders as Health Communicators'. New York, NY: UNICEF.

UNICEF (2004) 'Press release. South Asian religious leaders establish multi-faith Council to address HIV/AIDS, New York: UNICEF.

UNICEF (2005a) 'Press release. Children, the focus for Islamic solidarity', New York: UNICEF.

UNICEF (2005b) 'Press release. Investing in children in the Islamic world', New York: UNICEF.

UNICEF (2005c) *Investing in the Children of the Islamic World*, New York: UNICEF.

UNICEF (2000d) *Progress for Children: A Report Card on Gender Parity and Primary Education, New York:* UNICEF.

UNICEF (2006) 'Press release. UNICEF calls on religious leaders to work together for peace and development', 26 August.

United States Institute for Peace (2003) 'Special Report: Can Faith-Based NGOs Advance Interfaith Reconciliation? The Case of Bosnia and Herzegovina'. Available at: http://www.usip.org/pubs/specialreports/sr103.pdf Last accessed 1 February 2006.

US Department of State (2003) 'Mauritius'. Available at: http://www.state.gov/g/drl/rls/irf/2003/23741.htm Last accessed 18 December 2006.

USAID (2005) 'United States Agency for International Development Mission to Cambodia: Good health activities'. Available at: http://www.usaid.gov/kh/health/activities.htm Last accessed 18 December 2006.

Van Geest, W. (1998) 'The relationship between development and religion', *Evangelical Review of Theology.* 22, 1, pp. 61–77.

Varshney, A. (2003) *Ethnic Conflict and Civic Life: Hindus and Muslims in India,* New Haven: Yale University Press.

Venerable Nhem Kim Teng (n/d) 'Case Study. Santi Sena Organization'. Available at: http://www.wfdd.org.uk/programmes/case_studies/santisena.doc Last accessed 20 December 2006.

Ver Beek, K. (2000) 'Spirituality: A development taboo', *Development in Practice* 10, 1, pp. 31–43.

Vikram Sarabhai Foundation & World Faiths Development Dialogue (2004) 'Case study workshop, New Delhi, 9–11 February, Thematic summary'.

Vincent, J. and Ali, R. (2005) *Managing Natural Wealth: Environment and Development in Malaysia,* Washington, DC: Resources for the Future Press.

Vogler, J. (2001) 'Environment', in B. White, R. Little and M. Smith (eds) *Issues in World Politics,* 2nd edn, Basingstoke: Palgrave, pp. 191–211.

Warburg, M. (2001) 'Religious organisations in a global world. A comparative perspective', University of Copenhagen, Denmark. Paper presented at the 2001 international conference, 'The Spiritual Supermarket: Religious Pluralism in the 21st Century', April 19–22, London School of Economics, Houghton Street, London WC2A 2AE.

Weigel, G. (2003) *The Final Revolution: The Resistance Church and the Collapse of Communism,* New York: Oxford University Press.

Wolfensohn, J. (n/d) 'Faith and development'. Available at: http://web.world-bank.org/WBSITE/EXTERNAL/EXTABOUTUS/ORGANIZATION/EXTOFFI-CEPRESIDENT/EXTPASTPRESIDENTS/PRESIDENTEXTERNAL/0,,contentMDK:20091872~menuPK:232057~pagePK:139877~piPK:199692~theSitePK:227585,00.html Last accessed 21 December 2006.

Wolfensohn, J. (2004) 'Foreword', in World Bank, *World Development Report 2004: Making Services Work For Poor People,* Oxford: Oxford University Press for the World Bank.

Wolters, H. (2004) 'Summary'. 'Religion and Development' Conference, The Hague, The Netherlands, 3 November.

Woolacott, M. (1995) 'A Rage for Peace and Power', *The Guardian* (London), September 9.

Working from Within (2004) New York: UNFPA.

World Bank (1993) *World Development Report 1993: Investing in Health*, Washington, DC: World Bank.

World Bank (1997) *A New Agenda for Women's Health and Nutrition*, Washington DC: World Bank.

World Bank (2001) *World Development Report 2000/2001*, Oxford: Oxford University Press for the World Bank.

World Bank (2004) *World Bank Development Report 2004*, New York: Oxford University Press.

World Bank (2006) 'The Enhanced HIPC Initiative'. Available at: http://web. worldbank.org/WBSITE/EXTERNAL/TOPICS/EXTDEBTDEPT/0,,contentMDK:2 0260411~menuPK:64166739~pagePK:64166689~piPK:64166646~theSitePK:46 9043,00.html Last accessed 6 September 2006.

World Conservation Union (2006) 'Islam, environmental education and conservation in the MACP Conservancies of Northern Pakistan' Available at: http://www.iucn.org/en/projects/publ_um_religious.html Last accessed 15 December 2006.

World Council of Churches (2005) 'World Council of Churches statement to the high level segment of the UN climate change conference (COP11 and COP/MOP1)', Montreal, Canada, 9 December.

World Faiths Development Dialogue (2003) 'Seminar proposal: Faith leaders and global economics'. Available at: http://www.wfdd.org.uk/events.html Last accessed 2 September 2006.

World Faiths Development Dialogue (2004) 'The provision of services for poor people: A contribution to WDR 2004'. Available at: http://www.wfdd.org.uk/ programmes/wdr/WFDDWDR2004.pdf Last accessed 4 May 2006.

World Health Organisation (1997) 'Coverage of maternal care: A listing of available information', 4th edn, Geneva: World Health Organization.

World Prout Assembly (2006) ('Economy of the People, For the People and By the People! Put Economic Power in the Hands of the People!'), 'Arjun Singh hints action against RSS-run schools', 1 November. Available at: http://www.worldproutassembly.org/archives/2006/11/arjun_singh_hin.html Last accessed 20 December 2006.

Wuye, J. and Ashafa, M.N. (1999) *The Pastor and the Imam: Responding to Conflict*, Lagos, Nigeria: Ibrash Publications Ltd.

Wuye, J. and Ashafa, M. (2005) 'The Pastor and the Imam. Nigeria: From rivalry to brotherhood', *New Routes: A Journal of Peace Research and Action*, 10, 4, pp. 23–6.

Index

Abrahamic religions 15
accountability 45
Afghanistan 72, 73, 81, 105, 159, 188
Africa, sub-Saharan 3, 5, 7, 20, 22,
  28, 46, 47, 63, 65, 67, 77, 78, 86,
  91, 103, 111, 114, 119, 130, 153,
  154, 155, 159, 160, 170,174,182,
  183, 205, 211–12, 213
Aga Khan Development Network/
  Foundation 114, 119–23, 185
  See also the Coastal Rural Support
  Programme (Kenya)
al-Qaeda 57, 82, 83, 212
  See also bin Laden, Osama
Alliance of Religions and
  Conservation, the (ARC) 124
Ammar, Nawal 135–6
Anglican church 64, 171
Appleby, R. Scott 62, 78, 89
Argentina 88, 189, 191
Ariyaratne, A.T. 68
  See also Sarvodaya Shramadana
  Movement (SSM)
Ashafa, Muhammad Nurayn 96
Asia 5, 7, 20, 22, 28, 47, 63, 67, 77,
  91, 103, 111, 114, 119, 130, 155,
  159, 163, 182, 205, 211–12, 213

Bangladesh 21, 131, 178, 179
Basic Christian Communities (BCCs)
  69, 70, 71, 214
  See also liberation theology
'basic needs' 7
Berger, Peter 28, 57, 109
Bharatiya Janata Party (BJP; 'Indian
  People's Party') 195–8
  See also Hindu nationalism and the
  attempt to 'saffronise'
  education in India
Bhopal (environmental disaster 1984)
  125
Bhutan 19, 21
Bible, the 19, 20, 116, 188, 190

bin Laden, Osama 82, 83
  See also al-Qaeda
Bolivia 88, 193
Brazil 88, 131, 132, 154,170, 178,
  179, 190
Britain 8
Buddhism 5, 15, 37, 39, 54, 63, 67,
  69, 74, 88, 97, 98, 102, 106, 114,
  117, 124, 213
Buddhism: basic beliefs 18–19
Buddhism: education 198–204
Buddhism: environmental
  sustainability 136–7
  See also environmental
  sustainability
Buddhism, socially-engaged 19
Buddhism: health 163–6
  See also Buddhism in Cambodia
Buddhism in Cambodia 97–9, 163–6

'capitalist' development model 6
Cambodia 19, 25, 75, 81, 98–9, 103,
  119, 137, 153, 164, 202–4
  See also Buddhism in Cambodia;
  Khmer Rouge; Santi Sena
Carey, Dr George (former Archbishop
  of Canterbury) 11, 64, 111, 171,
  217
Caribbean, the 5, 7, 153, 154, 170,
  174, 193
caste 88
Chechnya 72
children 17, 25, 150, 178, 189
  See also maternal health and child
  mortality; women and girls
Chile 70
China 19, 113, 132, 153, 157, 178,
  179
Chipko movement 142
Christianity 5, 15, 37, 39, 54, 56,
  63, 74, 77, 79, 81, 88, 102, 106,
  114, 117, 182, 183, 213
Christianity: basic beliefs 19–21

Christianity: environmental
  sustainability   133–4, 139
  See also environmental sustainability
Christianity: ethics   20
Christianity: HIV/AIDS and health
  170–4
  See also HIV/AIDS
civil society   7, 15, 30, 32, 41, 45,
  48, 49, 51, 67, 180, 181
'clash of civilisations'   80, 81–4, 219
  See also Huntington, Samuel
clean drinking water   7, 25, 112,
  182, 206, 207, 210
climate change   104, 126, 127–30
  See also environmental catastrophes
  See also Stern Report on Climate
    Change
Coastal Rural Support Programme
  (Kenya)   121–2
  See also the Aga Khan Development
    Network
Cold War, the   2, 7, 8, 26, 33, 84,
  206, 207, 214, 215
Colombia   88, 93, 193
'communist' development model   6
Conable, Barber   206
conflict   12, 25, 28, 38, 48, 63, 72,
  75, 78, 90, 100, 217–20
conflict resolution and peace-building
  25, 28, 38, 63, 72, 79, 89, 90,
  91–100, 217–20
Congo, Democratic Republic of   86,
  92, 105, 157, 178, 183
consensus   43
corruption   18, 23, 40, 41
Costa Rica   132
Council of Religions, the (Mauritius)
  168
Cox, Harvey   27
Cuba   170
'culture wars'   76

Dalai Lama   18, 111
deforestation and desertification:
  impact on the developing world
  104, 127, 130–1, 138, 147
  See also environmental catastrophes
'developing world', modern idea of
  the   53

development agencies, faith-based
  24, 108, 117, 120, 150, 184, 214
development, secular and secular
  development agencies   1, 12, 17,
  18, 24, 37, 38, 50, 60, 61, 101,
  103, 106, 107
development aid   2, 40
development goals   1, 2
  See also spiritual capital and
    development
development: theory and practice
  5–7
Development Dialogue on Values and
  Ethics (DDVE)   11, 12
'Dhammayietra walks' (Cambodia)
  98–9

'Earth Summit' (1992)   114
economic development and growth
  25, 43, 59, 101–23, 214
ecotheology   44, 124
education   4, 7, 9, 17, 25, 38, 43, 48,
  63, 72, 74, 76, 114, 155, 176, 204,
  206, 207, 210, 214
Egypt   145, 178, 179
El Salvador   70, 170, 191, 193, 194
environmental catastrophes   104
  See also climate change; deforestation
environmental degradation and
  destruction   110, 146
Environmental Movement of
  Olancho (EMO)   139
  See also liberation theology and
    environmentalism in Honduras
environmental sustainability   63, 74,
  124–49
  See also liberation theology and
    environmentalism in Honduras
environmental sustainability and
  religious traditions   132–7
  ethics   13, 16, 23, 34, 36–8, 134
Ethiopia   86, 157, 186, 204
Ethiopian Muslim Relief and
  Development Association
  (EMRDA)   186
ethnicity and ethnic fragmentation
  and conflict   84, 85, 86, 87, 88,
  151
Europe   6, 20, 28

European Union, the   39
Evangelical Churches   129, 190, 213
'Evangelical Climate Initiative'   129

failed states   73, 81
faith-based organisations   1, 3, 4, 9,
   12,14, 15, 16, 17, 18, 26, 28, 34,
   35, 37, 42, 55, 59, 79, 84, 89, 90,
   102, 105, 114, 124, 146, 155, 174,
   212, 213
faith-based organisations and 'good
   governance'   46–51
   See also good governance
   See also development agencies,
      faith-based
faith-based organisations and
   education   181–4
faith-based organisations:
   pro-development' and
   'anti-development'   54–63, 68,
   71, 72
Father José Andrés amayo Cortez
   139–40
   See also liberation theology and
      environmentalism in Honduras
Federación Internacional de Fe y
   Alegría ('International Federation
   of Faith and Joy')   191–2
Food and Agriculture Organisation   103
Freire, Paulo   69
FRELIMO (Frente de Libertação de
   Moçambique)   94

Gandhi, Mohandas 'Mahatma'   68,
   69
gender   12, 38, 48, 74, 217
   See also women and girls; maternal
      health and child mortality
Gennip, Jos van   60
Germany   8
globalisation   2, 3, 25, 26, 30–3, 34,
   35, 36–8, 52, 57, 59, 60, 75, 76,
   82, 85, 127, 138, 212, 213, 215,
   216, 220
globalism   32
good governance   2, 25, 38, 39–52,
   59, 75
   See also accountability; corruption;
      transparency; responsiveness;

consensus; faith-based
   organisations and 'good
   governance'
green revolution   103
Guatemala   93, 190, 193
Gutierrez, Gustavo   20–1, 69, 216
   See also liberation theology

health and healthcare   4, 9, 17, 25,
   38, 43, 48, 63, 74, 113, 114,
   150–75, 210
Heavily Indebted Poor Countries
   (HIPC) initiative   65
Hindu nationalism and the attempt
   to 'saffronise' education in India
   195–8
   See also Bharatiya Janata Party;
      Hindutva
Hindu theology   136
Hinduism   5, 15, 38, 39, 54, 63, 69,
   74, 88, 106, 115, 124, 213
Hinduism: basic beliefs   21–2
Hinduism: environmental
   sustainability   136–7
   See also environmental
      sustainability
Hindutva ('Hindu nationalism')
   197–8
   See also Hindu nationalism and the
      attempt to 'saffronise' education
      in India
Hisbullah   77
HIV/AIDS   12, 72, 150, 151, 152–6,
   160, 165, 166–70, 171, 179, 217
   See also Christianity: HIV/AIDS and
      health
Honduran Association of Ecology
   (Asociación Hondureña de la
   Ecología, AHE)   138
Honduras   132, 170
   See also liberation theology and
      environmentalism in Honduras
human development   3, 4, 7, 15,
   16, 17, 23, 24, 25, 59–60, 62,
   118
human rights   24, 28, 41, 79, 203
hunger   25, 63, 101–23
Huntington, Samuel   81, 82, 219
   See also 'clash of civilisations'

identity politics 84–9
India 21, 77, 78, 86, 103, 115, 119,
 153, 157, 166, 178, 204
India: Hindu responses to
 environmental crisis 141–2
Indonesia 21, 81, 88, 178
industrialisation 29, 88, 127, 141,
 143, 213
Inter-American Development Bank,
 the (IDB) 13
International Conference on
 Population and Development
 (Cairo 1994) 154
international development policies
 111–14
international indebtedness 64–5,
 68, 112
 See also Jubilee 2000
International Islamic Relief
 Organisation, the (IIRO) 66
International Labour Organisation,
 the (ILO) 13, 64
International Monetary Fund (IMF)
 8, 13, 30, 34, 38, 39, 48, 49, 64,
 101, 107, 111, 112, 180, 207,
 215
*Investing in the Children of the Islamic
 World* 158
Iran 77, 95, 145
Iraq 72, 81, 83, 105
Islam 5, 15, 37, 39, 41, 54, 56, 57,
 63, 66, 74, 77, 79, 81, 88, 102,
 106, 114, 117, 119, 213
 See also Sunni Islam; Shia Islam
Islam: basic beliefs 22–4
Islam: environmental sustainability
 134–6
 See also environmental
 sustainability
Islamic Educational, Scientific and
 Cultural Organisation 158
Islamic environmentalism 44, 124,
 148, 149
Islamic extremism 212
Islamic fundamentalism 58, 81, 82
Islamic Party of Britain 65
Islamic schools (*madrasas*) in Africa
 and Asia 184–8
Israel 83, 85

Japan 19, 39
Jesus 20, 80, 116
Jubilee 2000 64–5, 68
 See also international indebtedness
Judaism 15, 21, 56, 67, 77, 79

Kashmir 72
Kenya 86, 88, 94, 125, 171, 185
 See also the Aga Khan Development
 Network
Khmer Rouge 97–9, 119, 202
Küng, Hans 16, 76, 219
Kuwait 135, 159

land use patterns 130–1
Laos 19
Latin America 5, 20, 28, 17, 48, 67,
 69, 70, 81, 150, 154, 155, 170,
 174, 182, 183, 190, 193, 211–12,
 213, 214
Latin America ChildCare 193–5
Lebanon 77
Lederach, John Paul 89
Liberia 73, 86, 91, 92, 105, 178
liberation theology 20–1, 115, 116,
 117, 139, 190, 192, 216
 See also Basic Christian
 Communities; Gutierrez,
 Gustavo
liberation theology and
 environmentalism in Honduras
 138–40
literacy 4, 176

Maha Ghoasananda 99
Malaysia 21, 131, 159
Malaysia: Islam and the natural
 environment 145–9
Mali 86, 159
Marshall, Katherine 11, 12, 13, 18,
 24, 36, 38, 46, 48, 50, 52, 111,
 152, 154, 186, 190, 191, 216
Marxism-Leninism 69
maternal health and child mortality
 156–8, 164
Mauritius 21, 166–70, 173
 See also Council of Religions
Mexico 88, 178, 193

Middle East, the   5, 22, 28, 46, 77, 130, 159, 218
Millennium Development Goals, the (MDGs)   9–11, 13, 24, 26, 38, 60, 63, 67, 102, 103, 114, 124, 149, 150, 158, 174, 176, 177, 180, 184, 204, 207, 210
Millennium Summit, the   16
modernisation   1, 7, 30, 59, 85, 140, 213, 214, 220
modernity and morals   6, 29, 34
morality   16, 23, 220
Mozambique   25, 75, 86, 91, 92, 93, 173, 174
Mozambique National Resistance (RENAMO)   93–4, 99
Muslim-Christian Dialogue Forum (MCDF)   96, 97
Muslim Supreme Council (Uganda) 161, 162
Myanmar (Burma) 19, 88

Nasr, Seyyed Hussein   23, 148, 215
National Council for Educational Research and Training (NCERT) (India)   195–6
National Forum of Fishworkers (India)   115–17, 123
natural environment   43, 124–49
   See also environmental sustainability
natural resources, protection and management of   38, 43, 114, 121, 203
Narayanan, Vasudha   141
   See also India; Hindu responses to environmental crisis
Nepal   21, 131, 132, 151
neo-liberal economic policies   8, 104, 206
Nicaragua   70, 75, 88, 89
Nigeria   25, 77, 78, 86, 91, 92, 94–7, 99, 145, 157, 178
Nigerian Civil War (1967–1970)   89, 94
Norway   41

'Operation Noah'   129
Organisation of the Islamic Conference (OIC)   95, 158, 159, 163

Palestinians   77, 85
Pakistan   21, 77, 78, 122, 123, 125, 131, 145, 151, 157, 178, 187, 188
   See also the Aga Khan Development Network
Pax Christi   91
Peru   88, 190, 191
Philippines, the   77, 81, 132, 151
political society   15
Pope John Paul II   33, 111, 134
poverty and the poor   9, 10, 12, 16, 17, 25, 37, 55, 59, 63, 72, 74, 101–23, 131, 187, 201, 203, 209, 210, 215, 217
Poverty Reduction Strategy Paper (PRSP)   49–50
Programa Integral de Educacion de Las Asambleas de Dios (PIEDAD) 194
Prophet Mohammed   22

quality of life   4, 55
Qur'an, the   37, 66, 120, 134–5, 136, 161, 163

Rastriya Swayansevak Sangh (RSS; 'National Volunteer Corps')   195
religion, definition and conceptualisation   13–16
religion and rational choice   54–7
religious experiences and globalisation   58
religious extremism   62
religious fragmentation   86, 88
religious fundamentalism and fundamentalists   34, 35, 58, 71, 80
religious ideas and development   57
religious practices   58–63
religious resurgence   2, 25, 27–30, 52, 55, 212
religious terrorism   81
Reproductive and Child Health Alliance (RACHA)   164–6
responsiveness   42
Roman Catholic church   41, 67, 69, 72, 115, 134, 183, 189, 190, 213

Roman Catholic social teachings 20, 50, 215
Roman Catholic view of development 20

Sant'Egidio 91–4
Santi Sena 117–19, 123, 202–4
See also Cambodia
Sarvodaya Shramadana Movement (SSM) 68, 71, 199–202
See also Ariyaratne, A.T.; Sri Lanka
Saudi Arabia 67, 77, 95, 135
Second Vatican Council ('Vatican II', 1962–1965) 115, 190
secularisation 1, 27, 28, 67, 214, 220
Sen, Amartya 55
September 11, 2001 (9/11) 30, 51, 57, 79, 82, 212
Shari'ah (Islamic law) 144 5, 148
Shia Islam 22, 77
See also Islam
Siddhartha Gautama (the Buddha) 18, 37
Sierra Leone 73, 91, 92, 93, 105
Singapore 7
social capital 13
social development 192
social harmony 23
social networks 106
social justice 12, 13, 28, 155
Somalia 73, 81, 85, 105, 178
South Africa 153
South Asia 67, 131, 151, 152, 157
South-East Asia 19, 130, 151
South Korea 7, 19
soft power 35
spiritual capital and development 108–10
spirituality 2, 62
Sri Lanka 19, 21, 50, 68–9, 72, 73, 77, 78, 198, 199–202
See also Sarvodaya Shramadana Movement
Stern Report on Climate Change 127
See also climate change
structural adjustment programmes (SAPs) 7, 8, 112, 113, 138

Sudan 72, 73, 78, 92
Sunni Islam 22, 77
See also Islam

Taiwan 7
Tanzania 41, 50, 85, 86, 183, 185
Thailand 19, 88, 98, 125, 132,137, 151, 152, 153
Thailand: Buddhist monks and environmental activism 143–5
See also Buddhism: environmental sustainability
theology 14
'third wave of democracy' 205
Thomas, Scott 29
Tibet 19
Tibetan Buddhism 18
transnational corporations 2, 3.', 114, 211
transparency 42
Truman, President Harry 2
tsunami (South Asia and South-East Asia, December 2004) 131, 199
Turkey 145, 185

Uganda 66, 86, 91, 160–3, 164, 177, 185
See also Muslim Supreme Council (Uganda)
underdevelopment 6
United Nations, the 3, 9, 13, 94, 100, 101
United Nations AIDS Global Strategy Framework 154–5
United Nations Children's Fund (UNICEF) 177, 179
United Nations Conference on the Human Environment, the (Stockholm, 1972) 125
United Nations Development Programme (UNDP) 4, 171
United Nations Economic Commission for Latin America 221
United Nations Educational, Scientific and Cultural Organisation (UNESCO) 177, 178, 179, 180
United Nations Environmental Programme (UNEP) 130

United Nations Fund for Population
Activities, the (UNFPA)   13, 64,
72, 150, 161, 162, 179
United States, the   2, 8, 9, 28, 39, 77,
83, 127, 158, 170, 194, 207, 212,
218
United States Agency for
International Development
(USAID)   164
urbanisation   29, 141, 173, 213, 214

Ven Phra Tuangsit   151
Venerable Nhem kim Teng   117–18
Venezuela   88, 189, 191, 193
Vidya Bharati Sansthan (VBS; 'Indian
Organisation for Education')
197–8
Vietnam   19
Voices of the Poor   55

'Washington consensus', the   9, 112,
207
welfare   43, 47, 113, 155, 208
Western technology   2
Wolfensohn, James D.   11, 49, 51,
64, 209, 217

women and girls   9, 40, 45, 61, 72,
161, 163, 177, 180, 186, 203, 207
See also maternal health and child
mortality
World Bank, the   3, 7, 8, 10, 17, 34,
38, 39, 48, 49, 51, 55, 101, 107,
108, 111, 112, 179, 180, 207,
208–10, 211, 215, 221
World Conference on Education for
All (EFA)   179–80, 181
World Council of Churches, the
(WCC)   11, 64, 135
World Education Forum (WEF)   180
World Faiths Development Dialogue,
the (WFDD)   11, 49, 51, 63, 64,
108, 181, 182, 216
World Health Organisation (WHO)
163–4
World Trade Organisation (WTO)   3,
33, 59, 215
World War II   5, 7, 9, 26, 71, 104,
190, 205
Wuye, James Movel   96

Zambia   50, 51, 172, 174, 177
Zimbabwe   94, 153